D1521208

Jury, State, and Society
in Medieval England

JURY, STATE, AND SOCIETY IN MEDIEVAL ENGLAND

James Masschaele

First published in 2008 by PALGRAVE MACMILLAN® in the United States - a division of St. Martin's Press LLC, 175 Fifth Avenue, New York, NY 10010.

Where this book is distributed in the UK, Europe and the rest of the world, this is by Palgrave Macmillan, a division of Macmillan Publishers Limited, registered in England, company number 785998, of Houndmills, Basingstoke, Hampshire RG21 6XS.

Palgrave Macmillan is the global academic imprint of the above companies and has companies and representatives throughout the world.

Palgrave® and Macmillan® are registered trademarks in the United States, the United Kingdom, Europe and other countries.

ISBN-13: 978-0-230-60779-8

Library of Congress Cataloging-in-Publication Data

Masschaele, James, 1961–
  Jury, state, and society in medieval England / James Masschaele.
     p. cm.
  Includes bibliographical references and index.
  ISBN 0-230-60779-9
  1. Jury—England—History—To 1500.   2. Governmental investigations—England—History—To 1500.   I. Title.
  KD7540.M37 2008
  347.42'0752—dc22   2008004028

A catalogue record of the book is available from the British Library.

Design by Westchester Book Group

First edition: November 2008

CONTENTS

ACKNOWLEDGMENTS

I have accumulated many personal and academic debts in the course of writing this book and it is a pleasure to acknowledge them here. Most of the research on which the book is based was conducted during a sabbatical leave from Rutgers University in 2001, and much of the writing was undertaken during a sabbatical leave in fall 2005. I am grateful to Rutgers for its support. I also want to thank several other institutions for inviting me to lecture on the material contained in this book prior to publication, including Fordham University, the University of Minnesota, the University of Toronto, and the École Normale Supérieure in Paris. The comments and questions offered at these presentations have helped me to think more clearly about the issues addressed in the book and have given me a clearer sense of how to frame the central arguments.

Numerous professional colleagues have offered feedback on the project prior to publication, including Alastair Bellany, Anne DeWindt, John Drendel, Maryanne Kowaleski, Samantha Kelly, Peter Larson, Francois Menand, and Katherine Reyerson. I am particularly grateful to John Hudson, Janet Loengard, and Rudolph Bell, who read and commented on an entire draft of the manuscript and offered many useful suggestions for revisions. Naturally, I bear sole responsibility for everything presented here.

My greatest debt is to my wife, Tia Kolbaba and my two children, Cameron and Elodie. Tia has listened to most of the stories and case histories discussed in the book, and her ongoing intellectual support and willingness to serve as a sounding board have profoundly influenced its shape. Along with Cameron and Elodie, she has created a warm and comfortable home environment, without which this book might have been finished earlier but not nearly as happily. I dedicate the book to her.

INTRODUCTION

This book is about the early history of the jury system in medieval England. It deals with the period from the middle of the twelfth century to the end of the fourteenth century, an era of momentous change that saw the birth of the Common Law, the origin of Parliament, and England's first experience as a major European power. The jury system played a central role in the country's transformation in this period, forming an institution—and more importantly a relationship between people and state—that shaped the nature of government at that time and still influences our world today. How this relationship began and what it meant to the people of that time will be the main focus of the following pages. Law and politics are central to the narrative, but so is social analysis; this book is ultimately driven by an interest in the people of medieval England, whose willingness to use and participate in the jury system ensured the institution's success.

Situating the jury system in the context of medieval society is sufficiently unorthodox to require some explanation. In its early days, this book was not really about the jury system at all. My original goal was to write about the process of state formation in medieval England. Historians have rightly pointed to the later Middle Ages as an important period in state development, particularly in England and France, where successful and expansive national monarchies developed in ways that defined much of Europe's subsequent political history. From tentative beginnings in the twelfth and thirteenth centuries, the major European states experienced an ongoing process of growth and expansion that, despite occasional setbacks, transformed them into the lumbering behemoths of the modern world, capable of dominating not just political and military life but social, economic, and cultural life as well. The general story of how states became such powerful entities has been well told in recent works such as Thomas Ertman's *Birth of the Leviathon* or in the multivolume series *The Origins of the Modern State in Europe,* commissioned by the European Science

Foundation.[1] But there is still much about the process that remains poorly understood, particularly its earlier phases.

My interest in state formation was oriented toward the period prior to the Black Death of 1347–49, when the brutal shock of plague caused a long hiatus in the forward march of the continent's political institutions, particularly north of the Alps. I was especially interested in studying developments in England, which was relatively successful in building a state apparatus in the twelfth and thirteenth centuries, so much so that words like "precocious" and "advanced" are often bandied about to describe its early political expansion. I happened to know a lot more about England than other parts of the continent because of my training as a graduate student and my early work in the fields of English social and economic history. The project thus seemed to be a reasonably good fit with my skills and interests.

The main issue I set out to explore was how the process of early state formation worked on the ground, and how people who were caught up in the state's orbit responded to their new political circumstances. Recent literature on state formation tends to adopt a centrist point of view, telling the story largely from the perspective of central governments and their internal institutional development. This is certainly an essential part of the story, without which many other parts would not make sense. Beginning in the later twelfth century, central governments succeeded in organizing and coordinating larger and larger budgets by appropriating more and more of their subjects' revenues. They succeeded in building more and more sophisticated administrations, with greater internal specialization and more effective means of communicating orders and supervising their implementation. And above all they succeeded in augmenting their military capacities, allowing them to engage in longer and more expensive wars that served to justify their policies of enhanced budgets and superior administrative capacity. All of these tendencies, first observable in the twelfth century, continued to drive the process of state-building into the modern era.

But there was a price to pay for these developments, and it was a price borne largely by peasants and others of lower social rank. One of the volumes in the European Science Foundation's series on state formation is, in fact, specifically dedicated to rebellion and resistance in the face of state expansion.[2] Its contributors emphasize repeatedly the contentious nature of state growth and the opposition it engendered among those forced to pay higher taxes and accept greater control of their lives, and their resources, by agents of the centralizing states. But the model associating burgeoning states and unhappy peasants does not work particularly well for England in the pre-plague era.

Opposition and resistance can certainly be found, but the level of violence and political disarray was typically much lower than in other parts of Europe, in spite of the fact that England's state formation was relatively fast and far-reaching in the twelfth and thirteenth centuries.[3] The growth of centralized government under the early Plantagenet kings led to protests and resistance among the political elites, to be sure, but it did not lead to the kind of large-scale social revolt that colors so much of the continent's history in its periods of rapid state formation. The divergence between the English and other European states struck me as an important question worthy of fuller investigation. How could early state formation in at least one part of Europe proceed so successfully without bringing in its train the ongoing hostility, opposition, and violence?

The answer, I felt, could only be found by looking directly at interactions between state agents and local society, including peasants, laborers, and others who were not part of any political elite, even at a local level. Some of the specific points of contact between state officials and local people were readily apparent and drew my early attention. Tax assessment was an obvious issue to examine. Even today, in far wealthier societies, taxes are often contentious and frequently serve as lightning rods for political resistance. In a world in which the majority of the population counted disposable wealth in pennies, and famine was never far away, taxes loomed much larger. Over and over again in European history, demands for taxes sparked revolt. Why had this not happened in pre-plague England? Why were English peasants and artisans, who clearly bore the brunt of taxation, so much more compliant and cooperative than their continental counterparts?

Intervention in the economy was another obvious part of the state-building process worth exploring. Europe as a whole experienced a commercial boom in the twelfth and thirteenth centuries, based on dramatic changes in textile manufacturing, increase in the availability of precious metals, and dynamic changes in business organization and entrepreneurship, among other things.[4] These, too, became grist to the mill of state-building. States asserted their rights to mint coins and monopolize the money supply; they asserted their rights to impose duties and other taxes on production and trade; they regulated markets and fairs and supervised the political life of towns. Indeed, economic historians have increasingly been inclined to treat state policies as major variables—if not the major variable—in determining paths of economic development, even in the Middle Ages. Why was there so little open opposition to economic intervention and regulation in medieval England?

Answers to such questions can only be found by looking at what was actually happening on the ground. In many parts of Europe, source materials for the medieval period are not rich enough to sustain this kind of detailed local study, but England is blessed with an abundance of suitable documentary material, beginning in the second half of the twelfth century.[5] There are virtual mountains of parchment in the National Archives in London that recorded governmental activity in minute detail: not just how much was collected in tax in a particular village in a particular year, but often the names of each taxpayer in the village, and sometimes even itemized portfolios of the property that served as the basis of each person's assessment. Similarly detailed evidence can be found regarding state expenditures. Sheriffs' accounts of the early fourteenth century, for example, documented a wide range of expenses related to military provisioning, including not just the total cost of sending food to armies fighting in Scotland and France, but also itemized details about where and from whom it was acquired, how it was processed and packaged, how it was transported, and so on. Indeed, anyone who comes into contact with these sources is bound to start wondering about the impact of state power on local societies.

Such sources are invaluable for documenting the objective circumstances in which state power operated, but their dry administrative form tends to make them less well suited for investigating qualitative responses to the state's demands. Observing the impact of state intervention in local societies does not necessarily illuminate the nature of the power relationship. Local people may have complied with state demands with great reluctance, employing the kind of foot-dragging tactics and stealthy opposition to external impositions so brilliantly described by James Scott in his account of Malaysian peasants.[6] Or they may have cooperated willingly, buying into the rationale offered for state expropriations and getting caught up in jingoistic war fervor. Or, more likely, they may have cooperated some times and in some circumstances but resisted and defied in others. Official administrative records occasionally give clues about local attitudes to state demands, but not as a matter of course nor in ways that are clear and straightforward.

My search for qualitative evidence regarding popular political responses to state demands led me to the records of the law courts, where disputes involving the application of state power were sometimes aired: opposition to the enforcement of regulations, for example, or complaints about the misbehavior or corruption of state officials. The medieval English legal system created mountains of parchment that rival the mountains of contemporary administrative records; equally important, the system's early commitment to case law meant that much of this early legal material was carefully preserved and has survived to the present day. The volume of surviving court material is so great that an interested reader could spend the better part of his or her lifetime working through the court records of the thirteenth century alone without managing to read every available source. There are lacunae in the records, to be sure, but they are overshadowed by the vast quantity of material that still remains.

Turning to the records of the courts to investigate local reactions to state demands is not, however, a straightforward task. Beyond the initial hurdles of working with arcane language and esoteric technical procedures, there are more fundamental issues of historical reliability. Is it reasonable to expect a legal system organized and managed by the central government to yield meaningful evidence about how people interacted with that very same government? Can the work of scribes and court officials beholden to the state truly represent local points of view when they are at odds with those of their paymasters? There are no easy answers to these questions, and readers of this book will have to judge for themselves whether I have paid sufficient heed to the issues in the following pages. They will not be front and center in what follows. I raise them here because thinking about the formal processes of court procedure and record production led me to change the focus of my research and ultimately write this book instead of the one I had originally planned.

One of the striking things about medieval English courts is the extent to which local people, other than those who were litigating or disputing, had to be involved in the process for it to work. Those others participated in a variety of ways but most of all through service as jurors. In many instances, it was a jury that was responsible for drawing a contentious local matter out into the open, by making accusations— presentments they were technically called—about abuses of power, or misguided or unacceptable responses to state demands. Furthermore, it was typically a jury that had to make decisions about the validity of competing or conflicting accounts of the circumstances behind particular disputes. Jurors had to operate within a framework imposed by the central government and they certainly did not have limitless discretion over how problems were resolved. But they had an extraordinarily active role in determining what the final outcome would be. Their verdict typically formed the official and binding resolution of a problem, even if bad blood and ill will were unlikely to disappear as soon as the jury made its pronouncement.

Juries are thus worth contemplating as an instrument of court procedure and a component in dispute resolution. But they are also interesting in their own right as articulation points between institutions and individuals and as places for interaction between central government and local society. In fact, they were a core part of the process of state formation. In medieval England, as in most of Europe, the power of the state was felt much more directly and continuously through the operation of the courts than through the operations of tax assessors or military recruiters and administrators.[7] Jury service constituted one of the state's biggest demands and one of the most intense forms of local involvement with the state. Simply put, the relationship between central government and local society in medieval England cannot be understood without full consideration of jury service and the nature of people's engagement with it.

Existing secondary literature dealing with medieval English juries has sometimes recognized the political nature of jury service, but relatively few works have explored the subject systematically. In 1933, Alfred B. White published an excellent short monograph, *Self-Government at the King's Command,* with the ambitious subtitle *A Study in the Beginnings of English Democracy.*[8] White's fundamental argument was that the regular use of juries put people in a position to exercise power on behalf of the state, and conditioned them to view political decision-making as an interactive process between center and periphery. He saw the relationship built around the jury system as having much in common with the political environment that produced Magna Carta, both manifesting a tendency for local notables to demand a share in governance. Perceptive though it is, however, White's book has some major limitations. He drew his evidence from a relatively limited number of sources and covered only the decades around the issuing of Magna Carta. His social analysis is also lacking by modern standards, since he limited his attention to knights and gentry and failed to consider less elevated social groups. It is nonetheless an important study, one that has never received the attention it deserves.

Thomas Green's *Verdict According to Conscience: Perspectives on the English Criminal Trial Jury, 1200–1800,* published in 1985, represents another significant landmark in scholarship on medieval juries.[9] Green provided a good historical overview of the institutional development of trial juries, but what made his work stand out was its treatment of the internal dynamics of jury decision-making. He was the first scholar to investigate systematically the propensity of medieval juries to exonerate large numbers of defendants.[10] They behaved in this fashion, he argued, because they had their own sense of justice that differed from the definitions of felony propounded by the state and its legal establishment. Where the law saw homicide in black-and-white terms, jurors tended to see it in shades of gray. In the eyes of most jurors, there were indeed acts of homicide that deserved capital punishment, but there were also some—most in fact—that did not. Jurors were willing to look beyond the act and take into account the circumstances surrounding the homicide and the preexisting relations between culprit and victim in ways that the formal legal establishment would not condone but could not prevent. Green's work popularized the idea of jury nullification to explain the phenomenon; by pronouncing a verdict of not guilty juries could overturn or nullify a legal process that otherwise seemed to be headed for a hanging. Even when the original indictment was made by the medieval equivalent of a grand jury, and even when many of the men who served on the grand jury also sat on the trial jury, indictments of felony were more likely to lead to acquittal than conviction.

Valuable as it is for understanding the behavior of trial juries, however, Green's work does not fully illuminate the interactions between state and local society inherent in the jury system. Any study of the jury that is limited to criminal procedure is bound to overlook essential parts of the story. As will become clearer in the course of this book, the criminal trial jury was one of the several different types of jury active in the period, and in many respects it was the least influential in terms of state formation. To understand the sociopolitical implications of jury service in the medieval world, it is necessary to look at all types of juries, not just those involved in criminal procedure. Green's study shows the considerable independence that one type of jury could display when implicated in the workings of the state, but it does not examine systematically the wider social and political context relevant to jury service as a whole. Still, by revealing the agency of jurors in criminal procedure, Green made an important contribution to our understanding of the medieval jury, one that complements the ideas in White's pioneering work.

In the quarter-century since Green's book appeared, there have been no major monographs devoted specifically to the medieval jury, but a number of important works exploring aspects of jury service in the context of broader general themes have appeared. In this light, mention should be made here of Edward Powell's study of criminal justice in the reign of Henry V, J. G. Bellamy's work on late medieval criminal trials, and Anthony Musson's works on public order and legal culture.[11] They all provide valuable insights into the workings and behavior of criminal trial juries; Musson's view that legal knowledge was widely disseminated in the thirteenth and fourteenth centuries is particularly relevant to the arguments developed in this book. But these recent works present the history of the jury principally, if not exclusively, from the perspective of criminal procedure and thus fail to elucidate the dynamics of the jury system as a whole, particularly as an element in the relationship between central authority and local society. Criminality is intrinsically interesting and the historical connection between medieval and modern types of criminal trial jury certainly explains why criminal juries loom so large in existing scholarship. Nonetheless, the neglect of other forms of jury procedure in recent scholarship has left a gaping hole in the secondary literature, hindering full appreciation of the social and political contexts in which juries operated.

Political historians have filled in some of the gaps in the story, but they too have typically failed to give the jury system adequate attention. W. L. Warren's biography of King Henry II (1154–1189) provides a good overview of the widening scope of jury procedure in a particularly formative reign, but recent surveys of politics in the twelfth and thirteenth centuries, such as Robert Bartlett's contribution to the *New Oxford History of England* or David Carpenter's contribution to the *Penguin History of Britain* deal with juries only as incidental parts of their narratives.[12] Susan Reynolds's influential work, *Kingdoms and Communities in Western Europe, 900–1300,* published in 1984, provides a valuable general framework in which to situate the emergence of juries and their relations with higher political authorities.[13] Reynolds argues that earlier historians had overstated the importance of vertical and hierarchical lines of authority associated with feudal relationships and in so doing had undervalued the role of horizontally-based collective groups in shaping political life. Her ground-up interpretation of politics drew attention to the role that collective associations played in determining and enforcing the period's laws and political norms. Larger political entities, including even kingdoms, accepted and respected the centrality of collective bodies as organs of government and were themselves deeply permeated by models of association. In Reynolds's formulation, English juries exemplify a broader characteristic of European political life as a whole, representing the kind of independent group decision-making process that could be found in other guises throughout the rest of

Europe. Reynolds overstates the similarities between English juries and other legal bodies vested with collective responsibilities over law enforcement, but her model of the medieval state as an amalgam of groups with strong horizontal bonds has obvious relevance for my attempt to situate juries in the context of state formation.

Recent studies of the political influence of knights and gentry also deserve mention here as aspects of jury history. Peter Coss's account of the formation of the gentry deals effectively with the growing importance of inquest juries in the thirteenth century, while Christine Carpenter's reconstruction of political relationships in fifteenth-century Warwickshire describes how the integrity of the jury system could be undermined in an era of weak kingship.[14] Both works emphasize the importance of juries in county politics, and both show that the higher echelons of county society were not only keenly aware of what juries were doing but also heavily committed to influencing how they operated. Their insights draw attention to the political nature of medieval jury service, but by refracting juries through the prism of relatively privileged political groups, even these studies have failed to address essential aspects of the jury's role. Jurors were, in fact, drawn from a wide cross section of society, routinely including social ranks below the level of the gentry. These lower social levels are a central part of the whole story; without them it is difficult to understand how the jury functioned as a link between state and local society.

Substantiating this argument is one of the main goals of this book, which focuses primarily on the implications of jury service for the base of society. At its heart are two related themes. The first is that demands for jury service were widespread and extensive from relatively early in the jury's history, much more frequent and recurrent than has hitherto been recognized. This theme is developed most consistently in chapters 1, 2, and 3. Chapter 1 looks at the early history of the jury in the form of royal inquests. The association between the inquests commissioned by the Norman kings of England and later jury forms has long been recognized, but what has been overlooked by most students of the jury is the survival of the inquest well past the birth of successor jury forms. Inquest juries were more than simple forerunners of court juries; they were an ongoing form of jury throughout the Middle Ages and after. Indeed, not only did they continue to exist but also they expanded dramatically, after the other types of court-based juries came along. Demands for jury service on royal inquests rose significantly in the thirteenth and fourteenth centuries along with demands for service on other types of jury. Jurors were thus nearly as likely to find themselves performing their duties in the context of an inquest as in the context of a legal tribunal.

Chapter 2 explores the emergence of court-based juries out of the inquest jury. Inquest procedure proved to be a fertile and adaptable form of decision-making and English kings made use of it in a wide array of circumstances. Three adaptations proved to be especially important in broadening the scope of jury procedure: presentment juries, assize juries, and trial juries. Presentment juries were medieval forerunners of the modern American grand jury. They were assigned responsibility for gathering evidence about crimes and other local problems, and using their knowledge about local conditions to make formal accusations before a royal justice. Their accusations served as indictments that required further legal process, typically in the form of a trial. Assize juries operated in the field of civil law following procedures set down in special laws that governed disputes over property. They had much in common with trial juries, except that they were required to operate according to the specific rules governing litigation over property. Trial juries operated within the context of specific cases presented in court. They were best known for their role in determining the outcome of criminal trials, but they were also frequently pressed into service to render verdicts on other matters, including allegations of trespass and other types of civil procedure.

As the range and frequency of jury decision-making increased, so did the practical necessity of drafting more and more people to serve as jurors. Chapter 3 is, accordingly, dedicated to the methods employed to set up juries and oversee their deployment. It focuses first of all on the duties of sheriffs and bailiffs who were responsible for selecting jurors and ensuring their presence in court. These two royal officials had responsibility for creating jury panels, lists of potential jurors who had to be available to serve when called upon by the courts. Sheriffs and bailiffs typically carried out their duties by writing lists of names of potential jurors on small slips of parchment, thousands of which still survive to provide evidence about the personnel of specific juries in the period. Chapter 3 also explores some of the efforts made to ensure that sheriffs and bailiffs constituted juries that were fair and reliable; fairness and reliability were obviously essential to the growing popularity of jury procedure. Some insight into the matter of fairness is provided by the special case of mixed juries, which were constituted when contending parties hailed from different religious or linguistic backgrounds, or even sometimes just from different parts of the country. In such cases, half the jurors were drawn

from individuals sharing the same background as one of the contending parties and half the other. The emphasis on fairness is also manifest in two related practices observed by the courts, one requiring
parties to acknowledge their willingness to accept the jurors constituted for the case; the other allowing parties to challenge jurors they
deemed to be partial or otherwise unsuitable to sit in judgment.

The second principal theme of this book—accompanying the
emphasis on the jury's expanding workload and competency—
addresses more directly the social dimensions of jury service. If it is
true that juries had a heavy workload from early in their history, and if
it is also true that their workload went up dramatically in the thirteenth and fourteenth centuries, then it follows that many more
jurors were needed in 1250 than 1150, and many more still in 1350
than 1250. In these circumstances, a symmetry emerged between the
growing emphasis on jury procedure in law and government and a
growing acceptance of jurors from less elevated social backgrounds.
Sheriffs and bailiffs inevitably responded to the demands for greater
numbers of jurors by selecting people who in earlier phases of the
jury's development would have been deemed unsuitable or ineligible
to serve. The net result was that by the second half of the thirteenth
century, and probably even earlier still, peasants were regularly drawn
into jury service and came to constitute a significant portion of all
jurors serving in the period.

Chapter 4 develops this argument by looking at the formal qualifications for jury service in the period. The central government's
expectations about juror quality can be reconstructed from routine
administrative documents, which emphasize that jurors had to be free
and lawful, as well as from statutes and other royal enactments, which
emphasize that jurors had to be men of substance and property. In
both cases, the assumptions about what made a juror suitable for service are worth probing for clues about how the system worked in
practice. Even more revealing, however, is the evidence in official
sources of problems confronted when jurors described as "useless" or
"impoverished" turned up. Royal officials were under such pressure
to find jurors that they often simply ignored the formal qualifications
altogether, implying that they were casting about for jurors, not just
among peasants but sometimes even well down into the ranks of the
peasantry.

Chapter 5 takes this social analysis a step further by examining the
surviving lists of jurors associated with particular cases or inquests. By
cross-referencing the individuals appearing on these lists with other
contemporary evidence about property and wealth, it is possible to

discern patterns in the composition of different types of juries. The chapter presents summaries of juror profiles associated with each of the four main forms of jury active in the period. This detailed profiling confirms that peasants frequently served as jurors, including in some instances peasants who were of modest means even by the standards of village society. But it also reveals that many juries were made up of several social levels, ranging from knights and wealthy gentry on one end of the spectrum to middling peasants on the other. The composition of individual juries fluctuated somewhat according to the magnitude or sensitivity of the issue set before them, but what is most striking about the juries discussed in chapter 5 is their social heterogeneity.

There are, of course, many other issues about medieval juries that would merit fuller investigation. The internal dynamic of jury deliberation begs for further research. One of the most interesting differences between the medieval and modern jury systems is that medieval jurors frequently brought detailed knowledge of cases to court with them, whereas modern jurors have minimal knowledge about cases before they hear evidence presented in court.[15] But the extent of this local knowledge and the role it played in guiding juror deliberations is hard to pinpoint, although it would obviously be worth knowing about. The matter is touched on several times in this book, but never in a sustained or systematic fashion. The same can be said for the relationship between judge and jury. Jurors were coordinated and supervised by royal justices, or other royal officials in the case of inquests, who instructed jurors on points of law and evidence, much as judges do today.[16] But medieval justices were more assertive and directive than their modern counterparts, and their ability to influence juries and shape verdicts needs more attention than it has hitherto received. Finally, it would be useful to compare the operation of juries in England with similar bodies elsewhere. Inquest and trial juries were known in medieval Scandinavia, for example, while assize juries played a central role in resolving property disputes in Normandy in the thirteenth century.[17] And yet, England was the only country to put the jury at the heart of its legal and administrative procedures; nowhere else did the jury system enjoy the vitality and longevity it enjoyed in England. The one exception to the rule is Scotland, where jury procedure was prominent in law and administration, but only after wholescale borrowing of institutional forms while the two countries were politically intermingled.[18] The distinction between England and continental Europe was clearly due to differences in state-building in different areas, but it would be worth knowing more about the specific developments that explain why different jurisdictions took different paths.

If these subjects seem worth pursuing, or at least worth thinking about from a different perspective, this book will have achieved its aim. My goal has been to situate the history of the jury system more directly in the context of medieval society and to explore the implications of the jury's growth for the people who lived at the time. Whether this enterprise has been successful or even worthwhile is now for the reader to judge.

CHAPTER 1

SWORN INQUESTS

In early April 1360, Henry Peverell, royal keeper of the town of Southampton, received a writ from Westminster instructing him to look into the state of the town's defenses.[1] War with France had broken out once again, and Norman ships had been spotted recently near Winchelsea. Southampton had suffered devastating destruction earlier in the Hundred Years War and suddenly seemed vulnerable once again: On a recent visit to the town, Thomas of Woodstock, the king's son and guardian of the realm, had come away with serious misgivings about the town's ability to withstand an assault. Combatants on both sides of the English Channel knew that without Southampton's extensive shipping and port facilities, England's military fortunes would be seriously impaired.

Upon receiving the writ, Peverell acted quickly and set up three juries of enquiry. The juries were diligent and within the space of about three weeks had reviewed the town's fortifications and developed a plan for addressing the most serious problems. They advocated thickening the walls in certain places, filling in some of the gateways, building sentry boxes in selected locations, and adding or modifying a number of other fortifications. The jurors also made several recommendations affecting the areas near the walls. Within the walls, property owners were to remove dung piles and other impediments that blocked movement along the adjacent inner path; beyond the walls, abutting houses were to be removed and all of the contiguous gardens and orchards were to be uprooted.

The recommendation concerning the houses and orchards outside the walls proved to be contentious. In a letter sent to Thomas of

Woodstock while the frenzied implementation of the jurors' recommendations was in full swing, Peverell described the difficulties he encountered while attempting to remove various apple and pear trees.[2] The owner of one of the extramural orchards threatened the workers who came to uproot his fruit trees, and the ensuing dispute jeopardized an essential part of the defensive plan; removal of the trees was deemed necessary to deny the French a source of building material that might be used to construct ladders for a siege. Though Peverell had been instructed to carry out all of the recommendations made by the inquest juries, the opposition he encountered on this key matter led him to request a further mandate dealing specifically with the orchards and gardens. His letter to Woodstock ends on a plaintive note: "If it please you, discharge me of this office and appoint others in my place, as I can no longer endure the labor."

In the end, the French did not attack Southampton; the Treaty of Bretigny was signed only a few months later, ending hostilities and ushering in a decade of relative peace. The fate of the town's orchards is unknown. For present purposes, the key element of the whole affair is not the specific measures that Henry Peverell implemented to confront the threat facing Southampton; of greater interest is the procedure used to deal with it. A striking feature of the story is the central role played by the three inquest juries. Confronting a situation of great military urgency and palpable danger, those in power deliberately chose to entrust the direction of policy to several local committees. Both Thomas of Woodstock and Peverell recognized the flaws in Southampton's defenses, and both probably had a good idea of what needed to be done to rectify the situation, yet neither acted by fiat. They opted instead to place their trust in the findings of local investigative juries, and both used the juries' findings as the basis for their actions. Peverell's letter was, in fact, written chiefly to explain why he had delayed in carrying out the recommendations recorded in the inquest verdict, a copy of which he was using to guide his actions.

While the circumstances that gave rise to the inquests in Southampton were exceptionally grave, the methods used to deal with them were part of a well-established routine. English kings made regular and frequent use of sworn inquests throughout the later medieval centuries; by 1360, they had nearly 300 years of experience with inquests and tens of thousands of precedents for what the jurors in Southampton were asked to do. During those centuries, the sworn inquest evolved from an occasional and irregular method of royal enquiry into a core institution of administration and law, one that could be used to make decisions in a truly remarkable array of circumstances.

This chapter presents an overview of the work performed by inquest juries in medieval England. Its basic argument is that the sworn inquest was both a forerunner of other better-known jury forms and a distinctive form of jury in its own right. The first part of the argument is not original to this book, although it is one that has often been overlooked by scholars interested primarily in the history of trial juries. The second part of the argument—that the inquest jury should be treated as a separate and ongoing form of jury even after the emergence of trial juries—is more original and will therefore be developed at greater length. This part of the argument is important for two reasons. First of all, it justifies the inclusion of a greater range of source material for studying the jury's development in later periods, a point that will be apparent throughout the course of this book. Second, it helps to explain how and why the other forms of jury developed as they did. Throughout the medieval period, and well beyond, the history of the jury is best told as a narrative of politics and law. A central part of the narrative involves the process of state building, which medieval English kings were particularly good at, and for these kings, the sworn inquest was a particularly valuable tool. If this perspective is adopted, then the work that trial jurors performed can be seen as an extension of the kind of work that the inquest jurors in Southampton did in 1360, and the history of all forms of jury service is enriched as a result. It is true that over the course of time, legal experts managed to draw distinctions between sworn inquests and other jury types, but for the vast majority of people who served on them, service on a sworn administrative inquest differed little from service on a jury constituted to resolve a property dispute or a question of guilt. Even in the courts, juries assumed several different forms, and the differences between the forms were at least as great as the differences separating each type from the kind of sworn administrative inquest put to use in Southampton in 1360. Indeed, though all jury forms were related to one another, only the sworn inquest can claim direct kinship with each of the other forms.

The chapter has three main sections. The first looks at the early development of sworn inquests and presents evidence for the quasi-judicial role of inquest juries in the twelfth and early thirteenth centuries. The second section explores the history of administrative inquests in the thirteenth and fourteenth centuries, the period in which they took on a mature form that then persisted well into the early modern period. This is the period in which the role of sworn inquests has often been overlooked by scholars, whose attention has focused on trial juries, particularly criminal trial juries, which rose to the fore in the court system. It is, however, also the period in which sworn inquests underwent dramatic expansion and became core features of English government and administration, with significant repercussions for society as a whole as well as for the king and other members of the political elite. For this reason, the second section delves into some of the uses to which sworn inquests were put. A key idea is that inquests operated as venues for information exchange between center and periphery. Acquisition of information became one of the central concerns of English government in the period and served to link the history of sworn inquests and trial juries: The information exchange that characterized sworn inquests essentially mirrored the more familiar exchange between trial juries and royal justices that occurred in a court of law. The third section develops the idea of information exchange further by looking at the frequency with which inquests were commissioned. It also returns to the issue of chronology, suggesting that sworn inquests went through three major phases of development between the eleventh and fourteenth centuries, phases that are of interest with respect to the development of other jury forms as well as to the history of state formation.

EARLY DEVELOPMENT OF THE INQUEST

The sworn inquest was the rootstock onto which other forms of jury were grafted. This seemingly simple and straightforward assertion, though widely accepted, has given rise to extensive debate and disagreement among historians. The first to assert it was Sir Francis Palgrave, a former Keeper of the Public Records, who wrote about the matter in 1832 with remarkable acuity.[3] Palgrave's observations on the relationship between sworn inquests and other forms of jury are still essential reading today, nearly 200 years after they were first published. Later in the nineteenth century, the German historian Heinrich Brunner built upon Palgrave's work, placing particular emphasis on the connections between earlier forms of Carolingian inquests and the forms of inquest that emerged in England after the Norman Conquest.[4] Both Frederic William Maitland and William Stubbs accepted the views put forward by Palgrave and Brunner, and in so doing, they helped to establish them as normative for much of the twentieth century.[5] When, in 1918, Charles Homer Haskins demonstrated the importance of inquest procedure in Normandy before 1150, the dossier appeared to be complete.[6]

In 1959, however, R. C. Van Caenegem issued a major challenge to the established model, arguing that Brunner and his supporters had overstated the importance of the inquest jury as a forerunner of the jury.[7] While acknowledging that inquest procedure had a role to play in shaping later forms of juries, Van Caenegem argued that the Anglo-Saxons had also employed a "popular" form of jury to settle disputes and that this popular jury continued to function after the inquest jury had been introduced. He thus advocated a double origin for the juries to be found in more settled form in the later twelfth century and suggested that one of the major achievements of the Common Law was the successful merging of the two anterior forms of jury, one stemming from continental forms of administrative inquest and the other from Anglo-Saxon forms of trial. Van Caenegem's views were in turn challenged by Doris Stenton, who rejected the argument that popular juries operated under the Anglo-Saxons in the way Van Caenegem depicted them.[8]

In recent decades,, a consensus on the subject has not materialized. Historians have, in general, been inclined to emphasize the sophistication of late Anglo-Saxon government and to recognize the extent to which it influenced early Norman administration.[9] There has been a corresponding tendency to downplay the role of the Normans in introducing the jury to England. Mike Macnair has, for example, recently drawn attention to continental parallels before and after the Norman Conquest and argued against a close association between the Normans and the adoption of sworn inquests in England.[10] David Roffe has similarly advocated a role for inquest procedure in the Anglo-Saxon period, although he also adumbrates the importance attributed to it by the Normans in making it a central feature of English government.[11] Patrick Wormald has written the most influential rehabilitation of Anglo-Saxon law, emphasizing the vitality of public peacekeeping as an aspect of kingship in the tenth and eleventh centuries and stressing the institutional continuity between Anglo-Saxon legal forms and those employed in the formal jury procedures of the twelfth and later centuries.[12]

In general, though, the recent debate about the origins of the jury has not been pursued with much fervor. Historians are, in general, more willing to recognize direct relationships between Anglo-Saxon and early Norman law and the forms of Common Law that crystallized in the later twelfth and thirteenth centuries, but they have also been inclined to heed Marc Bloch's famous admonition to steer clear of the "idol of origins."[13] It is, of course, always appealing for historians to look at the earliest forerunners of important institutions, but it is also important to keep in mind that these forerunners do not necessarily reveal very much about how the institutions actually worked in a later period. In the case of juries, one can certainly find antecedents in the tenth and early eleventh centuries, but if one wants to understand how juries became so central to English law and government, the answer must be sought not by looking at the nature of these early forerunners but by looking at what happened in the two centuries after the Norman Conquest.

Though no longer treated as the watershed event leading to the adoption of the jury system, the arrival of the Normans still deserves attention as an important step in that direction. Particularly significant in this regard was King William I's decision to use inquest juries on a grand scale to create the *Domesday Book* of 1086.[14] William had neither the resources nor the administrative skill to conduct such an extensive survey solely by means of royal officials who knew little or nothing about the villages they were scrutinizing. Instead, he relied on small groups of local people to provide the information he wanted for the survey. To minimize the risk of cheating and misrepresentation, he insisted that the people who provided the information swear an oath affirming the truthfulness of what they were saying, or, in other words, that they deliver a verdict to his officials. His limited staff of administrators could thus function more as supervisors and recorders of information than as primary investigators.

It is easy to overlook the central role played by juries in the construction of *Domesday Book*, because William the Conqueror's scribes skillfully recast the original returns about local assets and conditions into the form that was bequeathed to posterity, privileging the details about assets and conditions and eliminating most of the details about the juries used to furnish information.[15] There was nothing mischievous or malicious in their behavior; it was simply that the king and his officials viewed the method by which they learned about local conditions as incidental to the main purpose of crafting the survey and therefore as something that did not need to be carefully recorded or preserved. Later court records frequently display a similar mindset: The final verdict is often treated as the only part of the jury's work that merits preservation; accounts of how the jury operated, and often even the names of the jurors, are frequently omitted from the final record of events.

An inquest held by a Norman king largely as an accounting exercise might seem to have only a tenuous connection with a jury employed to determine matters of life and death in later centuries, but the connection is actually quite direct and important. For one thing, the formal components of inquests were closely related to the formal components of jury verdicts delivered in courts. Both were charged with deliberating on a specific matter assigned by a higher authority, usually the king himself or someone representing him.[16] Both deliberated collectively with the expectation that their deliberations would produce a consensus. Both acted as independent bodies that worked toward a consensus without the direct involvement of other officials, although the results of their deliberations were typically subjected to scrutiny and review. Even the Latin terminology used in official documents to refer to jurors throughout the Middle Ages (including *juratores, recognitores,* and *duodecim)* was common to both. Finally, both inquest jurors and other types of jurors stated the results of their deliberations under oath. The terminology referring to the oath (*sacramentum)* and to the sworn "verdict" (*veredictum)* was interchangeable, and the oath's purpose and meaning, as well as its structure and form, was common to both.

In addition to similarities in form, inquest procedure also often served the same purpose as a jury verdict. When the formal Common Law procedures emerged in the second half of the twelfth century, jury verdicts did not simply supersede the older form of the inquest; rather, the two coexisted as similar and related procedures that the courts would use depending on circumstances.[17] Indeed, the two were so closely intertwined that it is not always possible to distinguish between an inquest verdict and a jury verdict in surviving court records. Ultimately, the two did retain distinctive identities: Inquest verdicts were ordinarily delivered outside of court, whereas jury verdicts were ordinarily delivered to royal justices in the context of a court session. The distinction was usually maintained in terminology: Inquest verdicts were generally referred to as "inquisitions" (*inquisitiones)* whereas court-based verdicts were referred to as "verdicts" (*veredicta)* or "sworn statements" (*sacramenta,* a word that also means "oaths"). But the boundaries between what went on inside the courts and what went on outside of them were permeable. For one thing, much of the work that jurors did before delivering their verdict to a royal justice took place outside of the court session in which the verdict was delivered; unlike in our modern system, jurors were expected to know the details related to a particular case before they gathered in court. Though they sometimes learned things in court that influenced their final verdict, in most cases, their verdict was based on what they knew or learned before the formal trial began. For another thing, justices sometimes ordered that inquests be held on matters raised in court and treated the result of such inquests as equivalent to jury verdicts. In 1227, for example, justices in the king's principal court (the *Curia Regis)* decided that the way to determine if a woman in

Hampshire had been denied her dower was to conduct an inquest that empanelled jurors who had been present at the woman's wedding and thus knew what her husband had promised as dower; they postponed judgment while they waited for the results of the inquest to be sent to them.[18] ("Dower" refers to the property pledged by a husband for the support of his wife should he predecease her).[19] In cases like these, two of the jurors who served on the inquest were required to deliver the written verdict to the justices, and the document they delivered had to bear the seals of all of the inquest jurors.[20]

In other early property disputes, inquest verdicts sometimes awarded property rights directly. The record of a case heard in the King's Court in 1212, for example, rehearses the following series of events.[21] The prioress of Amesbury laid claim to 90 acres of land with pasture rights and two homesteads in the Wiltshire village of Barford, which had previously been held by a certain Beatrice. When Beatrice died, the sheriff seized the land, presumably because he thought that the king had an interest in the property, although the nature of the king's interest is not specified. The prioress made her way to the king to complain about the sheriff's seizure and to explain why the land rightfully belonged to her. After hearing her account, the king wrote to the sheriff, instructing him to put the prioress in possession of the property, with the proviso that he should do so only if he could verify her story. The sheriff held an inquest to look into the matter. The inquest supported the prioress's story, and the sheriff then put her in possession of the land. A similar procedure by inquest is also apparent in a dower dispute heard in the King's Court in 1196.[22] In that year, Roger de Leus filed a suit against his mother for taking a greater share of the family lands than was her right as a widow. The justices resolved the dispute by ordering the sheriff to convene an inquest to examine the family's property, stipulating that if the inquest found that the widow was, in fact, controlling more land than she was entitled to, then the surplus should be given to Roger.[23]

Inquest verdicts were particularly likely to serve as surrogates for court verdicts when the king had a direct interest in the case. They were used, for example, when someone called into question the boundaries of a royal forest; the resulting inquest jury would then conduct a perambulation of the forest to determine the bounds.[24] Similarly, inquest procedure was often used when the king's rights as a landlord were in dispute, as, for example, in disputes regarding the services of tenants who held land on the royal demesne.[25] Misconduct by royal officials was also often tried by means of inquest juries. In 1234, a plaintiff in Worcester claimed that the county's sheriff had beaten him up, tied his hands behind his back so tightly that he lost the use of his fingers, and detained him in prison for four days, solely as a result of a property dispute.[26] The plaintiff's suit sought damages for the sheriff's abuse of office. For his part, the sheriff claimed that the plaintiff had first committed an aggressive seizure of property and had then put up armed resistance when the sheriff tried to return the land to the previous holder. He acknowledged the incarceration but stated that he had not used undue force. The justices ordered an inquest jury to examine the conflicting accounts and postponed judgment until they had the inquest verdict in front of them.

Perhaps the most striking use of inquest verdicts in a judicial context is provided by cases involving excusable or justifiable homicides.[27] In the thirteenth century, and possibly already in the twelfth century, individuals arrested for homicide could petition the king for a speedy trial by alleging that they had killed unintentionally and accidentally or while defending themselves from mortal danger. These petitions were designed not only to shorten the period of incarceration but also to secure a royal pardon for an act of excusable homicide. If the king judged the prima facie evidence accompanying such a petition to be credible, he usually responded by commissioning a justice to convene a jury to look into the matter. But, he also sometimes chose to make use of inquest procedure rather than formal trial procedure to learn the truth of the matter. These special inquests were convened before a sheriff or a coroner and frequently led to a formal pardon.[28] In 1258, for example, Andrew Bucstan of Huntingdon was pardoned for the slaying of Richard de Freskeneye, who was in his service.[29] Freskeneye had been killed by a blow from Bucstan's sword, a blow that a jury deemed accidental: Freskeneye happened to be sitting beside a trestle that Bucstan was using to test the rigidity of a sword he had just purchased and was mortally wounded by a blow that glanced off the trestle. Bucstan was pardoned for the slaying.[30] The jury verdict that secured Bucstan his pardon was promulgated by inquest procedure; on the king's command, the inquest was held by the county coroners in the presence of the sheriff.

A related procedural method used when dealing with accusations of felony took the form of inquests *de odio et athia,* literally inquests "concerning hatred and malice."[31] By means of this procedure, individuals accused of felony, usually homicide, could have a special inquest jury render a verdict about the circumstances that led to the accusation. As in other forms of inquest, verdicts were rendered locally in the presence of a royal official and did not necessarily require the presence of a royal justice, although they were often held in front of justices assigned to oversee the proceedings. The jurors in these cases were asked to determine the validity of an accused person's claim to have been indicted spitefully by an enemy intent on harassment. The inquests are filled with remarkable anecdotes about the social dynamics of medieval villagers and townspeople. In 1276, for example, three carpenters were wrongly accused of murder by a man who had hired them to work on his house; the man accused them out of spite because they had quit before finishing the job.[32] A father in Cornwall accused a man of murder after he had run off with his eldest daughter and known her carnally.[33] An inquest jury in Kent rejected a man's claim of spiteful accusation, explaining that he was reasonably accused because his dog, who followed him everywhere, had been seen near the corpse, but went on to note that the canine was a false clue because someone else had committed the crime.[34]

These documents underline the close association between inquests and court-based jury verdicts, at a time well after the emergence of jury trial as the normative procedure for criminal cases. If an inquest *de odio et athia* determined that the felony accusation was justified, the accused remained in custody with a strong presumption of guilt. A jury verdict in court was necessary to hang the person, probably because the king and his justices were committed to the position that capital sentences ought to be imposed directly by the Crown. But trial juries usually agreed with the inquest verdict; Naomi Hurnard found that trial juries corroborated the inquest verdict in more than 80 percent of the cases that allow for comparison.[35] Even more significant, though, are the early examples (before 1215) showing that exoneration by an inquest jury was decisive on its own and did not necessarily require further trial.[36] This can be partly attributed to the fluidity in the forms of criminal trial that characterized the first decades of the thirteenth century, but it also demonstrates the comparability of sworn verdicts made by inquest juries and by juries acting in formal court settings.

The Ongoing Role of Inquest Procedure

As the inquests concerning hatred and malice suggest, inquests continued to play a significant role in court procedure well into the fourteenth century, when Common Law procedures had become relatively settled and regularized. The role of inquest verdicts had itself come to be more regularized over time. By the later thirteenth century, justices came to assert that while inquest verdicts could serve as acceptable surrogates for verdicts delivered in court, they carried less weight. They were treated, in effect, as initial solutions to problems or disputes, the import of which depended on the willingness of interested parties to abide by them. A disappointed party could challenge them by resorting to a higher procedural form, but they did so knowing that the first round of the dispute had been clearly won by the opposing side. The trend toward viewing inquests as a lesser form of verdict was part of a general process by which justices developed a hierarchical conception of jury verdicts, with inquest verdicts at the base and Grand Assize verdicts at the apex. A good illustration of this mind-set is provided by a case recorded in a Year Book in 1312, in which a woman expressed a desire in court to have a Grand Assize determine her right to a messuage.[37] Justice Scrope sought to dissuade her from doing so, stating that a messuage was such a small holding that an inquest verdict ought to suffice. As Scrope's exasperated comment indicates, inquest procedure was generally simpler and faster than other forms of trial, which no doubt explains its ongoing popularity with the courts.

In addition to its role as a surrogate for court-based jury verdicts, however, inquest procedure also continued to serve as a mechanism for gathering and conveying information to the king in a variety of nonjudicial or quasi-judicial contexts.[38] Kings employed it, for example, to investigate complaints of misgovernment and corruption. Many of these investigations were conducted on a broad national scale in the tradition of *Domesday Book*. Henry II, for example, sought to uncover the misdeeds of sheriffs by this means in 1170 when he commissioned his ambitious "Inquest of Sheriffs."[39] Each jury involved in the inquest was asked to report on multiple aspects of a sheriff's office: Had the king's manors in the county been managed appropriately? Had taxes been collected conscientiously? Were new laws being implemented effectively? Had the sheriff taken bribes? Information was also solicited on the misdeeds of royal messengers and forest officers, and, for good measure, the king wanted the juries to report the income of all lords in the kingdom. A contemporary chronicler referred to it as a "miraculous inquest" (*inquisitio mirabilis*), but unfortunately only a small number of the returns have survived to illustrate the conditions of government under the first Angevin king. The form of oath taken by the jurors is, however, distinguished in a surviving text commissioning the inquest, and some of the surviving returns are clearly described as verdicts (*veredictum*).[40]

A century later, King Edward I ordered a similarly sweeping examination of royal government in 1274–75, generating the series of records known as the "Hundred Rolls."[41] Edward provided the juries in the inquest of 1274–75 with a list of 45 different questions relating to the conduct of local government and instructed them to deliver their answers under oath. Juries were also invited to present information about any matters that did not fit under any of the supplied rubrics. A substantial number of the verdicts from the inquest have survived and they provide a remarkably detailed picture of the workings of English government in the 1270s. Complaints about the misdeeds of bailiffs are especially prominent in the returns but one can also find in them an extraordinary assortment of other matters, ranging from jurisdictional squabbles over obligations to attend local courts to economic concerns involving such things as the unauthorized export of wool and the collection of tolls.

Not content to stop with what he had learned in 1274–75, Edward I constituted an even more exhaustive enquiry into the state of the kingdom only a few years later in 1279–80.[42] This time around, Edward's primary aim was to compile a register of landholders in the kingdom, for reasons that are not entirely clear. Only a handful of counties have surviving returns from this inquest, but the level of detail in the surviving returns is staggering. In addition to the holdings of lords and knights, the returns document thousands upon thousands of smaller tenants, including many who held little more than a cottage or a few odd acres of land. Some sense of the magnitude of information supplied by the juries in 1279–80 can be gained from a comparison with *Domesday Book*. The village of Alconbury in Huntingdonshire provides a good illustration. In *Domesday Book*, the essential features of Alconbury are described in about 50 words of text; in 1279, the jurors' statement comprises somewhere in the neighborhood of 5,000 words.[43] The *Domesday* entry tersely notes that the village was home to 35 peasant tenants; the Hundred Roll entry names several hundred tenants individually and records the size of each one's holding and annual rent payment. One cannot help but admire the energy and ability of the jurors who reported on local conditions in response to the king's demand in 1279.

Many similar examples of the use of inquest procedure to solicit information about the state of the kingdom could be offered. Inquests were used to enforce the terms of the assize of arms in the later twelfth century; they were used to determine who ought to take on the obligations of knighthood in the later thirteenth; and they were used to investigate why the king had failed in his attempt in 1341 to institute a tax modeled on the tithes of the Church.[44] They were also particularly likely to be pressed into service during and after bouts of political turmoil. In the late 1260s, for example, Henry III made extensive use of inquests to determine who had joined the Barons' Revolt and what property belonged to the identified rebels; Richard II behaved in a similar fashion after the Merciless Parliament of 1388 and again at the end of his reign; and Henry IV also followed suit when his rule was challenged.[45] Though obviously more politicized than their counterparts in *Domesday Book* and the Hundred Rolls, the verdicts that informed the king about the activities and possessions of rebels were cut from the same cloth as those that dealt with property rights and the petty corruption of local officials.

Such large-scale applications of sworn inquests reveal how central inquest procedure was to the conduct of English government in the Middle Ages. But focusing on the instances when royal officials convened thousands of local juries in short order across the kingdom as a whole can distort as well as clarify the work these juries did on a more regular basis. The major national inquests constitute the tip of an iceberg; submerged beneath them is a tremendous mass of local inquests conducted as matters of routine. A good example of this more routine use of inquests can be found in the series of records known as inquisitions *post mortem*.[46] Individuals who held land directly from the king— "tenants-in-chief"—were obliged to pay certain dues to the king whenever their land changed hands, usually as a result of inheritance. Any heir of a tenant-in-chief who had not reached the age of majority (defined as 21 for men and 14 for women) also became a ward of the king, and the king took control not only of the ward but also of his or her property until he or she reached the age of majority. As guardians, kings were also entitled to negotiate marriage arrangements on behalf of their wards, an entitlement that was particularly worth having when property happened to descend to an heiress.

To capitalize on their position with respect to tenants-in-chief, kings needed reliable information about the status of specific tenants and holdings. They basically needed to know four things: Who was the nearest heir entitled to inherit the property? Had they attained the age of majority? What property were they entitled to inherit, and how much was it worth? At first glance, it might seem surprising that a government capable of producing surveys like *Domesday Book* and the Hundred Rolls did not simply keep a register that could be consulted as needed, but on further reflection, one can see how difficult it would have been to keep such a register current. The difficulties were innumerable: Holdings had to be divided among heiresses if no heirs could be found; marriages created new patrimonies as properties from both husband and wife came together; subsequent remarriages further complicated titles to property and lines of descent; and potential heirs and heiresses renounced their inheritances in favor of a religious life. The list goes on and on. Furthermore, the value of a tenant's holding might change substantially over the course of his or her lifetime, depending on unpredictable life events associated with inheritance and marriage. Yet, the king needed relatively specific information to enforce his rights. He needed to know the value of his tenant's lands, since the inheritance tax (the relief) was partly determined by value. He needed to know if the nearest heir was male or female, since land passed intact to an eldest son but had to be divided among daughters. And he also needed to know the age of the heir, since his entitlements as lord of a new tenant of majority age were very different from his entitlements as guardian of a minor.

Rather than rely on a written register, English kings made use of their living repository of information about local conditions, the sworn inquest. Whenever a tenant-in-chief died, the members of these juries drew on their personal knowledge of the family circumstances of the dead tenant-in-chief, supplemented by some detective work about the current condition of their property, to tell the king what he wanted to know. The royal commands ordering the inquests are known as writs of *diem clausit extremum*, literally writs of "ending one's final day," and they spell out the procedure with admirable precision.[47] The king states in the writ that he has learned of the death of a tenant-in-chief and so orders his official (usually an escheator) to take possession of the tenant's lands until the king issues further instructions. After seizing the land, the official is instructed to "diligently enquire by the oaths of upstanding and lawful men from your bailiwick through whom the truth of the matter can best be known" how much land the deceased held, how much it was worth, and who stood to inherit it.[48] The language used to refer to the jurors involved in the inquest essentially replicates the language used in judicial writs to refer to the empanelling of jurors to try a case.

The ensuing inquest was recorded in a second document that was sent to the king in response to the original writ. This second document, the inquisition *post mortem* proper, rehearses the instructions given in the original writ and then furnishes the details of the deceased's property and heirs. Because both the genealogical details and the property valuations are so rich in detail, the source of the detailed information can be easily overlooked, particularly if one is working with the printed calendars of the source. The original manuscript sources almost invariably state that the information is supplied "by means of an oath" (*per sacramentum*) and go on to name the men who took the oath. Following the listing of the jurors' names, the documents typically mark the transition to the description of the property by reiterating that the jurors "say upon oath" (*dicunt super sacramentum suum*) whatever is revealed in the remainder of the document. At the end of the verdict, reference is often made to the presence of juror seals, appended in accordance with the instructions issued in the king's writ. Historians have long paid heed to the role juror discretion played in determining the outcome of the inquests.[49] But, the form of the modern printed calendar tends to obscure the centrality of juror input to the whole process. First of all, the juror seals have seldom survived, so one of the most tangible expressions of juror involvement in the process has disappeared. Worse yet, the officials at the Public Record Office who compiled the standard calendars of the inquisitions decided to omit the names of the jurors, presumably as a means of saving space.[50] Thus, while it is clear in the calendars that the details were furnished by a jury, the role of the jurors in the process is muted and does not command the reader's attention as directly as do the original manuscript sources. The calendar format inadvertently augmented the role of sheriffs and escheators and downplayed the centrality of the work performed by members of the inquest jury.[51]

A second routine use of inquest procedure emerged from the Crown's willingness to intervene in situations involving potential rather than actual damages to property. In most jurisdictions today, problems involving future contingencies are commonly dealt with by permits and public hearings. In medieval England, the problem was typically handled by means of a special form of inquest known as an "inquest concerning specific damages" (*inquisitio ad quod damnum*).[52] The form and structure of these inquests mirrored those of other inquests, except that the jurors were specifically directed to investigate specific proposals for changes in the use of land, waterways, or public spaces. As in the case of inquisitions *post mortem*, the writ commissioning the inquest ordinarily specified how the assessment was to be carried out. Officials were to make enquiry "by means of an oath of upstanding and lawful men from your bailiwick through whom the truth of the matter can best be known," and they were to authenticate the document with their own seal and the seals of the men who served on the inquest.[53] The documents sent back to the king began with a brief rehearsal of the terms of the writ and went on to indicate that the inquest was made "by means of an oath" of a group of jurors, again usually named, "who say upon oath" what they believe would happen if the proposed changes were allowed.

These inquests concerning potential damages dealt with a remarkably wide range of issues. In 1291, for example, men from the town of

Grimsby approached the king with a plan to divert a waterway near the town to reduce the problem of silting in their harbor. The king ordered a local jury to investigate the situation, and the jury found that while the diversion would be beneficial for the town, it would also create problems for local mill-owners and landowners who had pastures abutting the watercourse.[54] A Hampshire jury reached a similar verdict in 1276 when asked to examine a plan to open the river Itchen to navigation between Southampton and Winchester; the proposed route would be so useful to merchants and traders, the jurors said, that "they could not in any way estimate its value," but the river could be made navigable only by tearing down a number of valuable mills on the river.[55] Even relatively mundane changes could require investigation by inquest. In 1302, for example, an inquest was held to determine potential damages if three stallholders in the marketplace in Norwich were allowed to enclose their stalls (the jury saw no problem with the plan).[56] Situations like these were amenable to private lawsuits, including suits of trespass, if the damage actually occurred. But, it was not always certain before someone acted whether others would be harmed. It was always possible that a river would still be navigable after a mill was built, or that a forest would still provide adequate forage even after part of it was cleared, or that an alternate path would be found when a familiar one was closed off. Preservation of the status quo was not an ideal in and of itself, nor was it deemed necessary or even desirable to prevent landowners from improving their property whenever the mere possibility of indirect damages arose.

A third category of inquisitions associated with a more nebulous set of governmental routines defies easy labeling or description. When the archivists of the Public Record Office sifted through the great mass of Chancery inquisitions in the late nineteenth and early twentieth centuries, they decided to arrange the documents into three principal groups, comprising the inquisitions *post mortem*, the inquisitions *ad quod damnum*, and everything else.[57] They termed this third group "inquisitions miscellaneous" and began to publish summaries of the documents in a series titled *Calendar of Inquisitions Miscellaneous*. In some respects, the name is well chosen, because the documents assigned to the class deal with an extraordinary range of public affairs. To be sure, certain types of inquests recur in the series, but the most striking feature of the series as a whole is the disparity of its subject matter. This diversity attests to the regularity and overall efficiency of the overarching procedure of conducting inquests as well as to its inherent flexibility. Inquests were such a common and familiar feature of English law and government that they could be routinely assigned to deal with novel, even bizarre, problems.

The bizarre featured prominently in a series of inquests held in Norfolk in 1347. In April of that year, the mayor of Lynn was ordered to conduct an inquest in his town to determine if there was any truth to the rumor that Thomas de Folsham had faked his own death and that his wife Joan and a group of accomplices had staged a fake funeral.[58] The mayor actually held four separate inquests into the matter on four successive days and sent all four to the king. They corroborated the rumors, describing when the funeral occurred, who attended, what property those in attendance held, and most importantly, that Thomas de Folsham was in fact still alive. (It was later discovered that Thomas and his accomplices even went so far as to procure a dead body from elsewhere, when they learned that the coroner was planning to exhume the body for an inquest.) The findings of the four inquests led the king to issue a judicial commission to examine the matter further, in the course of which the motives for Thomas's peculiar behavior emerged. Thomas had been involved in a lawsuit involving several properties in Norfolk. The jury in the lawsuit delivered a verdict in his favor, but the losing party had appealed it. Thomas must have expected a reversal of the original verdict, because he had faked his death to prevent the appeal from going forward. The four inquests were simply an intermediate step in sorting out the sordid affair, but their verdicts, and the detective work that went with them, were instrumental to the outcome of the subsequent judicial process.

An equally ingenious case of fraud was uncovered by a local inquest held in Northamptonshire in 1211.[59] In that year, Robert Trian filed a lawsuit against his aunt Juliana, alleging that she had been raising a stranger's baby as her own in order to prevent him from inheriting her land when she died. Juliana claimed that the child was her own flesh and blood, born while she was on a pilgrimage to Canterbury. The sheriff was ordered to conduct an inquest to determine the truth of the matter and to report the results to the justices hearing the case. The inquest itself does not survive, but the court summary of its findings states that "lawful men and women" (a rare instance of women being described as lawful) examined Juliana and concluded that she had not borne a child and, furthermore, that she was not pregnant when she departed on the pilgrimage.[60] Recognizing that she could not refute the findings of the inquest jury, Juliana then admitted that the child was not hers. She confessed that on her way back from Canterbury, she had come across a "poor little woman" (*quadam pauper muliercula*) in London who had agreed to give up her baby. Juliana wanted people to believe that she had given birth to the baby because she loathed her nephew and did not want him to inherit her property.

Even in circumstances that were not *sui generis,* inquest juries had to contend with problems that required careful investigation of unusual situations. These might include such disparate issues as the fate of lost falcons, the causes of riots, the treatment of treasure trove, the circumstances giving rise to abductions, prison breaks, suicides, floods, shipwrecks, acts of arson, and a bewildering variety of other problematic or contentious matters. Many of the issues now included under the rubric of miscellaneous inquisition arose through unique local circumstances, but some of the situations they document involve recurring problems. Questions concerning mental competency can be placed in this category of irregular but recurring inquest. Tenants-in-chief who lost their sanity, for example, became wards of the Crown, and inquest juries were given the task of verifying the tenant's mental state. In one such case in Cornwall in 1396, an inquest jury found that Elizabeth, daughter of William Chaumbernon, had been "continuously from her birth a complete fool and idiot," but her condition had for a long time been covered up.[61] The jurors reported to the king that three days after her father died, a certain William Polglass had married her to gain access to her inheritance; then, two days after Polglass died, a certain John Sergeaux married her for the same reason. In this instance, the king used inquest procedure to protect his own rights, since Elizabeth should have become a ward of the Crown.

Alongside these irregular and occasional sorts of inquest, one finds a handful of situations that gave rise to inquisitions on a more regular, even frequent, basis. Some of the common examples include disputes between landlords and tenants over rents and services; the causes of accidental deaths; the property of convicted felons; the exercise of borough privileges; the misconduct of local officials; the breach of parks, warrens, and fisheries; and, above all, the terms by which tenants of the king held their lands. But even when the root causes were similar, the circumstances revealed in the inquest were often specific to the individual case. In 1281, for example, the king ordered an inquest to be held into the status of a house in Southwark that was part of the ancient demesne.[62] Uncertainties about the current status of royal property gave rise to hundreds of similar inquests between 1200 and 1500. But none dealt with quite the same set of contingencies as in Southwark in 1281. The Southwark inquest jurors reported that the house had once belonged to Godfrey le Marbrer, who had died while on a pilgrimage to the Holy Land. Before leaving, Godfrey had gathered his neighbors together to inform them that his nearest heir was his nephew Simon Everard. Simon, who was living in Worcester at the time, came to the gathering so that his uncle could introduce him to the neighbors. When Simon inherited the house, he agreed to allow his aunt, Godfrey's wife, to stay in it as his tenant. When she died, Simon decided to dwell in it himself for a while but then sold it to Miles le Mareschal. Miles, after holding it for 16 years, had his title challenged in a royal court, and the court decreed that the house should be forfeited to the king because he had failed to acquire a charter recognizing his right of possession. One of the justices then rented the house to Henry le Vineter and his wife Margery and they were living in it at the time the inquest was taken. The record of the inquest does not indicate why the king wanted to know the history of this particular house; he later used it as a pretext for granting the house to Richard le Sauser, suggesting that a request from Sauser may have been the driving force behind the king's demand for a detailed history of the property.[63]

One of the most common tasks assigned to inquest juries was to assess and appraise the value of property that was under the king's control. This was done partly to guide the king's future patronage decisions, but mostly as a means of keeping tabs on the officials who were placed in custody of the property. Instructions about furnishing financial details were routinely included in the writs commissioning inquests, and the surviving inquests were full of assessments and evaluations: The forfeited goods of outlaws and felons; the chattels that caused accidental deaths; the confiscated properties of rebels; and the church lands that accrued to the king in his role as lord and patron of manorial properties had to be given values. Often, the central point of holding an inquest was to determine how much something was worth. In the case of Godfrey le Marbrer's house in Suffolk, the jurors cited the rent that Godfrey had paid to the king, the rent that Godfrey's wife had paid to Simon, and the rent that Henry le Vineter had agreed to pay when he took it over. The information was later referred to in the king's grant to Richard le Sauser.

Some of the inquisitions have remarkably detailed evaluations. A jury ordered to report on thefts from the king's forest in Worcestershire in 1292 itemized dozens of oak and ash trees that were cut down without license, giving different values to each tree.[64] In 1397, the jury charged with evaluating the property that Richard II seized from the Earl of Warwick in the town of Warwick itemized more than

300 belongings, ranging from hay and livestock to clothing and cooking utensils.[65] The earl's property in other counties came in for equally detailed assessment, as did the forfeited property of the Earl of Arundel. When entire manors came into the king's hand, as they did in 1397, every tenant on a manor was sometimes named in a manorial extent, with an individualized rent payment listed after each tenant's name.[66] The price attached to each item in a lengthy inventory must have often been conventional rather than market-based (although tenant rent payments were probably drawn from preexisting rentals or accounts), but the specificity of the language with which many items are described suggests that the jurors gave more than a cursory glance at the property they were evaluating.

GROWTH AND CHANGE IN INQUEST PROCEDURE

Considering the amount of work associated with the holding of most inquests, one cannot help but be impressed by the sheer numbers that were held. Providing an accurate count of the number of inquests held during a given period of time is actually a rather daunting task, because inquisition procedure was so common and could be used in so many different contexts. A figure encompassing all of the inquests held in medieval England would easily number in tens of thousands. Even the National Archives, where most of the inquisitions now reside, has had trouble dealing with the sheer volume of the records: The current archival classifications of the main series of inquisitions designate clusters of multiple documents affiliated with regnal years rather than single inquisitions.

A rough idea of magnitude can be gained from the printed calendars of the three main series of Chancery inquisitions (*post mortem*, *ad quod damnum*, and miscellaneous; the latter calendar includes most of the inquisitions *de odio et athia*). The first decade of Edward III's reign (1327–1336) is relatively well documented and makes a good frame of reference for an exercise of this nature. In that decade, juries participated in more than 600 miscellaneous inquests, in more than 1,100 inquests *ad quod damnum*, and in more than 1,600 inquests *post mortem*, or in more than 3,300 inquests in total.[67] As these figures suggest, the king's officials devoted an enormous amount of their time and energy to the holding of inquests.

As striking as these figures are, however, they do not tell the whole story. Documenting what is missing is difficult, but the circumstances surrounding the production and use of inquisitions made lapses in document survival almost inevitable: Sheriffs and escheators sometimes retained inquest results after they had been taken, and it is hard to imagine that every official returned every inquest held on his watch; Chancery officials sometimes sent them to the Exchequer as evidence related to an audit; and in later centuries, the bundles of inquisitions were subjected to the same unfortunate treatment accorded to most other medieval records.[68] Stray inquests can today be found in several archival classes in the National Archives, some in miscellaneous Chancery records, some associated with the Exchequer, and some residing among the records of the courts.[69] Inquests held by coroners are a good case in point. Coroners were obliged to hold inquests whenever a suspicious death occurred in their area of jurisdiction and while it is clear that they routinely did so, relatively few of their inquests survive, and those that do are not to be found in the three main Chancery series.[70] When all of these other possibilities are taken into account, it is not inconceivable that the figure of 3,300 inquests just calculated would have to be doubled to give an accurate tally of the total number of inquests held between 1327 and 1337.

At first glance, these figures seem surprisingly high, but when they are put in the context of what actually happened on the ground, one can readily see their feasibility. Inquests were commonly held at meetings of the county court, and even when they were held at other venues, they still often had a county focus stemming from the involvement of sheriffs and other county officials. One way to visualize the frequency with which inquests were held is simply to think of the number of inquests in the context of the 39 traditional English counties in which they were held.[71] Such an exercise suggests that the minimal figure of 3,300 inquests in a decade would be met if each county held a minimum of eight or nine inquests every year; even a doubling of this minimal figure would not have overwhelmed local administration. Of course, counties varied significantly in size so that averages can do little more than assist rudimentary contemplation of the phenomenon. One must also bear in mind that counties in the south were governed more assiduously than counties in the north with the likely result that counties near Westminster would have held inquests more often than those far away.[72] But as a general estimate of magnitude, it is reasonable to believe that most counties would have been called on to provide an inquest verdict about once every month. Viewed in this light, one might recognize that service on an inquest jury, while a common and recurring feature of public life in medieval England, did not require a Herculean commitment.

The first decade of Edward III's reign documents a mature phase in the history of medieval inquests, one that persisted with relatively minor changes into the sixteenth century and beyond. But, the decade also stands at the end of a period of growth and change that reaches back to the eleventh century. What, if anything, can be said about chronological development in this earlier period? When did the situation depicted in the second quarter of the fourteenth century come to the fore?

Answers to these questions are not easy to find. The story is greatly complicated, for example, by changing standards of record-keeping. In the twelfth century, royal business was frequently conducted orally without necessarily generating written records; by the fourteenth century, writing had become part of the governing routine, and even the most mundane administrative affairs frequently find their way onto a Chancery roll. There is an inevitable temptation for historians to equate writing with administrative effectiveness and to assume that changes in record production mirror substantive changes in the relationship between the ruling and the ruled. Writing and reality obviously cannot be directly related, although it is also true that quantitative changes in the use of writing often proceed from qualitative changes in governing procedures. Thus, while there is no necessary relationship between the two, it might still be useful to examine possible relationships between the volume of written evidence and the qualitative importance of inquest procedure. In this instance, it seems likely that changes in available documentation do reflect real changes in the use of inquests.

It is clear from the quantity of evidence, for example, that inquest procedure grew substantially in the later thirteenth century. The earliest surviving inquisition *post mortem* dates to 1236, and the standard procedure found in the fourteenth and later centuries came into use only in the 1250s.[73] The total number of such inquests was fixed by the relatively constant pool of tenants-in-chief, but even so, more than twice as many inquests survive for the 35 years of Edward I's reign (1272–1307) than for the preceding 35 years of his father's reign. Much more striking growth is evident in the other two main series of Chancery inquisitions. The series of inquisitions *ad quod damnum* begins in the early 1240s but takes off only during the reign of Edward I (1272–1307). Slightly more than 100 such inquisitions survive for the entire period between 1243 and 1272; by the end of Edward I's reign, that figure was being matched in a single year.[74] The series of miscellaneous inquisitions begins in 1219 and follows a pattern of growth somewhere in between the other two series. The presence of a significant number of undated inquisitions complicates any attempt to calculate averages, but it seems unlikely that more than

SWORN INQUESTS 37

a dozen miscellaneous inquests were held in any year before the
1260s.[75] The end of the Barons' Revolt in 1265 proved to be a real
watershed, as more than 300 inquests were held soon after the battle
of Evesham.[76] This was, however, an unusual response to an unusual
set of circumstances and was not immediately sustained. Conditions
similar to those found before the revolt characterized the last years of
Henry's reign before a pattern of rapid growth emerged in the last
decades of the century.

A second milestone can be found in the reigns of the first three
Angevin kings, Henry II (1154–1189), Richard I (1189–1199), and
John (1199–1216). Albert White long ago demonstrated the frequency with which these kings made use of inquest procedure.[77] The
1170 inquest of sheriffs discussed earlier in this chapter heralds this
development, and the period between 1170 and 1200 witnessed a
number of similarly ambitious undertakings. The Assize of Arms of
1181, for example, stipulated that inquest juries supply information
about the property and income of local people to determine what
kind of arms they ought to bear.[78] Four years later, inquests were used
to create an inventory of wards whose marriages belonged to the king
and also an inventory of the holdings of the Templars.[79] In 1188,
inquest juries were employed to resolve difficulties encountered in the
levying of the so-called Saladin tithe.[80] In the eyres of 1194, inquest
juries reported on the management of lands that had come into the
king's hand in the form of wardships and escheats.[81] Finally, Richard
I's land tax of 1198 (carrucage) also gave rise to a series of inquests
designed to elucidate individual tax burdens.[82] Though such inquests
harkened back to *Domesday* in terms of their scale, their narrower
focus and repeated use also look forward to the inquests of the thirteenth century.

Equally important in terms of future developments was the early
Angevin practice of commissioning "law-worthy" men to furnish
information about local matters of interest to the Crown.[83] These ad
hoc local committees dealt with a great range of business. They frequently supplied information about the current status of royal houses
and castles, sometimes with an eye to military preparedness but more
often to ensure that buildings and other assets received proper maintenance. They also clarified local privileges related to such matters as
attendance at courts, rights over markets and fairs, and the provision
of rents and services. They were even drafted to report on relatively
minor financial transactions in which the king had an interest, such as
the cost of carrying provisions through the countryside or the value
of wine acquired in various ports. In short, much of the same business

that one finds in the main series of Chancery inquisitions beginning in the 1220s can be found several decades earlier. English kings were clearly enamored with inquest procedure well before they committed themselves to the systematic preservation of written verdicts.

Moving back to the late eleventh and early twelfth centuries, one still finds inquests playing a role in royal government, although a greatly reduced one.[84] Henry I (1100–1135) commissioned more than a dozen local inquests during his reign, many dealing with issues that would later generate great business for inquest juries. In 1127, for example, he ordered 24 men to render a verdict about who was enti- tled to collect tolls and other port dues in Sandwich.[85] Similarly, in 1128, he commissioned an inquest into fishing rights in the Tyne river.[86] Other inquests were set up to define boundaries, determine tax liabilities, investigate royal property rights, and establish court privileges.[87] Procedural details are scarce, but the commissioning writs sometimes specify that statements were to be made under oath by local people knowledgeable about the matter at hand and were often coordinated by the sheriff.

But, while it is clear that Henry I sometimes used sworn inquests in ways that herald their role in later centuries, his use of them also differed considerably from that of his Angevin successors. For one thing, Henry appears not to have insisted that the results of the inquests be returned to him. For later kings, receipt of the informa- tion supplied in a jury verdict was an important part of the whole pro- cess. Unlike his successors, Henry I did not view the final verdict as something that necessarily belonged to the Crown. Inquests provided a way to resolve problems, including those associated with royal rights and privileges, but they were not as tightly bound up with the king's desire for information about conditions in the realm as they would be later on.

A related difference stems from the way inquests were commis- sioned. Henry I typically commissioned inquests to resolve problems brought to his attention by people with vested interests in a matter. Later kings often behaved in similar fashion, commissioning inquests in response to complaints presented to them. Complaints were some- times presented formally via judicial commissions or sessions of Parlia- ment, but they were more likely to reach the king through informal or personal channels, as appears to have been the norm in the early twelfth century. In effect, both Henry I and his successors saw the value of placing inquest procedure at the disposal of their subjects, and their willingness to do so accounts for the close kinship between inquest ver- dicts and jury verdicts when the latter emerged as a distinctive judicial procedure.[88] But, later kings also saw inquests as mechanisms for asserting and enforcing their own position. Inquests benefited the king directly: By determining, assessing, and preserving royal property and royal rights, they greatly enhanced his ability to exploit his land and jurisdictional privileges. This may be simply another way of making the obvious assertion that kings had a more expansive idea of royal authority in the fourteenth century than they did in the early twelfth, but it is worth pointing out that inquest procedure had a considerable role to play in this transformation.

A third major difference can be detected in the frequency with which inquests were held. We have already seen that well over 3,000 inquests were held in a single decade in the first half of the fourteenth century. Alfred White found 349 commissions for inquests in the seventeen plus years of King John's reign, not including inquests conducted in association with court procedure.[89] By way of contrast, the inquests of Henry I's thirty-five-year reign can be counted in the tens. The lack of a subject index to the standard edition of Henry's acts compounded by fluidity in the language of the acts themselves makes an exact count difficult, but the total is probably less than the number of Henry's regnal years (35). In the reigns of his Angevin successors, inquests were routinely employed by the courts and royal administration; in Henry's own reign, they were unusual measures used when other more common means of dealing with problems were not suitable.

This contrast in the regularity of usage is well illustrated by looking at some of the occasions when Henry did not commission an inquest in circumstances in which his successors routinely did. At some point before 1125, for example, the abbot of Ramsey claimed exemption from a customary service owed to the king's manor of Brampton.[90] An issue involving both royal property rights and customary services would almost certainly have given rise to an inquest in later centuries, but Henry I merely instructed his sheriff to consider the abbot's proof and to grant the request if the proof seemed reasonable. Or again a few years later, when he wanted to sort out the service owed to Rochester Castle, the king sent a writ of notification to the men of the archbishop of Canterbury, informing them that they should heed whatever the archbishop decided about their terms of service.[91] Similarly, in 1130, Henry notified the sheriff and barons of Nottinghamshire that the bishop of Lincoln could divert a royal road passing through Newark "in whatever way he pleases."[92] A century and a half later, the bishop's plan would automatically have given rise to an inquest *ad quod damnum*. But, perhaps the most revealing contrast involves the procedure adopted to settle a boundary dispute involving the royal manor of Torksey in Lincolnshire.[93] Perambulating inquests were common in the later twelfth and thirteenth centuries and were also a feature of Henry's own reign; the fact that royal property was involved added extra incentive for using an inquest on this occasion. Henry did, in fact, order his sheriff and three other men to lead lawful men of the county "to recognize and divide" the properties in question, but then, he added that if the sheriff had reservations about what the lawful men decided, he should compel the men to confirm what they said on oath. The core feature of later inquests was, in other words, something of a last resort early in the twelfth century.

The fourth and final distinction between the inquests of the early Norman kings and those of their Angevin successors lies in the use made of large-scale enquiries requiring verdicts from many juries on the same matter. *Domesday Book* set an audacious precedent in this regard, but it was one that stood isolated for almost a century after its crafting. Indeed, as Michael Clanchy has shown, William's great survey was seldom consulted before the later twelfth century and played only a minor role in the conduct of government under the Anglo-Norman kings.[94] A possible exception to the general rule occurred in the later 1120s and early 1130s when Henry I commissioned itinerant justices to travel through the kingdom hearing cases and looking into royal interests in the counties they visited.[95] Given the infrequent use Henry made of inquests in other contexts, though, one would be hard-pressed to argue that they featured prominently in the work done in these visitations; they certainly did not take on an entrenched role in royal administration in the following decades. And even if one were to view these traveling courts as venues for holding inquests, one would still be left with a striking contrast between the two halves of the twelfth century in terms of the number of major inquests held.

Viewed as a whole, the evidence related to sworn inquests between the eleventh and the fifteenth centuries suggests three major phases of development. The first phase extends from the late Anglo-Saxon and early Norman period into the second half of the twelfth century. In this period, inquests were used irregularly but just often enough to ensure continuing familiarity and an ongoing role for themselves. Many of the tools needed to use inquests as a regular feature of government simply did not exist at the time, nor, arguably, did a mind-set that emphasized their value. But, though they were peripheral to the overall structure of administration and justice at the time, they did establish models that shaped the future use of inquests. The key procedural features of later inquests were clearly derived from the forms current in this early period, and subsequent changes can be described as evolutionary rather than as revolutionary.

The second phase began during the reign of King Henry II and provides a backdrop for the assertion of royal power that characterizes the rule of the early Angevins. The period was characterized by a proliferation in the number of inquests and a renewed commitment to using inquests to gather information about the state of the kingdom, particularly the state of royal property and rights. Much more than their forerunners, the early Angevins treated inquests as tools that could be used to cut local officials down to size. Kings used them to demand greater accountability from their local officials, officials whose autonomy could now be circumscribed by the assessments, appraisals, and decisions furnished as needed by inquest jurors. Two major refinements of inquest procedure accompanied this development. The first was a growing emphasis on recording the findings of inquest juries. Although inquests did not develop into a separate genre of administrative document before the 1220s, enough fragments of earlier Angevin inquests survive to indicate that the writing down of jury verdicts was intimately associated with the new conception of how inquest verdicts functioned as tools of government. The second refinement worked hand in hand with the more consistent recording of jury verdicts. Jurors came to be named more regularly, their names providing a kind of preamble accompanying the verdicts they gave, and jurors began to seal the documents their work generated. These changes tended to heighten the role assigned to jurors as part of the inquest procedure. Jurors had, of course, always been an integral part of inquest procedure, but the new procedures emphasized both the autonomy of the jury as a corporate group and the responsibility each juror bore for the verdict that was returned to the king. Similar developments were transforming the role jury verdicts played in legal disputes at the same time, as will be seen in chapter 2.

The third discrete phase in the history of inquest procedure began during the reign of King Edward I and carried through to the end of the Middle Ages. The period was characterized by significantly greater use of inquest procedure, with a particularly dramatic increase characterizing the reign of Edward I. Some of the increase resulted from the use of sworn inquests in new areas of administration. The statute of mortmain (*De viris religiosis*) of 1279, for example, created a substantial volume of work for juries assigned the task of reviewing every request for an exemption from the terms of the statute.[96] But, most of the expansion occurred within the framework established under the early Angevins. Later kings were more assiduous in claiming

and managing their property and privileges and much more committed to intervention in local affairs. They were more likely to check
into the behavior of local officials, for example, including bailiffs and
higher officials such as sheriffs; sometimes, they even began to
demand two or more verdicts on the same issue as a check on the
jurors themselves. They were also more likely to use sworn inquests in
response to local demands to redress injustices, curtail violence, and
maintain public order, as the example of the fake funeral in Norfolk
intimates. Sworn inquests and petitions to the king were actually two
sides of the same coin, and the vigorous growth of petitioning in the
later thirteenth and fourteenth centuries brought in its train a corre-
spondingly vigorous growth in the number of sworn inquests.[97]

CONCLUSION

The history of sworn inquests in medieval England thus appears to
have undergone three major transformations, each building on the
preceding one. They were first employed by the early Norman kings;
they were moved to the center of government by the early Angevins;
and they were then vastly expanded by King Edward I. The situation
that emerged at the end of the thirteenth century then held stable
during much of the fourteenth and fifteenth centuries. To a considerable extent, the history of sworn inquests parallels the history of the
Common Law as a whole, as one might expect, given the intimate
relationship between inquests and other forms of legal procedure.
Legal historians have long viewed the innovations introduced by
Henry II as marking the genesis of the Common Law tradition, and
they have been equally likely to point to Edward I's alterations as constituting a second founding era.[98] In both periods, the elaboration
and extension of inquest procedure formed part of broader patterns
of assertive kingship and growing royal power.

The expansion of law and government is, of course, a leitmotif in the
history of the later Middle Ages. Appreciating the contribution of
sworn inquests adds texture and nuance to that history, highlighting in
particular the great appetite English kings had for information and the
ways they went about satisfying that appetite. The phenomenon of
growing state power in the period has often been described in terms of
burgeoning taxation and military ability. Alongside these two, one can
readily place the burgeoning ability of royal governments to develop,
process, and employ information, a transformation due in no small
measure to the success of inquest procedure. But, the story of the
sworn inquest can also be told from the perspective of local society.

Alongside the willingness of the king and his judicial officials to trust the work of inquest jurors, one needs to place the willingness of those jurors to engage in the king's work, to investigate the "truth of the matter," and to make fateful decisions. The remarkable expansion of inquest procedure brought with it an equally remarkable extension of civic duty and participation in royal government. Assessing how and why local people committed themselves to this enterprise will be a central concern in the following chapters.

CHAPTER 2

TRANSFORMING INQUESTS
INTO JURIES

When King Henry II ascended the throne in 1154, England was in
a state of disarray, the result of nearly two decades of debilitating civil
war and political infighting. In the ensuing 35 years of his reign,
Henry and his followers restored order and stability. One of the king's
priorities upon ascending the throne was to rebuild the links between
central government and local society that had been sundered in the
chaos of civil war. Henry threw himself into the art of governing,
a task that appears to have interested him almost as much as hunting
and war. His great insight into medieval governance was to recognize
that access to information was a form of power; in Henry's eyes, a
ruler could be served nearly as well by controlling flows of information as by controlling flows of money and soldiers. Hence his reign
was defined by the construction of a state apparatus intent on acquir-
ing and preserving information, particularly information that could
be used to enhance the rule of law.[1]

In his efforts to construct a state that could serve as the guardian
of peace, Henry and his inner circle found that the sworn inquest was
a particularly versatile and valuable tool. Inquests gave the king direct
and specific knowledge about the state of his kingdom and made
royal authority visible at a local level. Henry made much greater use
of inquest procedure than his predecessors, but his great political
breakthrough came through recognizing that inquests could be used
in a variety of innovative ways. He and his advisors enthusiastically extended inquest procedure to new areas of law and government, transforming the Crown's relationship with its subjects and inaugurating a

transformation in English political life. Their policy was driven by the realization that sworn inquests were well suited to enforce laws as well as provide information about matters of interest to the king. Inquests had sometimes been constituted to serve as judicial bodies before Henry came to the throne, but in Henry's reign they were transformed from occasional devices for exceptional problems into regular and recurring elements of legal process. Indeed, one of the key developments in the emergence of the Common Law tradition associated with Henry's reign was a growing emphasis on sworn inquests, or juries as they can also be called, as vehicles for combating crime and resolving disputes.

This chapter examines the expanding role of the sworn inquest by looking at three of its offspring. These children of the inquest include presentment juries, which reported on criminal activity (among other things, as will be seen); possessory assize juries, which resolved local property disputes using a distinctive form of civil procedure; and criminal trial juries, which determined questions of innocence and guilt. Each of these different forms of jury has a different history and different relationship to the sworn inquest, and each will be described in turn. Only the first two can be associated directly with Henry II's reign; ironically, the criminal trial jury, which is by far the most easily recognized modern descendant of the three forms, was a relative latecomer to the scene. It became a regular feature of English justice nearly half a century after the other two forms had been introduced. It is included in this chapter as a natural, though by no means inevitable, extension of the process that made presentment juries and possessory assize juries regular features of legal practice in the later twelfth century.

PRESENTMENT JURIES

Presentment juries were constituted to provide information under oath about specific matters assigned to them for deliberation. They loom large in the legal culture of medieval England because their brief included reporting on criminal acts, particularly felonies.[2] The term "presentment" is derived from the work the juries performed: They "presented" information to officials, including information about suspected felons. Their presentment served as a formal accusation or indictment, and it became the basis for subsequent trial. If a suspected criminal had not previously been apprehended, the presentment was also tantamount to an arrest warrant. A presentment thus initiated legal proceedings, but it did not end them: A subsequent trial was necessary to determine if the accusation was true.[3] Before 1215, the subsequent trial to determine guilt or innocence typically involved either compurgation (the swearing of oaths by credible character witnesses) or one of the forms of the ordeal (water or hot iron); after 1215, the subsequent trial generally involved a verdict by a trial jury. Presentment was thus a first step in the direction of conviction for felony but was not the equivalent of a conviction.

The origins of presentment have given rise to much debate. The great English legal historian F. W. Maitland thought that while "faint traces" of presentment could be found in earlier periods, the procedure was largely an innovation of Henry's reign.[4] Other scholars have, however, argued that earlier practices left more than "faint traces" on Henry's policy. Anglo-Saxon law made provision of information about criminal behavior a requirement of public life, and a relatively clear reference to a body acting much like later juries of presentment can be found in the late tenth century.[5] Certainty on this matter is hard to come by, but Maitland's view still has much to recommend it. Early references involving public accusation of criminals rarely give procedural details, making it hard to equate them with the specific form of the presentment jury that is well documented in Henry's reign and after. Maitland's dismissal of antecedents was undoubtedly too peremptory, but his general argument that presentment underwent great expansion in Henry's reign still seems sound.

The heart of Henry's effort to establish presentment as a core element of English criminal justice can be found in a legislative enactment in 1166 known as the Assize of Clarendon.[6] The first clause of the enactment stipulates that juries of 12 men should be constituted in every hundred to furnish information on oath to sheriffs and royal justices about robbers, murderers, thieves, and anyone who had aided and abetted them. (Hundreds were administrative subdivisions of counties; their size varied but typically covered between 50 and 100 square miles and included several thousand people dispersed in a dozen or more villages). In addition to constituting a jury that would speak on behalf of the hundred as a whole, the assize of Clarendon also stipulated that presentments should be made by groups of four representatives drawn from each village in the hundred. Both groups were instructed to present criminal acts that had already given rise to earlier public accusation, but both were also instructed to present people who were merely "publicly suspected" (*publicatus*) of having committed a felony. Subsequent clauses describe steps to be taken for the trial of those accused by the presentment juries and emphasize the wide competency of the presentment juries vis-à-vis other local courts.

The central tenets of the assize were updated a decade later in a document known as the Assize of Northampton.[7] For the most part, Northampton simply reiterated the form of presentment that had been outlined at Clarendon. The use of juries of 12 men drawn from each hundred was retained, as was the use of supplemental presentment from the four representatives of each village. More substantive changes were made in the forms of trial permitted to those who had been presented, as well as in the punishments meted out to those who were convicted. The most significant feature of the assize in terms of presentment was the addition of two new felonies—forgery and arson—to the four original felonies that had been defined at Clarendon. The addition of new responsibilities was a harbinger of things to come: In the following centuries, kings gave presentment juries more and more work to do, not so much by expanding the number of felonies on which they reported as by requiring them to provide information on a host of quasi-judicial matters.

In the Assizes of Clarendon and Northampton, Henry conceived of presentment as a standardized and widely disseminated procedure, but he did not insist on it as the sole device for bringing suspected felons to trial. Presentment was intended to supplement rather than replace other forms of accusation and indictment, and it functioned alongside these other forms of indictment throughout its subsequent history. Sheriffs and other royal officials were sometimes able to make what were essentially ex officio indictments after apprehending criminals, although their ability to do so was increasingly circumscribed over the course of the thirteenth and fourteenth centuries. More importantly, individuals could still bring private accusations, known as appeals, against people whose felonies had touched them personally. Private appeals of felony were common throughout the period covered in this book and were even expanded in the fifteenth century as a mechanism for prosecuting crime.[8] But while these alternate forms of prosecuting suspected criminals continued to operate, presentment took over an ever increasing share of criminal indictments in the centuries following the implementation of the Assizes of Clarendon and Northampton. This was partly due to an ongoing expansion in the number of crimes defined as presentable by juries, and partly due to a growing sense that presentment was a better and more efficacious way to bring suspected criminals to court.

Henry conceived presentment as procedure that would work in tandem with periodic visits to each county by traveling royal justices who were commissioned to review law enforcement and determine cases in each county they visited. These periodic itinerant courts, known as eyres, served as venues at which both presentments and trials took place.[9] Presentments about criminal activity were of two types in the eyres. The most common type was effectively an endorsement of an accusation that had already been made in some other venue, either in a local court or before a coroner. When functioning in this capacity, presentment jurors acted as a kind of review board, summarizing charges made by other bodies and presenting the essential details to the king's justices. Sometimes the trial itself had already been conducted in some other court, typically a more streamlined judicial gathering known as a gaol delivery. Eyre justices used these retrospective presentments to confirm that local officials had carried out their duties conscientiously and to monitor the performance of the judicial system since their last visit to the county. Since the justices had documents and other sources of information about earlier arrests and trials, retrospective presentments were also a test of the presentment jury itself, constituting what Irwin Langbein once termed a "grim spelling bee."[10] If the presentment jurors made an error in their summaries or omitted a case or otherwise covered something up that should have been presented, they were fined for their mistake.

The second type of presentment made in the eyres was known as a "private" or "secret" presentment.[11] These were presentments based on suspicions the jurors had about criminal deeds that had not already been acted on at some other venue. They were described as "secret" because of the confidentiality requirement imposed on the jurors who furnished the names of suspects to the justices. Secrecy was deemed necessary to prevent the flight of those who were accused. Even though trial juries regularly exonerated individuals who were accused by presentment juries, the accused often resorted to flight upon learning they had been presented. Confidentiality provided a measure of protection against flight, increasing the likelihood that a suspected criminal would be made to stand trial. These secret presentments could be based on the jurors' own knowledge and suspicions about criminal activity, but they could also be made on the basis of information supplied to the jurors by a third party, such as the village representatives who attended the eyre. Receiving and evaluating information from third parties would ultimately become the main preoccupation of presentment juries in later centuries, but it had become part of the work expected of these jurors by the early thirteenth century and may go back even to the twelfth century.[12]

An important variant form of presentment procedure that was often associated with the eyres came into existence when the office of coroner was created in 1194.[13] Coroners were associated with the holding of crown pleas; the name "coroner" is actually derived from the Latin *corona* meaning "crown." The category of Crown pleas was a somewhat arbitrary assemblage of matters defined as having immediate relevance to the authority of the king. Felonies formed a major part of the Crown pleas because they were defined as acts that disturbed the king's peace. Coroners were often referred to as "custodians" or "keepers" of Crown pleas because they were required to keep a record of such pleas but could not conduct trials related to them. In practice, their primary responsibility involved keeping a record of unnatural deaths, including homicide, suicide, and death by misadventure. Whenever someone found a body that showed signs of violence or raised suspicions about an unnatural mode of death, a coroner had to be called in to investigate. The coroner's investigation was part forensic and part detective. The forensic part involved an examination of the body to look for wounds or other physical marks that might suggest a cause of death. The detective part involved the holding of an inquest to investigate the circumstances that led to the death.

Inquests were conducted using sworn jurors who were likely to know something about how the death occurred. Coroners usually chose the jurors after arriving to inspect the body. In the early thirteenth century, jurors were chosen to represent the four villages or parishes nearest to the place where the body was found; in later periods, jurors tended to be drawn from the hundred at large, but were generally still made up of men from nearby villages or neighborhoods. The jurors had to view the body along with the coroner and their verdict typically included details about the wounds and other physical evidence they observed. After viewing the body, the jurors usually retired with the coroner to a more comfortable venue to hold the inquest. Like all forms of presentment in the period, the formal part of the inquest was conducted as a series of questions and answers. The coroner's questions were designed to elicit information about the circumstances leading up to the death, the presence or absence of witnesses, and the name or names of the suspected killer or killers.

The verdicts of inquest jurors were linked to presentment procedure in two ways. First of all, the verdicts in cases of homicide were themselves a form of presentment that could initiate a trial. If the jurors named a suspect or any accomplices, the coroner issued an order for their arrest. The trial had to wait until the coming of royal justices assigned to visit the county to hear felony cases. Justices sometimes held trials in the course of a general eyre, but they more commonly did so under the terms of a commission to "deliver" gaols, that is, to conduct trials of anyone who was in gaol, including those who had been indicted by a coroner's jury. R. F. Hunnisett suggested that the findings of a coroner's jury originally needed corroboration in the county court before the trial could be held, but by the end of the thirteenth century the presentments of coroners' juries were often sufficient on their own to lead to trial.[14] Reviews of the indictments made at coroners' inquests were common in the thirteenth century, however, and they form the second link with the development of presentment. These reviews occurred in the eyre courts as discussed above. The coroners' rolls documenting inquests that had been convened were one of the records used by justices to check up on the retrospective presentments made in the eyre.

By the end of the thirteenth century, the case load of the eyre courts had skyrocketed and legal procedures had become increasingly complex and time-consuming.[15] More and more people had also come to view the arrival of eyre justices as an opportunity to lodge formal complaints about local problems, and the justices found it more and more difficult to meet their obligation to conduct a general review of conditions in the shires in a timely manner. Adding to the problem was an upsurge in violence and crime, which not only added to the justices' workload but also complicated the smooth operation of the courts, as local feuds and rivalries made the work of juries and officials increasingly insecure.[16] In light of these problems, royal government implemented a series of reforms to reinvigorate the prosecution of crime.[17] After experimenting with several different configurations of justices, courts, and local administrators in the first decades of the fourteenth century, the Crown eventually assigned responsibility for hearing presentments to Justices of the Peace.[18]

Through all of the experiments in the first half of the fourteenth century, including the Justices of the Peace (JPs) and their forerunners, the Keepers of the Peace, presentment survived more or less intact. If anything, the role of presentment juries actually grew through this period of flux. Increasing the number and effectiveness of presentments lay at the heart of all schemes for reforming criminal law; the JPs rose to the fore mainly because of their ability to make the machinery of presentment run more smoothly. In the sessions held by JPs, presentment juries continued to make the accusations that gave rise to subsequent trials, and the juries continued to be drawn from individual hundreds. The changes to the system were far more noticeable at the top: Greater authority was given to local notables serving as justices, for example, and the sheriff and his staff gradually lost authority as a result.

From the perspective of the people who served on the presentment juries, though, continuity was much more evident than change. Presentment jurors convened by JPs continued to rely on a combination of personal knowledge about what went on in their hundred and information supplied to them by others.[19] They continued to engage in a sifting process before making their presentments. Probably the greatest change from their perspective involved the process of gathering information about matters they had not personally witnessed or been involved with. This had always been part of their work, but at some undetermined point in the fourteenth century, it began to crowd out other more direct and personal sources of information. The trend eventually turned the jurors into a body that reviewed written accusations, or bills as they were called, submitted by individual informants to the presentment jury in the hope of launching a prosecution.[20] Symptomatic of the change to a bill-reviewing body was a change in administrative geography: Presentment juries in the eyres had been drawn from each hundred in the county but bill-reviewing juries were usually drawn from the county at large. These "grand" juries, as they came to be called, continued to function in England until 1933 and in modified form still function in many jurisdictions of the United States today.

Making criminal accusations was always a central part of the work presentment jurors did, but it was by no means the only work they were asked to do. One of the reasons behind the success of presentment as an administrative procedure was its flexibility and adaptability. Between the 1160s and the 1350s, it found its way into a number of different kinds of courts and also came to be applied in areas other than criminal law. Throughout its medieval history, presentment remained true to its inquest origins, serving as a device for facilitating communication between local society and higher-level authorities. Like the sworn inquest, presentment was prized above all for its ability to supply information. It could transform the cacophony of local storytelling and gossip into a coherent narrative form that made sense to those in power. Royal justices, sheriffs, coroners, JPs, and manorial lords all understood the value of listening to these narratives, and all were eager to have them repeated in many different venues.

The expansion of presentment took place in two related ways. First of all, it entailed the addition of extra responsibilities within the traditional royal venues of eyre court and peace session. The addition of new forms of felony—included in the Assizes of Clarendon and Northampton—was part of this process, but of much greater consequence was a widening of the responsibilities of presentment jurors to include nonfelonious crimes, typically those involving disregard of royal statutes and ordinances. The second and related development was the extension of presentment to local courts, some of which were affiliated with the royal courts but some of which were not. Both of these changes were integral parts of the overall development of presentment in the period and both deserve a closer look.

The addition of responsibilities to presentment jurors in eyre courts and peace sessions was a natural extension of inquest procedure. Throughout its history, presentment was a method for furnishing information to a higher authority as well as a method for making criminal indictments. The close link between inquest and presentment is suggested by the language of the assize of Clarendon, which employs the Latin verb *inquirere*, "to enquire," to describe what the juries of presentment were supposed to do.[21] The same word was routinely used to describe what kings expected sworn inquests to do. A good overview of the uses of presentment for matters other than felony is provided by documents that enumerate the "articles of enquiry" assigned to presentment juries.[22] Before each court session involving the use of a presentment jury, one of the king's justices instructed the jurors about the matters on which they would be obliged to make presentments. Justices based their instructions on lists of questions that had been worked out by the king and his advisors as a prelude to a judicial visitation. The justices often gave copies of these lists, or articles of enquiry, to the jurors to keep with them while they deliberated on their presentments. As a result, the formal rendering of presentments before a royal justice typically took the form of a question-and-answer session, in which the justice went through his list of questions and the jurors presented their answers.

The question-and-answer strategy is implicit as early as the assize of Northampton, which instructed justices to enquire about escheats, advowsons, wardships, and the custody of castles in addition to felonies. The earliest surviving list of specific articles comes from an eyre held in 1194.[23] It includes 19 articles and indicates that the policy of using presentment to deal with infractions of royal statutes and ordinances was already current. In addition to questions about felonies, the 1194 list includes questions regarding infractions of the assize of wine, the disposition of chattels forfeited by Jews and usurers, and nonattendance at the eyre by individuals who should have been present, among other things. Similar lists survive for many thirteenth-century eyres. They reveal that questions were generally based on lists that had been drawn up for a previous visitation, with extra articles added in accordance with new legislation or new directives from the king. By the end of the thirteenth century, the articles dealing with administrative and regulatory law dwarfed the articles related to felony. A list from 1294, for example, includes articles dealing with the disposition of treasure trove, the imposition of tolls, the creation of new markets, and the fate of shipwrecked cargo; all told, the list includes more than 140 articles, of which only a handful involved acts of felony. The articles associated with sessions of the peace went through the same process of extension and elaboration in the fourteenth and fifteenth centuries, generating lists that were twice as long at the end of the period as at the beginning.[24] Articles might become obsolete and as a result were sometimes dropped, but a perusal of the lists associated with eyres and peace sessions suggests that those who drew them up operated under the age-old bureaucratic mind-set that it is easier to add than subtract.

The centrality of the articles in the formulation of presentments is readily apparent in the oaths taken by jurors. The wording of the oaths made explicit mention that jurors would tell the truth about the questions asked by the justices: "Hear this, ye justices, that I will speak the truth as to that on which you shall question me on the lord king's behalf" is the oath required of presentment jurors, according to Bracton.[25] "This here, ye justices, I shal truely enquire and truly presente almanere of pointes and articles that I shal be charged on the Kynges behalve at this tyme," is the form specified in an anonymous fifteenth-century tract describing proceedings before JPs.[26] Both accounts go on to note that the articles were read to the jurors immediately after they had sworn, reinforcing the notion that presentments were, effectively, responses to questions.

Surviving court records often show the imprint of the articles. This is often more readily apparent in manuscript sources than in modern printed editions or translations, because the latter either omit or standardize the extra spacing, thicker lettering, and extensions into the margin that could be used to mark the transition from article to article in the manuscript sources. Nonetheless, the transition from article to article is still often clear. In the presentments made by the hundred of Hirstingstone in the Huntingdonshire eyre of 1286, for example, there is a series of nine distinct presentments following the 63 presentments made about felonies. Each presentment begins with a brief note: "Concerning churches, etc. they [the jurors] say," or "Concerning wine sold against the assize they say."[27] If more than one presentment was made under any of the articles, the second follows on directly from the first with a "Likewise they say."

While the great increase in the number of articles assigned to presentment jurors was an important part of the overall expansion of presentment—and also, by extension, of the jury system—it was by no means the only cause. Equally important was the more or less simultaneous extension of presentment to other courts, specifically to local courts that were not directly managed by a commissioned royal justice. This second area of expansion is still poorly understood, although it is possible to capture some of the broad contours of the process. Of particular importance was the adoption of presentment in the courts convened locally in each hundred.[28] These courts met frequently, typically every three or four weeks, but presentments were usually made only at special sessions held once or twice a year. These special sessions, or "leets" as they were often called, were convened by the local sheriff, part of whose job it was to conduct a "tourn" of hundred courts in his county to receive presentments and take action in light of what the jurors reported.

Throughout much of England, the sheriff's tourn was associated with the system of mutual surety known as frankpledge.[29] A frankpledge was a group of households (the number varied according to place and time) who kept tabs on each other and took responsibility for maintaining public order. In some respects, the institution of frankpledge can be conceived of as a medieval neighborhood watch program, although a frankpledge group's responsibility for its members' behavior was considerably greater than even the most vigilant modern analog. Well into the fourteenth century, most peasants and townspeople were required to belong to a frankpledge, or at least to be in the household of someone who belonged to a frankpledge. Newcomers to a town or village had to be accepted into a frankpledge group within a few days of arrival or face expulsion. For the newcomer, entering a frankpledge meant agreeing to accept the public responsibilities assigned to frankpledge groups: contributing to fines and assessments imposed on the group; attending court when required; observing the rules governing the presence of strangers in one's home; and, most of all, working to maintain peace and lawfulness.

When a sheriff went on tourn, he worked closely with the frankpledge groups, or at least with the leading members of such groups, known as chief (or capital) pledges. He had two main objectives. One was to conduct a "view" of frankpledge that meant checking into the vigilance with which the membership rules had been observed since his last visit. Had any outsiders come to the village and if so had they entered into frankpledge? Had anyone hosted an outsider for an extended period? Had any sons of frankpledge members become old enough to take up frankpledge standing on their own account? Fines would be imposed if any of these rules were broken. The financial rewards stemming from such fines were certainly worth having, but the sheriff's watchfulness in this regard was also intended to preserve public order. People at the time associated crime with outsiders who had no stake in a local community.[30] Someone who either could not or would not take up the responsibilities of belonging to a frankpledge was suspect and so exclusion, even expulsion, made sense to both the sheriff and the local community.

The other objective of the sheriff's tourn was to hear presentments. From Anglo-Saxon times, frankpledge groups had borne a responsibility to maintain public peace and to provide information about those who had broken the peace. When the sheriff's tourn was instituted, probably as a result of the Assize of Clarendon, the frankpledge's general obligation for peace keeping was aligned with the sheriff's periodic visits.[31] The mechanics of the alignment can scarcely be glimpsed, but the net result was to turn the hundred courts into venues for making presentments. Presentments could be made about the current status of frankpledge membership, but they could also involve accusations of felony as outlined in the assize. Membership issues could be resolved locally within the confines of the court, but felony accusations ordinarily had to be dealt with by royal justices.

How juries came to take responsibility for the presentments delivered in the hundred courts is a puzzle. The clearest contemporary account of presentment in the sheriff's tourn is in the late thirteenth-century law text known as Britton, after the conjectured author of the text.[32] According to Britton, the presentment jury comprised substantial freeholders of the hundred who based their presentments mainly on information supplied to them by frankpledge groups and representatives of villages in the hundred. The jurors were supposed to sift the information provided to them and then make formal presentments to the sheriff. Historians have sometimes referred to this as "double" presentment because it involved two stages of accusation, a first stage involving the chief pledges and village representatives and a second involving a jury. The legal text known as Fleta, roughly contemporary with Britton, furnishes a similar account, and a few stray references in other sources can be found to suggest that these accounts reflect real practice in the courts. The mixing of local representatives with a formal jury is reminiscent of the presentment procedure outlined for eyre visitations in the Assizes of Clarendon and Northampton and it is possible that the similarities were more than coincidental.

For reasons that have yet to be fully explained, the frankpledge system went into decline in some parts of the country in the early fourteenth century.[33] The vitality of the hundred courts also began to erode reducing the effectiveness of the sheriff's tourn as a venue for making presentments. England went through a dramatic economic transformation over the course of the thirteenth century characterized by soaring population growth and burgeoning urbanization.[34] Workers moved to wherever jobs were available and many peasants left their meager plots of land to look for opportunity elsewhere. Perhaps the system linking frankpledge membership and hundred courts was simply overwhelmed by these changes.[35]

Before losing their importance as vehicles for presentment, however, the hundred courts gave birth to a more vigorous local venue for frankpledge enforcement, namely the manor court. From at least the twelfth century, lords had routinely held courts for their manorial tenants to deal with property transfers, agrarian practices, and minor local disputes.[36] Over the course of the thirteenth century, in a process still poorly understood, many lords also acquired the right to use the local court of the manor as a substitute for the hundred court. On such manors, the lord conducted the view of frankpledge directly, as a surrogate for the sheriff, and kept the fines that emerged from the business of the court.[37] Thus, the private court of the lord could be and often was turned into a public hundred court and the lord rather than the sheriff took responsibility for holding the tourn. How lords exercised their public rights varied from lordship to lordship, as did the extent of public jurisdiction claimed. Some lords, such as the bishop of Ely, maintained a relatively firm distinction between courts that exercised public jurisdiction and courts that conducted manorial business.[38] More often, lords simply held expanded sessions of the regular manorial court, at which they conducted the view of frankpledge and took cognizance of other business ordinarily reserved for the hundred court.

The intermingling of hundred court and manor court that occurred in places where lords had the right to hold the tourn raised a series of contentious questions about the duties of presentment jurors. Chief among them was the obligation of a jury to make presentments relating to a lord's authority over his tenants. Jurors were generally willing to accept responsibility for presenting felonies and other matters associated with the authority of the Crown. From the beginning, peasants played a role in formulating presentments in the eyres; the four men who represented each village according to the terms of the Assizes of Clarendon and Northampton must have been drawn mainly from peasant ranks. Likewise, many of the suitors to the local hundred courts must also have come from the ranks of the peasantry; even peasants who were not formally obliged to attend the local hundred court would have been familiar with how presentment worked there. Formally at any rate, there probably was not a great deal of difference between making a presentment of felony before a lord or his official and making a presentment of felony before a sheriff. Both were stepping-stones leading to trial before a royal justice, and both were easily construed as serving the interests of peace and security. But lords were often keen to stretch the limits of presentment and employ the jurors' knowledge and watchfulness for other ends. Since presentments often culminated in fines and since lords collected these fines, even small infractions of law or custom were worth hearing about. Even worse from the perspective of the tenants, lords began to insist that presentment juries enforce their manorial rights and their public rights. Had anyone shirked their obligation to provide labor to the lord? Had anyone tried to skirt the rules governing land transfers? Had anyone left the manor without permission? Bailiffs and stewards usually kept an eye on such things, but from the lord's perspective, it was far better to have the tenants themselves take a role in enforcement.

Complaints about using presentment to deal with manorial matters can be found on a number of manors in the later thirteenth and early fourteenth centuries.[39] In 1259, for example, a hundred jury in an eyre court in Kent made a presentment condemning the bailiffs of the archbishop of Canterbury because they had forced manorial tenants to make presentments at every manorial court, whereas traditionally they were only required to make them once each year (presumably at the view of frankpledge).[40] Two decades later, a bailiff in Lancashire was accused of forcing tenants to make presentments in his lord's court "where such things never have and ought not to be presented."[41] But in spite of what was probably fairly widespread opposition, the tide definitely flowed in favor of the lords, and on most manors the jury of presentment had become an entrenched part of manorial life by the early fourteenth century. Older forms of procedure that did not make use of presentment continued to operate in local courts throughout the period, but procedure involving jury presentment was ascendant in most jurisdictions.

In practice, tenants and lords must have reached informal compromises about how presentment could and could not be used in manorial courts. The jurors in these courts were generally chosen by the other tenants and they often used presentment to regulate matters that were in the interest of the local community.[42] Thus, jurors on

Ramsey Abbey manors often made presentments against people who abused common lands or who failed to clean their drainage ditches, issues that were of far greater concern to local villagers than to the lord.[43] Occasionally, one even finds the lord himself or one of his officials being presented for harming community interests.[44] Presentment could be, and sometimes was, made to work by imposing sanctions on jurors who refused to cooperate, but most lords probably understood the drawbacks of being too heavy-handed. Lords' interests were best served when presentment jurors cooperated in managing the local court and cooperation was much more likely when the jurors were treated with respect.[45]

The adoption of presentment at the level of a local village or manor has much to say about the emphasis all levels of government placed on the procedure. Presentment allowed people in positions of power to learn about what was happening on the ground in areas they were interested in controlling. Many forms of information were valuable. Information about criminality, deviant behavior, and challenges to authority were naturally valued most highly, but medieval rulers were enlightened enough to understand that provision of peace and stability had a public value as well as a personal one, and that attention given to public well-being had its own rewards. Presentment was, in the final analysis, a form of partnership between higher-level authorities and the local people who were called on to provide information under oath. The partnership could work effectively only if both parties were willing to invest in it. It is relatively easy to understand the investments that kings and lords were willing to make. The investments of presentment jurors are harder to discern, but are nonetheless worth pondering. While presentment jurors were effectively forced into a position of tattling on their neighbors, they also played a role in expanding public order and enhancing personal security. In a world in which public order and personal security were in chronic short supply, this alone may have sufficed.

Possessory Assize Juries

The dramatic expansion of presentment was a major step in the history of jury development, but it was by no means the only major step in the period, nor was it even necessarily the most important step along the way. A second influential development was the emergence of a form of civil jury designed to adjudicate disputes about the possession of land. Once again, the reign of Henry II stands out as a watershed era in the growth of the jury system, again less for its invention of something completely new than for its creative adaptation of procedures that had formerly operated piecemeal. A host of contentious problems greeted Henry when he assumed power, not the least of which involved the resolution of wartime seizures of property. Self-help had been the order of the day during the civil war and Henry and his supporters recognized that royal authority depended on the king's ability to deal effectively with the grievances of displaced property owners.[46] Whenever a quarrel over property rights arose, one party to the dispute was bound to lose something of great value. If the parties to the dispute—and equally important their peers and neighbors—could be made to agree that the adjudication process was fair and transparent, even if it produced an undesirable result, then the losers might find it difficult to use extralegal measures to undermine the judgment. And if this could be achieved in ways that allowed the king to stay above the fray but emphasize his role as guardian and enforcer of fairness, then there was even greater reason to be actively involved in resolving property disputes.[47]

Henry's search for a tool with which to achieve these goals led him to the sworn inquest. After gaining secure control of the kingdom, he and his advisors crafted the first of what are generally known as the "possessory assizes," putting jury verdicts at the center of the new procedures. To understand why they chose the sworn inquest for this purpose, a few words about the term "possessory" are necessary. English law, particularly as it developed in Henry's reign, recognized a distinction between lawful possession and absolute proprietary title—or "right"—to land, a distinction that has come down to modern times in the aphorism that "possession is nine-tenths of the law." To be in lawful possession of something, such as a house, meant having the right to live in it without necessarily being the ultimate and definitive owner. Medieval Common Law expressed this idea of possessory entitlement with the word "seisin." The person who was lawfully entitled to live in a house or to hold a piece of land was said to be "seised" of that property, even though someone else might have a higher right of ownership in the property. Seisin, which one might translate as "the right to possess lawfully" was a relative concept that took into account the fact that several people could have an interest in a piece of property without having the right to possess it at any given moment in time. The core relationship around which the doctrine of seisin developed was that between a lord and his tenant, the characteristic bond of feudal society.[48] When a lord granted land to someone of free status who became his "man" and who agreed to provide support and services in return for the grant, two people came to have an interest in the same piece of property. The tenant "held" the land without owning it: He or she might live on it, charge others for its use, build on it, and so on. But the land was held from someone else; every tenant had a lord to whom they were beholden for the land. Tenants had to pay rents and provide services to their lord and respect his authority. If a tenant reneged on the terms of tenancy, the lord might take the land back. Thus, while a grant might put a tenant in possession, it did not extinguish the lord's interest in the property. Often their respective interests in the use of the property were closely aligned, but there were many situations in which they were not.

Seisin thus has to be understood in the context of a society that saw property rights in the relative terms of lords and tenants rather than in the absolute terms of abstract ownership. Its definition was shaped by the presumption of titles to land that existed above the mere right of possession. The Common Law expressed this higher concept by reference to "right," a proprietary concept that approximated to the idea of pure and absolute ownership (saving only the Crown's theoretical superiority of title to all landed property). Someone who had proprietary "right" to a piece of land had unassailable and unencumbered authority over that land (again subject only to the Crown); as long as the land was kept directly in the hand of the person vested with right it could be used however the person saw fit: it could be denuded of all trees, for example, or sown with salt. There was no need for the person with right to consult or gain permission from anyone else when deciding what to do with the land. Like right, seisin also constituted a formal legal standing with respect to the use and transmission of land, but unlike right it assumed that the use and transmission would be encumbered with obligations to someone vested with a higher proprietary title to the land. One who held seisin of a piece of land had wide latitude in deciding how the land would be used but not unrestricted authority: The holder of seisin had to work within the limits imposed by the ongoing interest of the lord who held the land by right.

But while seisin presupposed the existence of a higher title, it nonetheless also embodied a relatively elevated stake in a piece of land. There were many ways of holding and using land that did not measure up to seisin.[49] An unfree (or villein) tenant, for example, might plant, tend, and harvest a piece of land for his entire life and never enjoy seisin of it because, in theory, the tenant's access to the land was based on the will of his or her lord. Technically, seisin of a villein's land belonged to the lord. In practice, villeins enjoyed considerable security of access on a day-to-day basis because of the deep-rooted sense of custom that permeated medieval society, but reliance on custom was a mixed blessing because it also imposed relatively strict limits on how villeins could use the land they worked. Villein tenure was not the only way to hold land without crossing the seisin threshold. Leaseholders and subletters also had rights that were inferior to those of freeholders vested with seisin. Leaseholders and subletters had an enforceable legal right to use land on the terms they had contracted (assuming the original contract was valid), but they did not enjoy seisin of the land they used. Seisin continued to reside with the lessor during the term of the contract.

The concept of seisin drew inspiration from both Roman property law and canon law, but it was effectively defined and elaborated by decisions made in the kingdom's courts. It was, in other words, a product of concrete and tangible case law rather than of abstract principles or theory; the relativity of seisin was a product of real situations rather than learned definitions.. Seisin had to be found rather than explained. It belonged to an individual and could not be understood without knowledge of the personal circumstances and relationships of every individual who had an interest in a particular piece of landed property. Seisin was what the courts ruled it to be, and most of the major developments determining its scope were made in the context of the assizes created to resolve disputes. The possessory assizes were thus instrumental both in enforcing the law of real property and in clarifying and amplifying the system of tenures within which seisin operated. Their success constituted not only a momentous step in the development of the jury system but also in the development of the Common Law itself. In a society in which land served as the primary economic asset, the main determinant of social status, and the formal basis of much legal and political authority, any procedure that could effectively find and award seisin would necessarily assume great importance.

Considering the centrality of case law in shaping the contours of real property law, it might be helpful to look at a few examples of how the possessory assizes worked in practice. A case litigated in 1233 involving property in Norfolk demonstrates the type of problem that could arise when multiple stakeholders held an interest in a single piece of property.[50] The dispute centered around 60 acres of land originally held by Robert de Crek' from Earl Roger Bigod, the most powerful man in Norfolk at the time. Earl Roger took control of the land when Robert died and seeded it with winter wheat before allowing Bartholomew de Crek' to enter into possession. Bartholomew was the eldest son of Robert de Crek's first marriage.

But Bartholomew's half brother Peter challenged the seizure by Earl Roger and subsequent transfer to Bartholomew. Peter was also Robert's son, but from a second marriage. He claimed that his father had conveyed the land to him years earlier, and therefore that Roger and Bartholomew had taken possession away from him. The jurors confirmed Peter's claim and added some interesting details about how Peter had come into possession of the land. They said that Robert gave the land to Peter because he wanted to make sure his second son was provided for (*voluit eum promovere*). Robert made a charter to this effect and went through a formal public ceremony at the hundred court to convey seisin to his son. Since Peter was only eight years old at the time, Robert also appointed a guardian for his son's land. When the original guardian died, Robert appointed another guardian. The two guardians managed the property on Peter's behalf for five years, until Robert died. Robert's death precipitated the dispute. Whose claim to possession was valid, the son of a first marriage who had the support of the superior lord, or the son of a second marriage who had been formally invested with the land by the legitimate sitting tenant? The jury was unequivocal in its verdict: Peter had enjoyed seisin for a number of years and had been unlawfully deprived of his rights.

A dispute in Suffolk in 1214 illustrates another situation in which an overlord and tenant could develop different ideas about possession.[51] In that year, Adam de Wikes and his son William filed suit against John, son of Bernard, in a dispute about lawful possession of land in three villages. In rendering its verdict the jury rehearsed the following details. Adam, a deacon, had once held the disputed land as John's tenant, but transferred his possessory rights to his son Peter, who performed homage for the land to John. Peter thereafter enjoyed the use of the land Adam had given him—we are not told how—but his father continued to reside on it. Peter happened to predecease Adam, however, and his death ushered in a contest over seisin of the land. His father Adam felt he had a claim to it because he had physically resided on it for a long time; Peter's brother William staked a claim as the presumptive heir of his deceased brother; but John, son of Bernard also claimed seisin as the superior lord who knew intimately the circumstances behind the transfer from Adam to Peter. The matter was further complicated by the fact that John happened to be away when Peter died and did not return home until six weeks later, during which time Adam continued to reside on the land. When John returned and discovered that Peter had died, he took control of the land, disregarding any claim Adam or William might have to succeed Peter. But he was not heartless in the matter; he offered to let Adam stay on the land, as long as he did so without his son William. John may have imposed this restriction simply because he disliked William, although he probably acted to avoid future disputes about seisin that might emerge if William were allowed to reside on the land. Adam refused John's offer, however, and decided to stake his fortunes and those of his son William on a lawsuit, which ultimately decided against him and his son and upheld the return of seisin to John.

As these examples suggest, the situations that could cause the property interests of lord and tenant to part ways were actually quite numerous. What if the tenant entered into a second tenancy agreement with another lord who was an enemy of the first lord? What if the tenant had a son to succeed him, but the son was of unsound mind? What if the tenant wanted to do something with the land that destroyed its future value? What if the tenant went on Crusade and was away for a number of years? What if the tenant gave the land to the Church? What if the tenant left the path of righteous living and could no longer requite his rents and services? In all of these situations, the lord was tempted to deal with the situation in a simple and immediate way: Seize the land back and find a more suitable tenant. But this form of self-help threatened public order and created exactly the kind of uncertainty—often tinged with violence—that had characterized the period of civil war. Henry decided to deal with the situation by emphasizing the principle that no one should be deprived of their land without judgment: Arbitrary seizure would not be tolerated. He zeroed in on the act of dispossession. Regardless of the ultimate right of the respective parties, regardless of the original cause of the dispute, a sudden ousting of someone from land they had occupied was not permissible and the king himself would intervene to restore the situation that had existed before the arbitrary seizure. Sitting property holders could be ousted only by due legal process.

Expelling someone from the property they occupied was akin to taking away their seisin, and so the expulsion came to be called an act of "disseisin." The procedure that Henry developed to deal with such cases is known as the "assize of novel disseisin." The term "novel" in this context simply means recent: As a practical matter, Henry did not want to get bogged down dealing with incidents that were no longer fresh in people's memory, so he placed a time limit beyond which the procedure could not be used.[52] The term "assize" means "enactment," although by association with the procedure set up by the enactment it also came to designate cases litigated according to its terms and even the courts that enforced it. As it happens, the actual ordinance setting up the assize has not survived. Ancillary references suggest that it was enacted no later than 1166 and probably goes back to the 1150s.[53]

The crucial issue Henry recognized, as he mulled over the problem of disseisin, was how to establish that an expropriation was unlawful.[54] Establishing the simple fact of expropriation was usually not that difficult. Some expropriations were forceful and violent and could not help but become immediately known. Even peaceful expropriations—moving into a house while a tenant had gone to market or removing animals from a pasture, for example—quickly came to the notice of neighbors and friends. But not all expropriations were unlawful. For example, a squatter might have moved into a house when the legitimate tenant died. Or an heir might have taken over a property that a tenant had leased only for a lifetime. Or someone might have posed as an heir—a bastard son for example—when in fact the property should have reverted to the lord for a lack of heirs. Or, as often happened, a tenant might have fallen behind in the rent or reneged on performing work services, in which case the lord might feel compelled to take action, including, prior to Henry's innovations, seizing back the property.[55] The crux of the problem was whether expropriation was justified, that is to say, whether it was the result of a proper judgment permitting expropriation. Unilateral seizure was not acceptable, even when the tenant had broken the bargain. That way lay chaos, as contemporaries had had ample opportunity to observe.

Since judgment was a public act, people who lived in the area could be reasonably expected to know whether or not the confiscation was based on prior judicial decision. Local people knew the properties and people involved in a local dispute as well as the circumstances surrounding a specific seizure, and their knowledge was essential to any ruling about the validity of the expropriation. Using a sworn inquest made a good deal of sense in this situation. It was not, however, the only option worth considering. Henry and his advisors could well have chosen to follow the model of Roman law, a rejuvenation of which was at the forefront of the intellectual and cultural revival taking place on the continent at that very time. The Roman model prescribed the use of judges who interviewed witnesses and other knowledgeable people and then rendered a verdict after sifting testimony. Henry decided to go a different route, giving far greater authority and responsibility to a group of local people constituted as a jury. It was a fateful decision, both for the local people who were asked to serve as decision makers and for the monarchy itself. Assize procedure created a legal system in which the welfare of the king's constituents was closely aligned with the welfare of his own position. The assize was a royal procedure, which meant not only that fees and fines associated with it flowed into the royal treasury, but also that people might be more inclined to associate the monarchy with justice and to see the king as an effective arbiter of disputes. But there was probably even more to the king's policy than that. The jury was particularly well suited to dealing with the divisions and prevailing mistrust that characterized a country that had experienced a long civil war. For one thing, it diffused responsibility across a relatively large group, which may not only have made the verdict more acceptable to the loser, but probably also made participation in the decision-making process less risky. But the great attraction of the jury may well have stemmed from what happened after the verdict had been delivered. By giving jurors a stake in how the verdict was reached, Henry also gave them a stake in seeing that the verdict stuck when his justices left the county. The jurors' duty to enforce the assize was often quite tangible, including the requirement of being physically present at the contested property to help readmit the tenant after judgment had been made.[56] In terms of rooting out self-help and promoting respect for the rule of law, the jury may well have been at its most effective in the days and weeks after the court ruling.

Over the course of Henry's reign, a number of similar forms of possessory assize emerged to complement novel disseisin, all related in that they focused on the issue of seisin and made use of juries. Each was designed to deal with a specific problem that frequently led to disagreements about where seisin was vested, just as the assize of novel disseisin dealt with the specific problem of expulsion without judgment. Three of these forms found frequent use in the period covered by this book. Two dealt specifically with property linked to the Church. One, known as the assize of "last presentment" (or "darrein presentment"), dealt with disputes over the right to nominate someone to hold an ecclesiastical position, such as a local rectorship. Since rectors were well remunerated and influential figures in their local communities, the right of appointment was well worth having. Most of the time, patrons made appointments without difficulty but the same ambiguous circumstances that could bedevil the possession of land could also bedevil the possession of patronage rights. Jurors in an assize of last presentment were asked to determine who had appointed the previous rector and then to establish how that patron's right had descended in the interval since the last appointment. The other assize related to church property was known as "utrum" (literally "whether"). It required a jury to give a verdict as to whether a specific piece of property was part of the patrimony of the Church or whether it was encumbered with secular obligations to a lord. The issue arose because churches often received their original endowments from secular patrons and continued to receive bequests from parishioners after their foundation. But the terms of such gifts were not always clear and transparent; questions sometimes emerged over whether the original grant had extinguished all secular obligations, such as the obligation to attend a lord's court or pay rents and services to a lord. Once again, local people were the ones most likely to know the status of a particular piece of property and its history, and so the matter was seen as well suited to settlement by an assize jury.

The third major type of possessory assize related to novel disseisin was known as *mort d'ancestor* (literally "death of a forebear"). It dealt specifically with contested inheritances and frequently required juries to intervene in complex family situations. In an assize in Norfolk in 1201, for example, four sisters accused Thomas of Gloucester of preventing them from inheriting 18 acres of land from their father.[57] The complex case involved two core issues. First, the right of the sisters to inherit the land at all was uncertain because their father had also produced two sons. According to the rules of succession observed in England, daughters could inherit land only when there was a failure of heirs in the male line. Second, even if the daughters were entitled to inherit their father's land, it was not clear how it should be divided between them; the law required that each receive an equal share. In the course of pleading, Thomas explained that he had come to an earlier understanding with one of the sisters to buy the entire property. The other three sisters insisted, though, that the selling sister could only make a deal for her fourth of the estate, and they pressed a claim that the remaining three-fourths belonged to them. Thomas countered with the argument that the deceased father had had two sons in addition to the four girls. According to Thomas, one of these sons had married and fathered children of his own and the other was still living. He presumably brought up the issue of other children in order to undercut the daughters' claim to be the true heirs of their father. The three sisters contended, though, that their two brothers had died before their father and that neither had produced any surviving children. The jurors thus had a convoluted set of family relationships to contend with in the assize. They ultimately decided that the sisters' version of their family tree was more accurate and awarded the property to them.

There were many circumstances that led jilted heirs to opt for the assize of mort d'ancestor. Uncertainty about lines of descent was endemic in the period. Questions of legitimacy were often tricky to determine in a world that lacked birth certificates and marriage licenses. But problems associated with illegitimacy formed only the tip of an iceberg; the base comprised myriad tangles of multiple marriages and premature deaths, situations that were so common that the smooth transmission to an eldest son from a father who was also an eldest son seems to have been the exception rather than the rule. The jury's job was to sort out the competing claims of half brothers, stepchildren, and uncles and cousins, problems that were wont to rise to the surface following the death of a forebear.

In addition to the four main possessory assizes, a fifth type of assize also emerged late in Henry's reign, but it was more a cousin than a sibling of the others. The four possessory assizes required juries to make decisions about seisin rather than about right. There were occasions, however, when people wanted to contest right directly. These generally involved disputes between people of higher social standing at odds over more substantial properties. Disputes about right typically encompassed disputes about lordship itself, and thus often had profound repercussions for the power and status of the disputing parties. A decision about right was appealing in some circumstances because it was more definitive than a decision about possession; it could not be overturned by a further verdict, for example, as might happen with one of the possessory assizes. Before Henry's time, disputes about "right" to land that did not end in a negotiated compromise had generally been decided by battle between the contesting parties. But by the 1170s battle was no longer seen as self-evidently apposite for settling conflicts. Not only had the success of the possessory assizes drawn people's attention to the viability of alternatives, but it is also possible that the growing rationality characterizing the twelfth-century renaissance made people more receptive to procedures that privileged reason and argumentation over brute strength. Henry thus crafted the "Grand Assize," probably in 1179, as an alternative to battle. The tenant/defendant had to ask for a jury verdict to settle the dispute; if they did not the case could still proceed to a resolution by battle. But most defendants did want to avoid battle, and as a result even among the privileged classes who staked everything on the outcome of the case, procedure by sworn inquest became normative.

Within the space of about twenty-five years, Henry and his advisors had fundamentally changed English civil law, with profound consequences for the future. Land was the overwhelmingly dominant source of wealth and power in the period and the assizes ensured that henceforward people would look to the Crown to protect their property rights. By instituting a mechanism for bringing royal government into regular contact with the localities, Henry reinforced the idea that the king and his subjects were partners in attaining peace, good government, and the protection of property. There were plenty of occasions when this community of interest seemed ready to dissolve, but the fact that it so rarely did testifies to the strength of the relationship created and sustained by the frequent use of sworn inquests to resolve property disputes.

Frequent use was the key. Administratively, the assizes provided a template that could be used over and over again in just about any circumstances. Compared to the alternatives, they were streamlined, efficient, and effective, even in situations in which one of the litigating parties was weaker and more vulnerable than the other. Already within Henry's own reign they attracted a lot of business. Formal court records do not survive before the 1190s, but references to fees and fines collected from the workings of the assizes abound in the Pipe Rolls of the 1170s and 1180s.[58] These Pipe Roll entries have too many ambiguities to allow a meaningful count of the number of cases, but the court records from the 1190s and early 1200s give some idea of magnitude. Civil pleas survive for three counties visited by eyre justices in 1198, for example. In those three counties (Hertfordshire, Essex, and Middlesex), justices heard 19 cases of novel disseisin and 35 cases of mort d'ancestor.[59] Assuming the counties were typical, one can extrapolate that well over 500 plaintiffs across the country as a whole used the two assizes in that year. A substantially higher figure is suggested by evidence drawn from the eyre of 1202. In Bedfordshire, 48 cases of novel disseisin and mort d'ancestor are recorded, suggesting that for the country as a whole a figure approaching 2,000 can be contemplated. In all of the examples given here, four years has passed since the previous eyre visitation, so the numbers cannot be taken to represent annual averages. Even distributed over several years, though, the figures reveal the early popularity of assize litigation.

The popularity of the assizes continued to grow, as did litigation during the thirteenth century as a whole, as Paul Brand and others have documented.[60] But the high regard with which people viewed the assizes was clearly one of the engines driving this growth, as shown in the eyres, where the number of assize cases climbed steadily over the course of the century.[61] But the eyres tell only part of the story. Speed and efficiency were central features of the assizes and the eyres made a poor fit in this regard, particularly as the thirteenth century wore on and the intervals between eyre visitations increased. The alternative of requiring litigants to travel to Westminster for every assize was equally problematic; even if the principals accepted the need to make the journey, such an arrangement would have imposed a real burden on the jurors and without their active support the assizes would have bogged down. The whole point of the assizes was to lower the bar for people wanting to use the king's law and that meant allowing the cases to proceed locally rather than centrally.

At some point early in the thirteenth century, two alternatives to the eyre emerged to facilitate local handling of the cases.[62] The first involved commissions to knights and local notables issued on an ad hoc basis and authorizing them to act as royal justices for the purpose of deciding a single possessory assize. To date there has been little study, unfortunately, on the operation of these special commissions. They may have emerged as a stopgap measure necessitated by the growing popularity of the assizes. They had the great advantage of allowing cases to be dealt with promptly. And since most local notables had experience managing courts of their own, as well as prior observation and experience with the operation of the assizes, they undoubtedly had a good sense of how to see cases through to a resolution. In some ways they prefigure the role local JPs came to play in the fourteenth and later centuries. And as has often been asserted with regard to the JPs, the drawback to the arrangement was the forfeiting of some degree of central control over the assizes.

The second method used to respond to the demand for assizes was to increase the frequency with which professional royal justices visited the counties. This entailed a narrowing of the terms of commission typically used for an eyre visitation, so that the justices could limit their work to the hearing of assizes alone. Using these distinctive assize commissions, one or more justices could be authorized to hear all of the assizes pending in a particular county. Their narrower focus allowed the justices to go on circuit more frequently than justices traveling on an eyre circuit, and this in turn allowed for the quicker dispatch of pending assizes. Their early history is, however, no better understood than the early history of the ad hoc assize commissions. Records of their sessions can be found as early as 1225, and it is clear from the inclusion of two clauses dealing with their activities in the original Magna Carta of 1215 that their history goes back even earlier.[63] Both of the Magna Carta clauses reveal the popularity the assizes had attained by 1215: Chapter 18 incorporates the demand that assize justices should visit each county at least four times a year, and chapter 19 stipulates that if the justices could not get through all of the cases on the day of their visit, it was permissible to continue them on the next day even if the professional justices could not be present.[64]

These two alternates to the eyre—ad hoc commissions to local notables and general commissions to traveling royal justices—coexisted for several centuries. Early on, the use of ad hoc commissions was particularly common, but professional justices gained the upper hand in the later thirteenth century and retained it thereafter. The eventual triumph of the general assize commissions was marked by more careful defining of the circuits and frequency of the justices' visits and ultimately formed part of the system of quarterly assize sessions, or "quarter sessions," that was a mainstay of English law for many centuries.[65]

These innovations in procedure were fuelled by high popular demand for the assizes, particularly the assize of novel disseisin. Some idea of the magnitude of this demand can be gained by examining the record of commissions issued to justices authorizing them to hear assizes. A litigant who wanted to make use of one of the assizes had to acquire a writ from the Chancery specifying the form of assize he or she wanted and outlining the property in dispute. The writ was given to the litigant upon payment of the requisite fee and the litigant conveyed the writ to the sheriff to begin the suit. Chancery clerks ordinarily did not keep a duplicate of the writ, but during much of the thirteenth century and the first few decades of the fourteenth century, they made a corresponding entry on the Patent Rolls summarizing the essential details of the case and appointing justices to hear it.[66] Thus by combing through the Patent Rolls, which are available in a good modern calendar, one ought to be able to find every assize initiated in any given year in the relevant period.

In practice, the task is not so easy. The number of assize commissions is, in fact, so great that Henry Maxwell-Lyte, when Deputy Keeper of the Public Records, opted to exclude them from the modern calendar. His decision was based on a prior attempt to calendar the commissions, made by a Public Record Office clerk named Frank Haydon, portions of which were published as appendices to the Deputy Keeper's Annual Reports to Parliament in the 1880s.[67] Haydon's calendar covers the first nine years of Edward I's reign (1272–1281) and includes every assize commission. As he sought to condense the entries into calendar form, Haydon noted with some exasperation that "At least seven-tenths of the roll [for 1272–73] are filled by appointments of justices to try assizes."[68] He estimated that somewhere between

2,000 and 3,000 commissions occur in the roll for Edward's first regnal year, and that similar numbers can be found in the rolls of subsequent years.[69] Soundings of Haydon's calendar corroborate his estimate: In Edward's seventh regnal year (1279–80), for example, approximately 2,300 assize commissions can be found.[70]

The remarkable growth in the popularity of assizes had two important consequences for jurors. The first, and most obvious, was a marked increase in the demand for jury service. Many litigants reached settlements with their adversaries before a formal trial took place, and many others failed to pursue their cases after securing the initiating writ. In the county of Huntingdonshire in the years 1279–81, for example, only about a third of the cases with commissions entered on the Patent Rolls can be traced in surviving assize rolls.[71] But this can be seen as a minimal figure with respect to jury service. For one thing, assize rolls were not systematically preserved in the later thirteenth century; indeed, assize justices were not formally required to turn their rolls in at all before 1325.[72] Furthermore, assize jurors were actively involved in cases well before the final trial stage; one cannot safely assume that jurors played a role only in cases that were heard by justices. There is, unfortunately, no sure way to know for certain what proportion of cases begun with the acquisition of a writ and appointment of justices gave rise to a body of jurors. A figure somewhere between one-third and two-thirds of all commissioned cases seems plausible. This would suggest that by the 1270s, assize cases would have called for the services of somewhere between 8,000 and 24,000 jurors in any given year.[73] When one considers that similar numbers were needed year after year, and that the assizes constituted only one form of jury service, one begins to get a sense of how heavy the demands placed upon jurors were in the period.

The second major consequence of the growing popularity of assize procedure involves the social dynamics of litigation. By the 1270s, and probably a good deal earlier, the assizes had become a form of litigation popular with the peasantry, or at least the upper echelons of the peasantry.[74] There really is no other way to explain the issuing of 2,000, or 3,000 assize commissions every year without including peasants and modest town dwellers. Even a casual perusal of the assize records reveals the frequency with which litigation turned on relatively small amounts of property, holdings one regularly encounters at the village level.[75] Similarly, the circumstances giving rise to dispute can only be associated with people of modest social background, for example, plaintiffs and defendants who had inheritances comprising only a few acres. It is even possible in some instances to trace litigants in local manorial court records, such as Benedict Clere, who sought to recover by mort d'ancestor a tenement in the Ramsey Abbey village of Houghton, Huntingdonshire, in 1279.[76] Clere was cited three times in his local manor court for defaulting on work services owed to the Abbey for his free tenement, and his wife Emma was fined for breaking the assize of ale and several other offences.[77] Assize litigation never lost its appeal for members of the gentry and others of higher social standing, but the procedures that were originally designed with their interests in mind had clearly trickled down the social hierarchy in the space of just a few generations. Such trickling down had significant repercussions for jury service. The social background of jurors will be examined more fully in chapters 4 and 5, but it bears emphasizing at this juncture that one of the most common types of jury service developed in tandem with legal procedures that were notable for social inclusiveness rather than exclusiveness. One of the hallmarks of jurors serving on assizes was their familiarity with the local context in which litigation arose. As peasants and more humble residents of towns began to avail themselves of the king's promise to protect freehold property, the social ranks of the jurors drafted to determine and enforce the outcome of the cases also inevitably changed.

The success of the assizes had implications for the development of the jury system that went far beyond the procedure itself. Its early development, combined with its popularity, provided a solid rationale for the use of juries as decision-making bodies in other contexts. The assizes demonstrated that juries could be trusted and that they were preferable to other modes of judgment. Sworn inquests probably tended in the same direction, but presentment, the other major extension of jury service in the later twelfth century, was far more ambiguous because presentment jurors were regularly forced to report on things they would rather have ignored or left uncovered, and were often fined for failing to comply with what the Crown demanded.[78] The assizes presented a more favorable image of what juries could achieve and brought home immediately and more forcefully to a wider cross section of society, the benefits of using juries. Over the course of the thirteenth and fourteenth centuries, the Common Law vastly extended its scope, spinning off new procedures and new areas of competency.[79] As it did so, the popularity and evident success of assize procedure provided a powerful motive for the extension of the jury principle to other areas of law and government.

TRIAL JURIES

Like the presentment and assize jury, the trial jury developed out of the sworn inquest, but its period of transformation and expansion occurred about a half-century later. Most people today think of the trial jury as its quintessential form and so it takes some historical imagination to picture it as a latecomer to the scene, the last chapter of the story rather than the first. Like its predecessors, the trial jury underwent a period of rapid dissemination and extension soon after its introduction and in less than a generation had established itself as the default procedure for deciding issues of innocence and guilt and had also made substantial headway in other areas of adjudication.

The widespread application of trial by jury to criminal matters in England happened in response to a decree promulgated by the Church at the fourth Lateran council held in 1215. Among the many sweeping changes in christian life instituted at the council was a stipulation that members of the clergy could no longer participate in judgments that led to the shedding of blood, including judicial ordeals.[80] For centuries, the ordeal had been widely used in England and throughout Europe to resolve questions of guilt and innocence in serious criminal cases, particularly in difficult or contentious cases that were not amenable to other forms of resolution.[81] As appeals for God's help in sorting out difficult problems, they were conducted as religious rituals including fasting, vigils, prayers, and sometimes even specially blessed water. Priests were intimately involved with the ritual preparation for the ordeal, and their withdrawal effectively undermined the social logic that gave the ordeal its credibility: Without the clergy there could be no ordeal.

This presented the English Crown with a real dilemma. The assize of Clarendon, which had greatly expanded the Crown's role in prosecuting crime a half-century earlier, had specifically stipulated use of the ordeal to determine the veracity of accusations made by juries of presentment. Resort to the ordeal in the aftermath of Clarendon did not automatically follow the presentment of a felony, but ordeals were the default procedure applied by the courts and they were certainly common enough to make a deep social impression. Hence the dilemma: By 1215, presentment was ensconced in the king's courts and the king's subjects had come to associate royal authority with the adjudication of felonies and the preservation of the peace. But presentment needed a mechanism to conclude the process started by the jury's formal accusation. Judicial ordeals had provided closure for nearly 50 years, but Lateran IV had done away with that option. What could be used instead?

Resort to a second jury verdict, pronounced specifically on the veracity of the accusation and leading directly to a hanging if guilt was established, was the solution hit upon. In hindsight, given what we know about the longevity of trial by jury, it seems like the natural and obvious choice, but things were not quite so transparent at the time. All across Europe, the banning of clerical participation in ordeals posed a similar problem, yet England alone chose to solve it by using jury verdicts. Elsewhere, tribunals of professional judges, trained in the inquisitorial methods assimilated from Roman law, were handed responsibility for deciding the outcome of criminal cases. Nor, as Roger Groot has demonstrated, was the turn toward a different path entirely sure of foot. The decision to commit to jury verdicts was not taken until 1220, nearly five years after news of Lateran IV reached the country, and even then implementation was halting and uncertain.[82] Vestiges of the uncertainty and the expedients adopted to deal with them, were to linger for centuries thereafter.

Had the ordeal been banned a few decades earlier (at the third Lateran council held in 1179, for example) jury trial would probably not have emerged as the standard procedure for determining guilt. But much had changed in England between the 1170s and the 1210s, and these changes explain why the king and his advisors eventually made the choice they did in the aftermath of Lateran IV. Above all else, the jury system had by then established a successful track record. Its success in other areas was the driving force behind the decision to extend the use of jury verdicts to the determination of criminal cases. The Crown had come to rely upon the verdicts of sworn inquests to investigate contentious matters and furnish reliable information on a wide array of topics. Ascertaining the facts related to an act of felony was not that much different than ascertaining the facts related to the behavior of a royal official or many of the other specific tasks assigned to inquest juries. Perhaps more importantly, the assizes had become firmly entrenched in civil law by the 1210s. By then, not only had the king's subjects come to see them as a desirable and effective method for dealing with property disputes, but also their popularity and frequent use created a large pool of people who had served as jurors and so understood from personal experience what it meant for such a body to have responsibility for making a crucial decision.

Within the more direct field of criminal procedure, juries had also made a deep impression by 1215.[83] First of all, presentment itself had built a solid bridge between jury deliberation and assessments of criminality. This was implicit in the whole procedure, but there were also specific practical features of the presentment process that bore more directly on the matter. For one thing, felons who fled after committing a crime could be and often were presented for their offense in their absence. When this happened, a presentment could set in motion the process of outlawry, carrying with it the presumption of guilt and the denial of the king's peace to the one outlawed. In this respect, the determination by presentment jurors that they had sufficient cause to accuse someone of the felony was tantamount to a conviction; further process was necessary but not any further deliberation or judgment. Furthermore, even if the suspected felon was apprehended, the presentment jury exercised considerable discretion over the subsequent mode of trial.[84] In some cases, the jurors expressed reservations about the quality of the evidence that underlay their accusation or singled out some extenuating circumstance that made them uncertain about felonious intent, and when this happened the justices often called for a second jury (sometimes referred to as a "medial" jury) to review the case before deciding whether or not to send the suspect on to the ordeal. These reviewing juries often included the presentment jurors, but also incorporated others with better knowledge of the case. In practice, accused felons went to the ordeal only when the presentment jury had good reason to suspect their guilt.

Juries sometimes had an even more direct role to play in deciding the outcome of a criminal case while the ordeal was still in force. In some instances, individuals accused of felony were able to secure the privilege of a jury trial after they had been accused but before a justice ruled how their case would be determined. This could be done in at least two ways. One way was to secure a writ "of spite and malice" which created a jury to examine the motives of the person responsible for the accusation. As discussed in chapter 1, these sworn inquests regarding the circumstances of the accusation were not formally determinative in the way that verdicts of trial juries came to be after Lateran IV, but in practice inquests that swore that the accusation had been motivated by spite and malice were very nearly equivalent to full acquittal.[85] The second way was simply to request that the king allow a jury to determine the validity of the accusation plain and simple. These requests were generally accompanied by a proffer of cash to persuade the king to accede to the request, so that people in effect bought the right to be tried by a jury.[86] Verdicts that originated in this way were fully determinative. As these cases make clear, having a jury determine one's fate was viewed as a privilege well before it came to be viewed as a right.

With these models and precursors in front of them, one might legitimately wonder why the Crown was not more decisive about prescribing jury trials as a substitute for the ordeal. There is no simple answer to this question. Several extenuating factors need to be taken into account. The presence of alternative modes of resolution certainly complicated the decision-making process. In addition to the inquisitorial method of resolution, which would have been familiar from England's continental possessions, the canonical procedures of the English church, and the general intellectual climate of the day, Henry and his advisors had to consider two alternatives with established track records in determining the outcome of felony prosecutions, trial by battle and compurgation. Trial by battle pitted an accuser against the one accused in a vicious and desperate brawl to determine who was being truthful.[87] If the accuser won, the accused was convicted and usually hung straightaway; if the accuser lost, the accused was judged to be not guilty and the accusation was treated as malicious. Trial by battle shared with the ordeal the underlying ideology that God would intervene to ensure that the truthful party emerged victorious, even if the laws of nature suggested that one party had greater strength and fighting ability than the other. But trial by battle was not really a suitable candidate to replace the ordeal. It was disliked by the judicial establishment of the day, which tended to see it as irrational and capricious, but also could not be easily accommodated to the system of presentment, in which there was not a single readily identifiable accuser who could be made to fight. When the situation arose and a defendant demanded the right to fight following an accusation by a presentment jury, the presiding justice curtly told the defendant that presentments were made on behalf of the king and the king could not be required to fight one of his subjects.[88] Even after the trial jury rose to the fore, trial by battle continued to operate in cases that were brought by private accusation (known as appeals), but it was not a realistic solution to the problem posed by the banning of the ordeal.

Compurgation was better suited to a world in which presentment occupied a significant part of the criminal justice landscape. Compurgation involved the formal swearing of oaths by friends and neighbors of the principals in a case. The word itself is a compound of the Latin word *cum*, meaning "with," and *purgatio* meaning "a cleansing or purifying," and the original idea behind the procedure was that an individual could be "cleansed," or cleared of an imputed flaw or misdeed by declaring his or her innocence under oath and finding others who would swear in support of the oath. The compurgators, those who swore with the principal, were effectively akin to character witnesses, in that their oath attested to the credibility of the principal swearer.[89] In some respects, compurgation was well suited to function as a response to presentment, a sworn accusation made by people from the area where the crime occurred, but who were not necessarily direct witnesses of the act that gave rise to their accusation. Compurgation could, in theory at any rate, have become the single unifying mode of resolution used by the courts, equally applicable to cases initiated by private appeal or presentment.[90] It retained a role for God's intervention in the judgment process and was no more difficult from an administrative perspective than was trial by jury.

The feasibility of this line of development is suggested by the history of trial procedure in a number of towns which acquired the right to use compurgation to determine the outcome of felony cases before 1215 and continued to do so after trial by jury had become normative in the rest of the country.[91] In London, compurgation in a felony trial was last used in 1276, for example, and in some of the Cinque Ports it survived into the sixteenth century.[92] The English Church likewise continued to rely on compurgation in its own courts for centuries after jury trial became normative in secular courts, including cases involving clerics accused of committing felonies.[93] But the intellectual climate of the thirteenth century was, on the whole, not favorable to compurgation, and the justices and other royal officials who implemented the law tended to see it is as a vestige of an irrational past that needed to be restrained rather than expanded. Soon after the adoption of jury trial in criminal cases, for example, royal justices began to insist that clerics accused of felonies be subjected to a jury verdict before being transferred to the ecclesiastical courts.[94] Such verdicts were not binding and had no bearing on the conduct of the subsequent ecclesiastical trial; they appear to have served no purpose other than scoring points off a rival by showing that jury verdicts were more accurate and reliable than compurgation.

While trial by battle and compurgation both lacked appeal as general replacements for jury trials, the Crown was unwilling to push for their elimination during the revamping of trial procedure that followed Lateran IV. Trial by battle was a particularly tough issue to address because it was so well established as a mode of trial within the royal courts themselves, not only in criminal cases initiated by private accusations but also in civil litigation conducted according to the terms of the Grand Assize. The king took a safer, more conservative route to legal reform, substituting trial by jury for cases that earlier would have gone to the ordeal, but not imposing it in cases that had earlier been settled using trial by battle. Essentially what the courts did was to give defendants accused by private appeal the option of choosing how their trial would be conducted, the options being the traditional method of trial by battle and the newer method involving a jury verdict. Allowing defendants a choice in the method of their trial was not without precedent. As discussed above, some defendants before Lateran IV had been permitted to buy the right to have a determinative jury verdict; they, too, exercised personal discretion over the nature of their trial. Similarly, in civil law, the justices who held property assizes often sought to have a defendant agree to abide by the terms of the assize before proceeding to a verdict.[95] By 1215, these practices had deep enough roots that the king was wary of digging them up to plant his sapling and he decided that a graft was more likely to produce a fruitful tree. Thus, jury trial was—and would be for centuries to come—cast as an option available to a defendant, who had to agree to be tried by a jury before a jury trial could be held. In the common idiom of the courts, one had to "place oneself upon the countryside" (*ponit se super patriam*) before the court could proceed to take a verdict. Even suspects who were manifestly guilty were ordinarily given the right to reject a trial that would be decided by a jury verdict.

Adhering to tradition, though, left a glaring problem: What could be done if the accused withheld consent? A defendant who was manifestly guilty and could be almost certain that the final verdict would lead to a hanging had, after all, little reason to give consent. This scenario presented itself to the courts many times during the thirteenth and later centuries and led the king's justices to develop several strategies to address the problem, none of them very satisfactory.[96] One solution was to refer back to the older method of trial by battle. A defendant who would not agree to be tried by a jury could be forced to fight his accuser. The justices preferred to have a jury verdict, but since the law insisted on the need for consent, they were willing to resort to the more primitive method when the need arose. But this option was available only when the accusation had been made by a private appellor, and even then it was not permitted if the appellor was elderly, or a woman, or a cleric, or unable to fight for some other reason. Moreover, it could not solve the knotty problem of what to do when the indictment had been made by a presentment jury. In these cases, a justice's first recourse was persuasion. Judges might tell the accused that jurors were often inclined to be merciful and remind him or her that a verdict of not guilty would liberate them from prison. Snatches of these conversations can sometimes be found in contemporary narrative accounts of cases and procedure.[97] A certain

William, accused of stealing a mare, engaged in the following exchange with a steward entitled to hear his case on behalf of the king:

> *William:* Sir, I disavow this mare, and never saw I her until now.
> *Steward:* Then, William, thou canst right boldly put thyself upon the good folk of this vill that never thou didst steal her.
> *William:* Nay, sir, for these men have their hearts big against me and hate me much because of this ill report which is surmised against me.
> *Steward:* Thinkest thou, William, that there be any who would commend his body and soul to the devils for thee or for love or hatred of thee? Nay verily, they are good folk and lawful.[98]

In a similar account, an accused rapist named Hugh asked for legal counsel before deciding whether to allow a jury to determine his fate.[99] The justice told him that accused felons were not entitled to counsel and that he should simply tell the truth and rely on the jury: "Hugh, you must answer," said the judge, "Here is the alleged deed that has been charged against you and you are capable of answering whether you committed the deed or not without counsel. If, contrary to law, we allow you counsel and the jury finds on your behalf, which it may do with God's assistance, then it will be said that you were delivered through the favor of the judges." Hugh then raised several other objections about proceeding to a jury verdict, but the judge kept turning the conversation back to the issue of consent: "Hugh, if you are willing to consent to them [the jurors], with God's intervention, they might work on your behalf." In the end, Hugh finally did consent and the jury found that the alleged rape had occurred but that Hugh's men had committed the act without Hugh's participation or knowledge, and so Hugh was set free.

Judges sometimes even resorted to verbal trickery to gain consent. A late thirteenth-century advice manual for lawyers and court officials, known as *Placita Corone* ("Pleas of the Crown") advised accused felons to refuse consent and discussed some of the steps a judge might take to obtain it.[100] The author refers to an earlier case he had witnessed at which the judge opened proceedings by saying to an accused thief: "My good friend, you are indicted by the country of such a thing: How do you wish to acquit yourself of such a theft?" The accused thief offered to undergo trial by battle, but since the indictment was brought by a presentment jury, he was told that battle was not feasible. The judge then "wondered how he could bring the thief to give another reply" and said "Are you a good and honest man?" The accused thief replied, "Yes, indeed, and I am ready to defend myself by my body [i.e. by battle] against this accusation." But the justice persisted: "I say are you good and honest?" The suspected thief again answered "Yes, sir, I am." "How," asked the judge, "do you wish to prove it?" "By the country, to be sure," replied the accused thief. The judge then used this answer as grounds for proceeding with a jury verdict on the original indictment; the jury found the suspect guilty and he was hanged. "And in such a way," the author of the text concludes, "he was tricked."

No matter how cunning the judge, though, some defendants clung tenaciously to their refusal of a jury. Judges sometimes rode roughshod over refusals and ordered juries to deliver their verdict regardless of the suspect's unwillingness to agree.[101] More scrupulous judges remanded the accused to prison, probably hoping that the many months of miserable confinement that would pass before the case could be heard again might change a suspect's mind about trusting to a jury verdict.[102] This habit of relying on imprisonment in noisome conditions ultimately led to the bizarre legal process known as *peine forte et dure* (literally "strong and harsh punishment").[103] When an indicted criminal refused to accept a jury trial, he or she could be sentenced to undergo severe physical deprivation and even torture to change his or her mind. The core punishment involved what was essentially a starvation diet, with the prisoner allowed to eat a modicum of coarse bread without any drink on one day and then to drink water without having any food on the next. Some sources add that the water should be drawn from a fetid standing pool rather than a running stream. By the early fourteenth century, infliction of physical pain accompanied the emaciating diet. Prisoners who refused to accept a jury trial were forced to lie on the floor wearing minimal clothing while heavy weights were piled on top of them. Prisoners who continued to withhold consent were sometimes crushed to death. Modern commentators have suggested that some prisoners accepted death in this manner because, unlike convicted felons, those who perished in prison awaiting trial normally did not forfeit their land when they died.[104]

Sentences of *peine forte et dure* were not common, but neither were they entirely rare. The record of the Northamptonshire eyre in 1329–30, for example, refers to its use on two and possibly three occasions.[105] One prisoner was sentenced after refusing to accept three different juries that were offered to him; a second entry notes that a coroner was instructed to examine the body of someone who had died while undergoing the punishment (possibly the prisoner sentenced in the earlier entry). The third reference describes a felon who initially refused to accept a jury verdict but then changed his mind when threatened with the *peine forte et dure*. Such about-turns must surely provide the rationale for instituting and maintaining such a cruel procedure. A judge's ability to persuade someone to consent to a jury trial was much greater if he could threaten the prisoner with something that was conceivably as bad as a hanging. If the choice confronting an accused felon was certain death by starvation and crushing or possible death by hanging, then consenting to a jury must ordinarily have seemed the better course to take. The case of the accused rapist Hugh, whose reluctance to accept a jury trial is discussed above, certainly seems to corroborate this view: Hugh finally consented to a jury when the judge described the *peine forte et dure* to him and counseled that "it would not be good to die in that manner and would be much better to consent to the jurors."[106]

The *peine forte et dure* survived in English law until 1772 and even made it to America, where it was used in one of the Salem witchcraft trials in 1692.[107] By the sixteenth century, it had become something of a legal curiosity, but well into the fifteenth century it was alive and well. Both its longevity and its severity are difficult to account for. One cannot help but wonder why a legal system that looked askance at such nonrational procedures as trial by ordeal and compurgation and that showed such great reluctance to condone judicial torture in other circumstances, clung so tenaciously to the *peine forte et dure*.[108] Why was the principle of giving consent to a jury trial so highly cherished that even torture was worth accepting to maintain it? Or to put the matter another way: In all of the sweeping changes made to the legal system during the thirteenth and later centuries, why was there never any legislation designed to do away with the consent requirement? It does not take great imagination to conjure up an Edwardian statute with a provision that all felony trials (or at least all trials initiated by presentment) be determined by a jury regardless of whether or not the defendant consented to such a trial.

Certainty on these matters is hard to come by, but several plausible explanations can be advanced to account for the legal system's steadfast retention of the consent principle. First of all, a tentative policy incorporating choice probably made sense in the early going, when the mode of criminal trial procedure was in a state of flux. Experimenting with procedure when an individual's life was at stake could not have been undertaken lightly, particularly in cases that began as presentments and thus were open to influence by hearsay and indirect evidence. Negotiating consent gave the accused an opportunity to argue against the presentment before his or her life was on the line. Judges and jurors may have seen this as a fairer—and possibly more effective—way to navigate the choppy waters between initial indictment and final judgment.

It is also possible that the judicial establishment saw the consent requirement as a useful part of their strategy of developing a more comprehensive public sphere for law enforcement. The rise of presentment procedure in the later twelfth and early thirteenth centuries was part of a general reordering of government and social life characterized, among other things, by an emphasis on "public" order and "public" responsibility for preserving the peace.[109] In order to succeed, presentment had to make inroads into earlier patterns of behavior that were overwhelmingly local or familial and that treated crime as primarily a private act that brought two individuals and/or two families into conflict.[110] Before the expansion of presentment, most legal process in criminal matters aimed at bringing the affected parties to an agreement about compensation for the ill effects of the deed. Even an intentional killing could be amenable to private resolution (in the form of *wergeld*) if the right terms of compensation could be agreed upon. The idea that public order was threatened by a criminal act can certainly be found well before the second half of the twelfth century, but usually only indirectly, as a consequence of failure in private negotiations.

Presentment did not do away with the belief that crime was a private matter between victim and perpetrator, but it shifted the balance between public and private interests. One of its central premises was the idea that crime victimized public order as well as individuals and families. It forced presentment jurors to address criminal acts that were not amenable to compensation because the perpetrator was unknown; even if little could be done to bring the culprit to justice, the act of making a presentment reinforced the notion that the crime itself was a public matter. Whenever a private suit was feeble because the victim and his or her family were poor or powerless, the presentment jurors were supposed to step into the breach and ensure that the culprit was prosecuted, again as a matter of public well-being. The whole ethos of presentment was permeated by the view that crime was a matter of public concern and should be dealt with as a public responsibility.

Requiring consent, fit into the strategy of constructing a public sphere of law enforcement in two important ways. First of all, as Thomas Green has suggested, it helped to frame the trial as a process that could potentially lead to reintegration into local society.[111] Giving consent meant entrusting one's life to a social group that was effectively a community surrogate, and agreeing to abide by community standards of justice and morality. It meant accepting the community's right to bring forward the accusation that led to the current predicament, and it meant accepting that further communal action was the only way out of the predicament. When crime came to be seen as a breaking of the bonds joining an individual to his or her society and not just as an act that harmed another individual, the consent requirement constituted a mechanism that allowed the severed social bonds to be rebuilt. The jury might well decide that the criminal act had severed the bonds so completely that meaningful reattachment was no longer an option, but more often than not juries were willing to believe that the bonds could be rebuilt. Expressing a willingness to accept the verdict of the community probably predisposed the jurors to be merciful, since the defendant was, in effect, taking the first step toward reintegration.

Consent probably also eased the way for juries to convict. The burden of deciding whether or not someone should live or die is heavy at all times, but it may well have borne more heavily on medieval jurors than their counterparts in other eras. Contrary to popular belief, medieval English people did not thirst for more hangings. According to Thomas Brinton, Bishop of Rochester (1373–89), people were reluctant to condemn even manifestly guilty thieves and murderers and he alludes to common arguments that aimed to exculpate criminals because of their youthfulness or because of the shame that would be heaped on their families, if they were hanged.[112] Popular attitudes were permeated with ideas that reached back to the period when compensation was the preferred mode of resolution and execution was a last resort. Prior to 1215, even cases that were sent to the ordeal because the presentment jurors expressed strong suspicions about the likelihood of guilt rarely led to a conviction: Of 275 documented ordeals between 1194 and 1208, only eight yielded convictions and seven did so because the accused person confessed before the ordeal was held.[113] According to Margaret Kerr and her colleagues, the ordeal was "an instrument of mercy" designed "to spare the lives of the guilty."[114]

The Crown, however, pushed strongly in the opposite direction. When the prosecution of crime came to be redefined as a matter of public order, the issue of how to make amends for crime inevitably rose to the fore. Greater reliance on capital sentences was not the only possible outcome of the process, but in practice it was the path chosen by Henry II and his successors.[115] The legal establishment throughout the medieval period had no doubt that widespread use of capital punishment was an effective method of protecting public order.[116] The Crown's conviction on this score stemmed partly from the sense that its own authority and legitimacy were augmented whenever it imposed the death sentence.[117] A policy of extending capital punishment was also helpful, though, in fostering the sense of public responsibility for crime. A policy of hanging rather than seeking fines and compensation was a fitting symbol of the transformation the Crown aimed to bring about.

Trial jurors thus found themselves caught between two worlds. On the one hand was the older tradition of private negotiation and compensation; on the other the newer conception of felonious crime meriting the death penalty. From the perspective of the judicial establishment, jurors needed to be weaned away from the more lenient approach, and having them operate in the context of a consenting suspect must have gone a long way toward achieving this goal. Consent did not necessarily push juries to find more defendants guilty, but it probably did make them more willing to consider the option. A trial that was forced on the defendant would have operated as an impediment to conviction; a trial based on consent removed one of the hurdles that had to be overcome on the way to returning a guilty verdict. This dynamic may have been important in all cases, but it was probably particularly important when the evidence was ambiguous and uncertain, as it often was when presentment was the route to trial.

Conclusion

The history of the jury system is often told from the perspective of the criminal trial jury, but it bears emphasizing that even as a form of trial jury, it constitutes only a single type. In addition to making judgments of life and death, medieval trial juries decided a host of other more prosaic affairs: whether someone was free or serf; whether a lord had imposed unfair new burdens on his peasant tenants; whose version of the terms of an endowment was most accurate; whether a charter was genuine or false; whether someone had abused his right to collect tolls and so on. Examples of these and many other matters can be found even before the trial jury became normative in criminal cases and they proliferated in subsequent decades and centuries. From the middle of the thirteenth century, jury trials became standard in cases of trespass (a nebulous category of "wrongs" that would later be treated as misdemeanors and torts) and the rapid growth in trespass litigation in the later thirteenth and fourteenth centuries gave rise to a substantial increase in the demand for trial jurors.[118] By the second half of the fourteenth century, trespass litigation was so common that jurors were more likely to be pressed into service to determine a case of trespass than to sit in judgment on an accused felon.[119] The adoption of jury procedure in criminal trials was certainly an important step in the overall expansion of jury responsibility, but it was only one among a number of such steps. The criminal trial jury is best understood not as a model that other forms of trial jury emulated but rather as an example of the tendency of royal justices to use sworn inquests whenever they sought to establish the relative truthfulness of conflicting versions of events.

An appreciation of the different forms of medieval juries—not just trial juries but also presentment and assize juries—calls attention to the extraordinary range of responsibility assigned to jurors in the period. It also suggests how heavy the demands for jury service must have been. Royal judges and administrators continued to develop new procedures making use of jury verdicts over the course of the thirteenth and fourteenth centuries, but they rarely, if ever, reduced the scope of earlier ones. New areas of responsibility were simply added to those already in existence. Indeed, just like the sworn inquest discussed in chapter 1, the early forms of jury continued to expand at the same time as newer forms were spun off. Thus, in the case of presentment, the number of articles to which presentments were made grew substantially over the course of the thirteenth century, as did the number of venues in which presentments were made. In 1166, presentment was designed to operate chiefly before itinerant royal justices; a century later, while still flourishing in its original capacity, it had also teamed up with coroners conducting inquests, sheriffs holding tourns, and lords holding manor courts. In the case of the assizes, the widening scope of jury procedure is evident in both a widening of the clientele making use of the procedure and a widening of the definition of seisin to include such things as common rights and officeholding. During the fourteenth and fifteenth centuries, the refining of earlier forms of jury procedure came to take precedence over the creation of new applications, but only because the prodigious expansion of the later twelfth and thirteenth centuries meant that there were relatively few areas of law and government left for the jury system to infiltrate.

Finally, it is important to remember that every new application of jury procedure meant an increase in the demands for jury service. This chapter has focused mainly on legal and administrative developments that influenced longer term historical processes, but these developments were also important in terms of the experiences of people living at the time. The great expansion of the jury system brought in its wake a major transformation of people's contact and interaction with law and government and fundamentally reshaped what it meant to take part in public life. It also inevitably drew an ever widening circle of society into its orbit, so that even local villagers became familiar with the workings of juries. The story of developments in procedure is, in other words, also a story about proliferating demands for jury service.

CHAPTER 3

CHOOSING JURORS AND
CONSTITUTING JURIES

The rapid expansion in inquest and jury procedure described in chapters 1 and 2 created an extraordinary challenge for royal government and administration. The king's administrators always had plenty of work to do simply to ensure that the principals in a case and relevant county officers were present in court when the king's justices needed them. But the emergence of the jury system demanded that they have many dozens, sometimes hundreds, of jurors in attendance at royal court sessions. To meet this challenge, local officials had to create and oversee a workable process for selecting jurors and guiding them through their assigned tasks. On the whole, they carried out their duties well, with a remarkably small staff and remarkably little help from the central government. There were chronic problems to be sure: Jurors frequently failed to show up for their appointed court date; they often complained about the method of their selection; and charges that officials used their power to appoint jurors in partisan or corrupt ways were common throughout the period. But when the frailties of premodern forms of communication and the intricacies of cooperative ventures are taken into account, one cannot help but be impressed by the accomplishments of the officials responsible for administering the system.

This chapter will focus on how the process of choosing jurors and constituting a jury worked in practice. It begins with a look at the role of sheriffs and bailiffs as the administrative links between the central government, which organized and coordinated the functioning of the legal system, and the population as a whole, or at least the population implicated in the workings of the legal system. The work of sheriffs and bailiffs in this regard gave rise to a special type of document, the jury panel, and the purpose and uses of these panels will be investigated in the second part of the chapter. In part three, various special forms of jury will be considered, particularly forms that required the appointment of jurors from specific social groups, including "mixed" juries, or juries with half their members drawn from one specified group and half from another. Such juries were often pressed into service when the principals were of different faiths, languages, or political allegiances. The fourth section of the chapter will probe the issue of consent, not just to the principal of a jury trial as discussed in chapter 2, but also to the specific group of jurors responsible for rendering the verdict. Then as now the courts were willing to give principals and litigants a role in the selection procedure, primarily by giving them the right to challenge individual jurors. The circumstances in which challenges were allowed reveal a good deal about the assumptions behind the process of jury formation as a whole. They draw particular attention to the issue of fairness in the selection process and to the even larger issue of legitimacy, issues that will be addressed directly in the fifth and final section of the chapter.

SHERIFFS AND BAILIFFS

The sheriff was the linchpin of the administrative machinery dedicated to creating juries. As the top ranking royal official at the county level, he bore direct responsibility for implementing the steady stream of legal directives from the king and his justices.[1] With the great expansion of the jury system in the later twelfth and thirteenth centuries, he confronted seemingly unending demands to have qualified people available to serve on inquests, assizes, and juries. One of the chief virtues of the jury system was its effectiveness at tapping into local knowledge needed for the fair resolution of a dispute. Local tribunals had always had access to such input, but local knowledge and decision-making were not easily reconciled with the urge to develop a legal system that sought uniformity and consistency across an entire kingdom. The key to making this system work resided at the level of county administration, or, in effect, with the office of sheriff. From Anglo-Saxon times, sheriffs had been the primary conduit through which information and resources flowed between central government and local society. Henry II had thus naturally turned to the sheriffs as he sought to develop a legal and governmental system that brought local knowledge of circumstances into close alignment with centrally administered procedures and forms, and his successors, impressed with his success in this area, eagerly built on his foundation.

Assigning responsibility over the creation of juries to the sheriff and county administration as a whole made even more sense in light of the Common Law's emphasis on providing direct justice in the localities. While jury verdicts could be, and often were, delivered in the central courts in Westminster, it was recognized early on that requiring 12 people to travel to the capital every time a case needed to be resolved presented tremendous logistical difficulties and would result in a judicial system that was unwieldy and probably unworkable. Jurors sometimes did trudge all the way from Northumberland or Cornwall to deliver verdicts in Westminster and one cannot help but admire their willingness to do so. If all went well, such a trip might be accomplished in a week or so, but if the roads were in poor shape, or, as was far more likely, if the case had to be delayed on procedural grounds, then the demands on a juror's time and pocketbook would be much more onerous. Had English kings and justices insisted on having jury verdicts delivered in Westminster on a routine basis, the Common Law would have become unworkable soon after its inception and a profoundly different system than the one known to us would have emerged.

The delivery of jury verdicts in Westminster was, however, the exception rather than the rule throughout the Common Law's long history. From very early on, most jury verdicts were delivered in the counties at judicial sessions conducted by traveling royal justices rather than in the central courts. It made much more sense to have a relatively small number of justices travel from county to county to hold courts, where many verdicts could be delivered in succession than to expect large numbers of jurors to undertake the journey to Westminster on a routine basis. As a practical matter, the Common Law sought to foster cooperation between central government, which supplied judicial expertise and overarching coordination, and county administration, which hosted the itinerant justices and ensured that everything they needed for the dispatch of legal business was ready and available when the justices arrived.

Communication between the central government and the local administration headed by the sheriff was effected through the use of writs, brief and simple stylized orders in Latin conveying information and mandates for further action. In the case of jury formation, writs generally took one of two standardized forms. The most common writ ordering the formation of a jury is known as a *venire facias*, meaning "make come" or "cause to come." The name is derived from the key phrase in the text of the writ indicating what the sheriff was supposed to do. A writ to the sheriff of Kent in 1230, for example, specified that he should "make come twelve from the hundred of Milton who best know and who are willing to speak the truth" about the circumstances governing a disputed wardship.[2] Similarly, a writ sent by justices assigned to determine criminal cases in Hertfordshire in 1315–16 ordered the sheriff to "make come before them in Royston on Saturday, January 2, all the prisoners in Royston gaol. . . . and as many knights and other free and lawful men of the area" as would be needed to determine the truth of the indictments.[3] The second common writ form related to jurors took its name from the command "summon" or, in Latin, *summoneas*. This form was usually associated with assize juries. A good example is furnished by an extant writ relating to a case of mort d'ancestor heard in the 1248 Berkshire eyre. Among other things it ordered the sheriff to "summon by good summoners 12 free and lawful men of the neighborhood of Newbury to be before our justices" when the justices arrive to hear the case.[4]

Writs ordering the creation of a jury could be sent either by the king or by the justices who had been assigned to try a particular case or set of cases. Very often sheriffs received writs from both relating to the same matter. The system of assembling jurors before itinerant royal justices revolved around three related procedures. First of all, the king issued a commission to one or several people constituting them as royal justices, specifying the type of authority they were allowed to exercise, and delimiting when and where their commission was to be in effect. These commissions could range from specific mandates to hear and determine a single case, known as *oyer and terminer* commissions ("hear and determine"), to the broad ranging commission that constituted eyre justices to hear and determine all types of pleas. Between these two extremes one can find numerous other types of commissions, the most common of which were commissions to determine all pending criminal cases in a particular county, known as commissions of gaol delivery, commissions to determine all pending property assizes in a particular county, and commissions to receive criminal indictments. As a matter of course, whenever the king commissioned justices, he also took the second step toward constituting a jury, sending a writ to the sheriff informing him that the royal justices named in the writ would soon be visiting his county to hear certain types of cases and indicating that further details about the session would be sent by the commissioned justices. These writs often noted that the sheriff should "make come" all people who would be needed at the upcoming sessions, but usually referred to the jurors only indirectly or in general terms. The third procedural step was taken when one of the justices sent a writ to the sheriff providing details about when and where the upcoming session would be held, and stipulating what the sheriff should do to prepare for their arrival. The justice's writ, or judicial writ as it is often called, typically included a *venire facias* clause ordering the presence of jurors and other people needed to conduct the trials (coroners and bailiffs, for example, or representatives from nearby villages) and sometimes added a clause or two elaborating what sort of jurors the justices expected to be available.

The arrangements for summoning jurors to be present when traveling royal justices held their sessions in the county could be easily modified to constitute juries for other purposes. When justices required jurors to deliver a verdict in Westminster, for example, they issued a writ, usually in the *venire facias* form, that specifically called on the sheriff to send the jurors there. When they needed specific information derived from a jury verdict but did not require the jurors to be physically present in Westminster, they sent a writ to the sheriff ordering him to take the verdict locally and send the results to them in Westminster. Over time, they came to rely heavily on a procedure that combined central and local procedures in the form of *nisi prius* verdicts.[5] The term itself translates literally as "unless before" and refers to an arrangement governing civil pleas in which pleading, first conducted at Westminster to establish the central issue in dispute, was followed by the taking of the jury verdict in the county where the dispute arose. Under this arrangement, a sheriff was ordered to send jurors to Westminster "unless before" they set off on their journey a royal justice came to the county vested with the authority to take verdicts. Naturally, juries seldom left their county once the justices had ruled that their verdict could be delivered according to *nisi prius* procedure.

Kings, too, could adapt the standard writs sent to the sheriffs to craft juries for special purposes. When a king wanted a jury to serve as an inquest body of the sort discussed in chapter 1, for example, he sent a writ specifying the information he wanted a jury to supply, sometimes even specifying the sort of jurors he expected to participate. But the writ almost always left the ultimate choice of jurors and execution of the commission in the hands of the sheriff. Similarly, a king might assign a trusted royal official to examine a sensitive matter in the county by means of a jury, in which case the three steps used to create juries for an itinerant judicial commission would be duplicated, with the royal administrator assuming the role of a justice. Many jury verdicts actually fell somewhere in between a formal judicial decision rendered in court before a royal justice and an inquest verdict on an administrative matter delivered before a sheriff or other royal minister. Most of the thousands of special *oyer and terminer* commissions that constituted local notables or royal officials to examine problems that had been brought to the king's attention fall into this category.[6] The king's standard response to petitions for intervention in a contentious matter was to appoint someone to examine the situation on the ground. In most instances, the examination was actually conducted by a jury constituted for the purpose with the appointed official serving in a supervisory capacity. Once again, the procedure closely paralleled the one used to create juries for visiting royal justices.

Sheriffs thus faced constant demands to provide the king and his designated officials with reliable and knowledgeable people who could serve as jurors. Not surprisingly they in turn fell back on their own staff and delegated much of the responsibility for finding qualified jurors to lesser officials. Occasionally, sheriffs were instructed to participate personally in the process of forming a jury, but as a matter of routine sheriffs processed rather than implemented the demands for juries embodied in royal and judicial writs. Implementation was usually assigned to the sheriff's staff of bailiffs, who made most of the decisions about who would be empanelled and did most of the legwork involved in ensuring the appearance of the jurors. Delegating the selection to bailiffs made a good deal of sense. Typically, bailiffs were responsible for managing the administrative subdivisions of counties known as hundreds or wapentakes, and their jurisdictions were generally small enough to allow them to have personal knowledge of the background and social circumstances of the people they put on a jury panel. Furthermore, the courts themselves often treated hundreds and wapentakes as the main functional entities with respect to court procedure in such matters as presentment and criminal trials, so it was natural for the chief administrative officer of the hundred or wapentake to assume responsibility for the oversight of juries.

A few examples of the correspondence between sheriffs and their bailiffs have survived to give us a glimpse of how they coordinated responsibilities.[7] Ordinarily, the sheriff simply copied the text of the writ he had received and then added a sentence or two ordering the bailiff to execute the king's command and stipulating when and where the jurors should appear. On at least one occasion, though, a sheriff omitted the language of the writ and wrote in more direct terms to the bailiff to tell him what needed to be done. The letter in question can be found among a file of documents stemming from an inquest held in Essex in 1279.[8] In that year, Christina de Valoniis sought to give some of her land to a chantry, and, in order to persuade the king to sanction the gift, bought property of equal value in another place. The king wanted reassurance that the purchased property was really equivalent—a recent statute had forbidden bequests to the Church that seriously diminished the grantor's estate—so he sent a writ of *venire facias* to the sheriff ordering him to hold an inquest at which jurors could state under oath how much the properties were worth.[9] The sheriff, in turn, wrote to the bailiff of Harlow hundred. Following a general salutation, the text of his letter went as follows:

> On behalf of the king we command you upon penalty of ten pounds to make come (*venire facias*) before the beloved and faithful men of the same king, William de Birlay and Geoffrey de Rothinges, his Justices, at the manor of Lady Christina de Maule of Scheering on the Monday after the feast of St. Martin [November 13], 18 knights and other free and lawful men from the aforesaid neighborhood to hear and do those things which William and Geoffrey will enjoin them to do on behalf of the king. Make sure, however, that none belong to the homage of the said Christina. Farewell.

On the back of the letter is a list of 16 names, 12 of which have a small, circular, ink pricking immediately before their name. This list of names represents the bailiff's response to the sheriff's letter. He did not quite manage to find the full complement of potential jurors requested by the sheriff, but he had chosen well enough so that the justices were able to constitute a jury of 12—whose names were pricked—to conduct the inquest.

JURY PANELS

The steps taken by the sheriff and bailiff are unusually well documented in this instance, but the procedure they outline was a matter of routine for all of the parties involved, from the justices through the county officials to the jurors who delivered the sworn verdict. Lists of names similar to the one entered on the back of the sheriff's letter by the bailiff of Harlow hundred in 1279 can be found in many of the archival classes now used to organize the remains of medieval justice and government. As will be discussed more fully in chapter 4, other historians have noted the existence of these panels and used the lists of names to study the social composition of medieval juries, but to date only Michael Clanchy has paid heed to what they reveal about the working practices of jury formation. In addition to drawing attention to their importance as working documents, Clanchy unraveled some of the procedural steps associated with their use. His conclusions, though, were tentative and restricted mainly to the jury panels of a single eyre.[10] A fuller study, using a wider range of source material, substantiates many of the points Clanchy sketched out and also allows greater insight into how the documents were used in practice.

Jury panels existed in a variety of different forms depending on how they were used by the courts or county administration. Their core feature is a simple list of names, as in the example from Harlow hundred. The list was often written on the back of a letter or writ ordering the formation of a jury but was also commonly entered on a separate slip of parchment, frequently sewn to the writs ordering the formation of a jury. Like the writs and other ancillary documents related to court and inquest administration, the panels were practical working documents, although they could also serve as evidence when disputes about jury conduct emerged. Scribes sometimes copied the panels at the beginning or end of a document recording the proceedings of a court or inquest session, but they were not required to do so, and did so inconsistently.[11] Many panels are still extant in their original form—perhaps several thousand all together—but because their value as evidence was only temporary the vast majority has not survived.

Many of the surviving panels bear annotations and abbreviations in addition to the list of juror names, and these additional markings provide important evidence about the process of jury formation. One of the most common annotations is the abbreviation *jur'* written as a marginal note beside some of the names on a list. The abbreviation was short for *juratus,* meaning "sworn," and indicates which of the people on the list were actually put on the jury and participated in the sworn verdict. A typical panel has between 16 and 20 names on it, though both smaller and larger panels can be found.[12] In the case of larger panels, the additional names were essentially a form of insurance, a precaution against illness, shirking, or the need to remove a juror who was challenged for partiality or proved to be otherwise unsuitable. Justices and higher level administrators presumed that if 16 or more potential jurors were included in the panel, 12 could be counted on to take the oath and deliver the verdict. Modern courts take similar measures to ensure that sufficient numbers of potential jurors are available to ensure that cases proceed in a timely manner.

The inclusion of extra names on a panel was sometimes a source of contention, because jurors who were named on the panel but failed to appear in court were liable to be fined for nonappearance. The second statute of Westminster (1285) prescribed a limit of 24 names per panel, and other sources suggest that this was treated as a customary limit.[13] Both this statute and a clause in the "Articles upon the Charters" issued in 1300 indicate that such a limit was needed because sheriffs and bailiffs often nominated large numbers of people to serve on the panel in order to collect fines or bribes from people who did not want to serve.[14] Similar complaints can sometimes be found in inquests into the misdeeds of royal officials. In an inquest held in Cheshire in 1331 to examine the behavior of the county's bailiffs, for example, the people of the county complained that the bailiffs put "an unlimited number" of people on the panel and then took bribes from many of them in order to be relieved of the obligation to serve on the jury. It was later asserted that the "unlimited number" was actually in the vicinity of 60, but even this less exaggerated figure went well beyond acceptable practice.[15]

After the bailiff had chosen the people who would be put on the panel, he ordinarily returned the list of names to the sheriff, who was responsible for handing the panel to the justices or other authorized officials.[16] A statute of 1368 notes that sheriffs traditionally handed the panels to the king's justices when they arrived to conduct trials, but stipulated that henceforth they should have the panels finalized four days before the court date.[17] The change was sought to allow litigating parties an opportunity to learn who had been put on the panel before the case was heard, presumably in case they wanted to challenge the panel in court. It is not clear, though, if the sheriff did anything with the panels other than transmit them to the justices. As will be discussed more fully below, sheriffs were sometimes directly involved in the selection of jurors, but they probably did not tinker with the panels assembled by the bailiffs on a regular basis, although they may well have reviewed them before giving them to a judge or a royal official.[18]

The division of responsibility between bailiff, sheriff, and justices with regard to the final selection of jurors is difficult to discern from the annotations on the panel, nor is it easily diagnosed from other sources. Some insight into the matter can be gained by considering the annotations more directly. The entry of "jur'" before or after a name has already been noted. It was by far the most common annotation on the panels. Usually the abbreviation occurs beside 12 of the names on the list, though other numbers are also encountered, particularly on the panels derived from inquests rather than court proceedings. Many jury panels are, however, entirely devoid of the annotation. A comparison of the panels that are not annotated with the actual court record of the case for which they were empanelled reveals that such jurors were not marked as having sworn because the case with which they were involved did not terminate in a jury verdict.[19] Cases could be terminated before reaching the jury for a number of reasons: through withdrawal of a plaintiff; because the parties agreed to settle out of court; or because the justices rendered judgment on procedural grounds during preliminary pleadings. Since they did not deliver a verdict in these circumstances, they were never formally sworn and thus they do not have a jur' entered beside their names. The jur' annotation was used only for people who were actually sworn in to give a verdict. This in turn suggests that a court official must have had the panel to hand while the court was in session, making the jur' annotation while the case was in progress, probably when the jurors actually took their oath.

Another common abbreviation on the panels is a small cross, again usually entered before or after a name. These crosses indicate that a juror who had been nominated to serve on a case or inquest failed to appear when required. The meaning of these crosses is less transparent than the jur' annotations, but support for the interpretation offered here is provided by three different types of evidence. Occasionally, sums of money are entered beside the names of the individuals marked with a cross, the sums representing the amount due as fine for nonappearance.[20] Fines for nonappearance of jurors were also sometimes entered on a separate piece of parchment known as an estreat, and on at least one such occasion the names marked with crosses on the jury panels can be found on an estreat roll with the heading "because he did not come."[21] Similarly, fines for non-appearance are sometimes noted in the record of a case on the court roll, and when these can be compared to a surviving jury panel, the people so designated on the roll appear on the panel with a cross beside their name.[22] The meaning of the cross symbol is, however, complicated by the fact that some individuals marked with a cross also have a jur' written beside their name. The crosses in these instances may refer to jurors who failed to appear for an earlier stage of the trial process, or perhaps to jurors who came late to court, and thus were absent when the court was called into session but were later sworn in.

A third common annotation is the one noted in association with the panel from Harlow hundred, namely a circular ink mark, or pricking beside a name. These marks are often found on panels that also have crosses and jur' abbreviations and appear to be particularly common in the later fourteenth and fifteenth centuries, particularly on the panels associated with inquests.[23] Although people whose names were pricked often did not swear, they were much more likely to swear than people whose names were not pricked. The prickings, in effect, appear to designate a pool of preferred jurors. It is tempting to see them as a form of notation used by a sheriff to indicate his preference for who should be put on the jury. If that is the case, then the procedure for constituting a jury could be reconstructed as follows. In response to a writ from a sheriff, a bailiff established a pool of potential jurors, wrote their names on a panel, and sent the panel to the sheriff. The sheriff reviewed the panel, and occasionally designated those he thought were best suited to serve, indicating his preferences by pricking the relevant names. The justice or other official convening the court or inquest took the panel from the sheriff and reviewed it either at the start of a session or before hearing a particular case. A court official kept the panel while the court or inquest was in session, entering crosses beside the names of jurors who did not show up and then later entering jur' beside the names of the jurors when they took their oath to deliver a true verdict.

The importance of the jury panels is demonstrated by two cases involving their use that came to light in the trials of corrupt royal officials conducted between 1289 and 1293.[24] Both alleged that a justice had misused a jury panel, and the accounts of how they did so shed considerable light on the creation and use of the panels. In the first case, Ralph of Ditton (a village in Cambridgeshire) complained that he had been put on an assize jury by William de Saham, justice, against his wishes and without prior summons to serve on the case.[25] Ralph felt particularly aggrieved because the verdict he had participated in was later overturned and he had been imprisoned with the rest of the jury for delivering a false verdict. The accused justice rejected Ralph's allegations of wrongdoing and asked to have both the official record of the assize and the jury panel brought before the inquisitors reviewing the matter. The two documents were duly produced and a transcript of the assize record was entered on the inquisitors' roll. In addition to recording the details of the dispute, the transcribed record states that eight members of the jury panel failed to appear when the assize was taken, one of whom was Ralph of Ditton. Justice Saham, represented by an attorney, said that both the record and the panel, which is appended to the inquisitors' roll, proved that Ralph had been duly summoned and sworn. He sought judgment accordingly.

Ralph of Ditton asserted in response that the record and panel examined by the inquisitors did not contradict his complaint, and defended his position on two grounds. The first was based strictly on the evidence in the hands of the inquisitors: The record of the case showed that he had been fined 40s. for failing to appear, thus presupposing his absence when the assize was taken, but the panel included his name and indicated that he swore the juror's oath. Thus the record and the panel were at variance, and he sought judgment on this basis. But he went on to say that even if it could be established that he had taken the juror's oath, he had not been properly summoned and thus his inclusion on the jury had been unjust. He went on to explain how it might happen that someone could unjustly find himself serving on a jury:

justices used to resort to the following practice on assizes and jury cases, namely, that if there was a shortage of jurors caused by a challenge to the panel or for some other reason, the justices told the sworn jurors to choose [other jurors] from the lawful men present before them in court until they had a full complement of 12. The justices would also say to their clerks that they should put the names of those chosen on the panel and join them to the names of those originally put on the panel, but on this account it does not follow that those chosen in this manner were sworn even though they might be entered on the panel.

Ralph stated that he had been placed on the panel in this fashion and had objected at the time, only to have Justice Saham brush aside his objections.

The extant jury panel that now forms part of the inquest record appears to be the same one that was used for the original assize that gave rise to Ralph's problem. It contains 21 names. The first has no marginal notations of any kind, suggesting that the individual was present in court but was rejected as a juror. Ralph of Ditton is the second name on the list. Beside his name is a cross in the left margin with the additional notation "20s." in Roman numerals, and the abbreviation jur' in the right margin.[26] Of the remaining 19 names, 11 have jur' abbreviations in the right margin and eight have crosses in the left margin. One of the eight with a cross also has the notation "one mark" (equal to 13s. 4d.), while a second is struck through (striking through usually designated that a juror was sick or otherwise excused from jury duty). Excluding the name that is struck through, the other eight names that have a cross in the margin (including Ralph of Ditton) are the names entered in the court roll as failing to attend. Interestingly, they occur on the roll in the same order as on the panel, suggesting either that the scribe who wrote the record used the panel to compose his text, or that the justice or some other court official actually read the names in court while the scribe composing the record took notes.

Pleadings broke off without any resolution, but the specificity of Ralph's allegations and his eagerness to have the sheriff verify his story imply that he was telling the truth. The practice of drafting "talesmen" from the people present in court in order to round out a jury has been discussed by J. B. Post for the later fourteenth century and Ralph's account suggests that the practice was not uncommon a century earlier.[27] The unusual opportunity to compare a descriptive account of how a jury panel was used in court with the record of a case and the panel for the case also raises some other intriguing possibilities. It intimates not only that the courts expected all the people entered on the panel to be present in court when the time came to strike a jury but also that court administrators methodically checked attendance. It also raises the possibility that someone was coordinating the jury between the time that the original panel was struck and the time the case was heard. It is possible that Ralph of Ditton's problems all stemmed from the one juror whose name was struck through. One can legitimately wonder how a list that probably originally included 19 names yielded the presence in court of 11 jurors and one person who happened to be sick or otherwise unavailable.[28] Coordination of this kind could have been done by the bailiff, the sheriff, the summoners, or perhaps even by the jurors themselves. Jurors, particularly assize jurors, did much of their work outside of court before the trial or inquest was held, so positing some sort of advance planning about who would actually attend the court session seems reasonable.

The second case of judicial misconduct involving the empanelling of jurors heard during the inquests of 1289–93 involved the royal justice William de Brompton, a notoriously corrupt judge. Among the many serious complaints raised against him was one lodged by Roger of Thornton, who gave the inquisitors a long and sordid story of Brompton's manipulation of legal process, much of which involved tampering with jury panels.[29] Thornton stated that he had contested possession of certain lands in Cambridgeshire with a certain Hugh, son of Henry, only to discover that Brompton was in cahoots with his adversary. Specifically, Thornton alleged that Brompton had refused to accept a panel given to him by the sheriff and had instead arranged for a panel of partisan jurors to be turned in. As Thornton told the story

when the sheriff returned his writ along with the names of the jurors on a panel, not once but twice, William [de Brompton] did not permit the jurors named in the panel to swear because he did not think that they had been procured by him or by Hugh. Moreover, when for a third time the sheriff returned a jury panel of thirty men, including knights and others, he [Brompton] did not allow five or six of them to swear and ordered the jurors to return to their homes. And afterwards he . . . caused to be enrolled the names of jurors he wanted and who had never been summoned by the sheriff.

Brompton followed this up with yet other procedural tricks. Not surprisingly, the litigation terminated in a judgment against Thornton and the loss of the lands he was claiming.

The inquisitors made a serious effort to look into the substance of Thornton's allegations. Some they readily dismissed, but the tampering with the jury panels attracted considerable attention. At least two further sessions were held to examine the allegations, at the second of which Thornton elaborated on his original complaint. He told the inquisitors that after rejecting the third panel and telling the jurors to go home, Brompton sent a panel to the sheriff along with a threatening letter ordering him to cooperate. According to Thornton, Brompton's letter demanded that the sheriff put the people he had named on the jury. Again according to Thornton, when Brompton got wind that the sheriff had added some other names to the panel, he sent threatening letters to each of the additional jurors ordering them to decide the case on behalf of Hugh.

Brompton responded to Thornton's charges with a series of technical arguments that did not require a direct denial. His chief defense was that the sheriff was a royal official and that if any tampering was done with a jury panel, it was the sheriff who bore responsibility. Since the sheriff had not been convicted of any wrongdoing in the matter, it was, in Brompton's view, not permissible to entertain charges against a possible accessory. As for threatening jurors, which Brompton characterized as bribing rather than threatening, Brompton argued that Thornton needed to state exactly who had been bribed in order for his allegation to be sustained. Since he had not identified any of the jurors by name, the court could not, in his view, entertain the allegation. In any event, Brompton concluded, the case was ultimately determined on procedural grounds and not by the verdict of an allegedly corrupted jury, so the issue of jury tampering was not material to the outcome of the case.

The inquisitors' decision about Thornton's allegations is not recorded on the roll. In the course of the proceedings they exonerated Brompton of some of Thornton's other charges, and their stated rationale for doing so makes it clear that Thornton had embellished his story. But they did not address the issue of jury tampering in the surviving text, and so the truth of Thornton's allegations cannot be determined. What is clear from the case, though, is that Thornton had told a credible story about how a justice might abuse the process of empanelling juries. Both sides accepted that the panel would govern the process of juror selection and both assumed that the sheriff would be responsible for assembling the panel and conveying it to court. The inquisitors, too, apparently viewed Thornton's allegations on the matter as plausible, and, unlike some of his other claims, pushed to have the details brought out in pleading.

Mixed Juries

The methods that sheriffs and bailiffs used on the ground to assemble jury panels are poorly documented and for the most part are obscure. Glimpses of their activities are, however, afforded by some of the procedural requirements of the courts. While sheriffs and bailiffs were given considerable latitude over the formation of a jury panel, they were not given *carte blanche*. They had to work within a framework of basic rules and assumptions about who could and could not be asked to serve, and their choices were subject to review by justices and other royal officials. Similarly, writs ordering the formation of juries might specify certain traits required of jurors in a particular case, allowing the sheriff or bailiff to choose but narrowly defining the boundaries within which choice could be exercised. In some forms of civil procedure, notably the possessory assizes, the litigants themselves might be given a role in the initial selection process, and in both civil and criminal procedure, litigants and defendants had the right to challenge individual jurors and even entire panels if they were dissatisfied with what a sheriff or bailiff had done. Modern jurisdictions tend to assume that all jurors are equally qualified to make decisions and therefore that a random selection of people is likely to yield a viable jury. These were not the assumptions of the period treated in this book. In the Middle Ages, it was widely accepted that the pool of jurors had to fit the needs of the case, and that the pool would differ depending on the type of decision the jurors had to make. Bailiffs and sheriffs were thus expected to make their selections in light of the matter at hand, limiting their choice of prospective jurors to people with personal backgrounds suited to the demands of particular cases. Many matters decided by juries were generic enough that the issue of personal background was relatively muted, but some cases required more specialized types of jury. These more specialized cases shed considerable light on the broader principles governing juror selection in the period as a whole and therefore merit a closer look.

The principle that the pool of jurors should correspond to the case at hand is most apparent in the case of mixed juries constituted to deal with cases in which one of the principals was not fully integrated into the social order.[30] Civil cases pitting Jews against Christians, for example, often went to a jury half of whose members were Jews.[31] An interesting example is found in a case heard in 1219–20, in which an executor of William, earl Marshal, claimed repayment of a debt allegedly owed to the earl by the Jew Samson Furmentinus.[32] The latter denied owing the debt and offered to prove his assertion "as a Jew against a Christian" in the manner the court prescribed. He also stated that an earlier inquest jury comprising both Jews and Christians had looked into the matter while the earl was still alive and that the Jews on the inquest jury had stated that they had no knowledge of such a debt. Furmentinus's claim about the earlier inquest was called into question, though, and the judges hearing the case decided to order the sheriff of Gloucester to conduct a new inquest, unless he had proof that the earlier inquest had indeed rendered a verdict. The outcome of the case does not survive, but the writ to the sheriff ordering the new inquest stipulates that it should be taken "by the oath of lawful Christians and Jews" and a note added to the entry on the court roll states that the parties agreed that the jury should consist of four Christians and four Jews.

A similar form of jury determined a dispute in 1272 involving some houses in Worcester, claimed by the king as an escheat (by law the property of a Jew escheated to the king when the owner died).[33] Aaron, son of Hake, and his brothers contested the king's claim and their title to the properties was upheld by two inquest juries, one made up of six Jews and six Christians and the other made up of six Jews and 12 Christians. It is not entirely clear why two verdicts were needed in the matter; the second was taken several months after the first and was more detailed, suggesting that the first verdict was viewed as deficient. Both of the documents recording the two verdicts have signatures of the Jewish jurors in Hebrew at the bottom of the document.[34] Both juries concluded that Aaron and his brothers had purchased the disputed houses from Christians with their own funds and had not inherited them from their father.

While these mixed juries of Jews and Christians usually dealt with civil litigation, a similar procedure might be used in criminal cases. In 1290, for example, two royal officials were ordered to constitute a jury of Jews and Christians to look into an accusation made by William le Convers that he had been assaulted by Jews in Oxford.[35] An unusual record of a murder case heard in the king's court in 1224 gives considerable detail about the role Jews might play as jurors.[36] In that year, Martin, son of William, a Christian, formally accused two Jews, Bonenia and his wife Aunstera, of murdering his father. He asked for a trial in the form of a Christian versus a Jew, by which he presumably meant that the trial would involve a mixed jury. Bonenia denied the charge and stated before the justices that the murdered man had not come into his house on the day of his death. Asked if he was willing to put himself on a jury of 12 neighboring Christians and 12 neighboring Jews, Bonenia rejected the proffered jury, citing King John's charter to the Jews in support of his rejection (the charter stipulated that a Jew accused of a criminal offense by a Christian was entitled to judgment by his fellow Jews).[37] Bonenia's rejection appears to have caught the justices off guard. They first ordered an inquest to be held by 18 Christians, divided into three groups of six. The subgroups gave similar but not identical answers. They all stated that they suspected the members of Bonenia's household rather than Bonenia himself, but two of the subgroups testified that Bonenia had dragged the body out of the house and into the street. One of these witness/jurors—it is hard to know how to describe those serving on the inquest—added that Bonenia was seen dragging the body from the house, and a second concurred but added that Bonenia had said to him at the door of his house that William (the victim) was still alive when he was removed from the house.

In spite of Bonenia's rejection of a jury amalgamating Jews and Christians, the court also asked a number of Jews from the neighborhood to make statements in court. In the document, 12 Jews are named. The first is described in the document as "the first juror" (*primus jurator*). He said that he knew nothing about the death, and that William was not killed in the house of Bonenia, and that he did not suspect Bonenia, his wife, or anyone in Bonenia's household. He also said that William did not work in Bonenia's house the day he was found dead in the doorway and that Bonenia was not home at the time William was found. The other Jews, likewise described as "jurors," responded individually and said that they agreed with what the first juror said.

The record of the case breaks off abruptly after the twelfth juror's testimony and gives no hint as to the final verdict. One plausible reconstruction is that William suffered some kind of health crisis or life-threatening accident while working in Bonenia's house and that Bonenia, or someone in his household, fearing what would happen if a Christian died in a Jewish home, carried him into the street to die. Such an interpretation would make sense of a scribal emendation that changed the first Jewish juror's testimony. Initially, the scribe wrote that the juror had testified that William had been "killed" (*occisus*) when found in front of Bonenia's door, but then changed the entry to read that William was found "dead" (*mortuus*) in front of the door. Whatever the truth of the matter, the case reveals a surprisingly strong commitment on the part of the justices to the principle that a mixed jury of Jews and Christians was the best mechanism for getting at the truth. Even when the defendant rejected the procedure, the justices saw no alternative but to proceed as though he had accepted.

Jews were not the only minority group to be accorded the right to a mixed or special jury. The courts often treated cases involving a Welsh or Scottish principal in the same fashion.[38] Foreign merchants also had their right to a mixed jury with representatives from their native land enshrined in the Carta Mercatoria of 1303 and elaborated in several fourteenth-century statutes, but precedents can be found as early as 1251.[39] A particularly interesting example of foreigners serving on a jury can be found in an inquest into piracy in the English Channel held in Yarmouth in 1317.[40] It had long been customary for inquest jurors to affix their seals to the written verdict, but on this occasion the Flemish merchants refused to comply because "it is ordained in Flanders that no man unless a knight should affix his seal to any such inquisition outside the county under forfeiture of life and limb." Since the inquest found that the count of Flanders had commissioned the pirates and was chiefly to blame for their deeds, the caution of the Flemish jurors was no doubt well advised.

The use of mixed juries is particularly striking when one of the parties was a foreigner or somehow otherwise marginal, but the same practice can often be found when the parties were both English but hailed from different jurisdictions. The prototype for all mixed juries was probably the special inquest set up to perambulate boundaries, a particularly early form of jury. On these early perambulating inquests half of the jurors were sometimes explicitly chosen to represent the interests of one of the contending parties and half to represent the interests of the other; such a jury was struck, for example, to resolve a boundary dispute between two lords in Hampshire settled by 1162 at the latest.[41] Similar types of mixed juries were sometimes set up to fix the boundaries between counties or between areas that fell under the forest law and areas that did not. In such cases jurors were usually drawn equally from the neighboring counties rather than from competing lordships.[42] In 1212, for example, the king ordered an inquest into the boundaries of a marsh used as common pasture by people in three adjoining counties and stipulated that each county should have six representatives on the jury.[43] The overlap between perambulations and other forms of mixed juries is particularly striking in a dispute over a wooded area on the border between Shropshire and Wales in 1229. The Welsh disputant claimed that the woods formed part of his property on the Welsh side of the border and the English disputant claimed them as part of his manor in Shropshire. To resolve the matter, King Henry III ordered the sheriff of Shropshire to conduct a perambulation of the woods with a jury made up of 12 Welshmen chosen by the English disputant and 12 Englishmen chosen by the Welsh disputant.[44]

Mixed juries were also frequently prescribed when the central issue involved jurisdictional rather than territorial boundaries.[45] Two powerful lords squared off in 1208 when the abbot of Bury St. Edmunds claimed that his jurisdictional rights in the hundreds surrounding his abbey had been undermined by the bishop of Ely.[46] The abbot told the court that the bishop had entered his lands to retrieve the body of a murder victim and had proceeded not only to bury the corpse but also to arrest the suspected murderers. Such shame (*pudor*), the abbot said, could not be endured. The bishop, however, shrugged off the abbot's shame, and said that a jury had already issued a verdict defining their respective rights. He went on to specify that the jury in the case had comprised six men chosen by him, six by the abbot, and six by the archbishop of Canterbury. The abbot's attorney did not dispute the bishop's claim and went on to argue, not very convincingly, that the bishop had failed to respect the terms of the original verdict. A variant form of mixed jury can be observed in a jurisdictional dispute between the abbot of Cirencester and Ralph le Moyne in 1223.[47] Ralph exercised lordship in the manor of Shipton near Cirencester and had recently erected a gallows and a tumbrel there. He had also recently had the ear of a thief cut off in his manor court. The abbot protested that these actions infringed the judicial monopoly that he exercised on behalf of the king in the hundred, and he filed suit to have his monopoly restored. The justices hearing the case called for a jury to be made up partly of men drawn from within the hundred and partly from men from a neighboring hundred. They clearly felt that the abbot's control of the hundred precluded a jury that would be fair to le Moyne, whose main property interests were in another county. In the end, however, the jury did not determine the case: The justices ruled on the basis of le Moyne's charter and statements in court that he did not have the judicial rights he claimed.

ACCEPTING AND CHALLENGING JURORS

Mandates to have a panel of jurors fitting a particular description obviously limited the discretion a sheriff or bailiff could exercise when empanelling jurors, but they were only one among a number of similar limitations designed to ensure that jury panels were chosen in ways that were fair and evenhanded. Mixed juries provide a particularly clear illustration of how juror pools might be limited in the interests of fairness to the parties whose lives and property hung in the balance, but the principle itself can be seen in many other procedures and practices. Two related practices were particularly important and will come in for special attention here: the policy of securing consent to the jurors presented in the pool, and the policy of allowing litigants and defendants to challenge the impartiality of the jurors chosen by a bailiff or sheriff.

The principal of requiring consent to a jury trial from a defendant in a felony case was discussed in chapter 2. Similar principles also operated in some types of civil litigation, particularly in litigation associated with the possessory assizes. Assize juries were regularly described in court documents as having been constituted with "the consent of the parties" and there is plenty of evidence to show that this was more than an empty formula. The practice is hinted at in the late twelfth-century text ascribed to Glanvill, which notes that assize jurors should be chosen in the presence of the plaintiff and defendant, and then goes on to discuss what should be done if one or the other of the contending parties was unable to attend.[48] Descriptions of direct participation in the selection of jurors also occur in the law text ascribed to Bracton, and in the account of a dispute over warren rights in 1240 given by the chronicler Matthew Paris.[49]

The point of having the litigating parties attend the selection was to ensure that the jury pool was constituted in an acceptable manner and also, perhaps, to give the parties some input into the bailiff's choices. Since assize jurors did most of their work on a case before they appeared in court, and since their impartiality could be challenged when the case came before the court, there were good reasons to give the litigating parties a say in the selection process early on. The extent to which this actually occurred is difficult to discern; it probably depended on the inclinations of individual bailiffs and on the circumstances of the case. But the underlying principle that jurors had to be acceptable to both parties was central to the process of juror selection, regardless of whether or not it occurred in the presence of the litigants. A case of novel disseisin heard in Lincolnshire in 1219 illustrates particularly well the lengths to which a bailiff might go to come up with suitable jurors.[50] The case revolved around the behavior of an assistant bailiff, who had, allegedly, given the plaintiffs a bogus trial date so that they would default on the day of the trial. The plan did not quite work, however, and the aggrieved plaintiffs eventually gained the ear of the justices, who decided to look into the matter more fully. Among other things the justices asked the chief bailiff of the wapentake—the supervisor of the corrupt assistant bailiff—to account for his behavior in assembling a jury. The bailiff gave a very informative response. He knew, he said, that the case was bound to be a difficult one because it involved a dispute over access to common pasture, with multiple plaintiffs and multiple defendants. Many of the people who lived nearby had a vested interest in the case, and many were kin to one or the other of the litigating parties. In order to come up with a body of jurors who did not have a direct, personal stake in the outcome of the case, the bailiff decided to convene a meeting of the three wapentakes over which he had jurisdiction, at which the jurors for the case were elected. The plaintiffs, he added, were in attendance at the meeting and the defendants had also been invited but had declined to come. After the jurors had been chosen, the chief bailiff told them when they were expected to appear in court to deliver their verdict.

The procedure outlined in Lincolnshire in 1219 would not have been practical on a regular basis, although there is some evidence to suggest that sheriffs and bailiffs sometimes used ordinary gatherings of county courts and hundred courts as recruiting grounds for jurors.[51] What makes the Lincolnshire case so interesting, though, is not so much what the chief bailiff did, but the matter-of-fact explanation he gave to explain why he did it. He operated on the assumption that his job required him to create a panel that could deliver a verdict that was not only well informed but also fair and impartial, and thus necessarily one that could not include men who might use their power as jurors for personal benefit or to reward someone to whom they were personally bound. Similarly, his decision to invite the plaintiffs and the defendants to attend the selection process indicates that he made a genuine effort to create a jury that both litigating parties would find acceptable. But what is most remarkable about this story is the fact that the bailiff's activities would never have come in for discussion at all had there not been a problem with another aspect of procedure. The chief bailiff was describing something he had done in the past, before he had any reason to think that there would be special scrutiny of the steps he had taken. His behavior suggests that he had internalized a general ethos in which the provision of fair-minded jurors was standard operating procedure. Bailiffs (and sheriffs) often flouted the rules and used their power to tilt the jury toward one or the other of the litigating parties, but on the whole they respected and implemented the standards of fairness and responsibility without which the jury system could not have succeeded.

That is not to say, of course, that sheriffs and bailiffs were always able to pass up the temptation to subvert the process of juror selection in return for bribes or other forms of reward. Inquests into the behavior of royal officials in the period are full of complaints about abuses of office and concrete examples of bailiffs and sheriffs using their positions to line their own pockets. Abuses related to jury composition are not the only, nor even the chief, issue singled out in these inquests, but they are common enough to indicate that fair dealing could never be taken for granted.[52] Ultimately, the main guarantor of the integrity of jury procedure was not the integrity of the officials who formed the jury panels; it was instead, the right of a defendant or litigant to challenge any or all of the jurors who had been drafted for the case. Juror challenges were probably built upon a foundation set in place by the witness challenges that were a feature of both Germanic customary law and Roman and canon law of the twelfth and later centuries.[53] They are, of course, also an integral part of modern trial procedure, albeit one that has come in for a good deal of criticism in recent years. The differences between medieval and modern challenges are striking and far reaching but the principle underlying both is fundamentally similar, namely, the belief that a fair judgment cannot be rendered by people who are predisposed to favor a particular outcome. The primary difference is that the predisposing influences underpinning modern challenges tend to be sociological, whereas in the Middle Ages they were direct and personal.

Juror challenges were permissible in all of the principal forms of jury procedure with the exception of presentment. The exclusion of presentment was due principally to the fact that the jurors did not sit directly in judgment on the people they presented, meaning that the issue of bias against a defendant could be handled more effectively when the case reached the trial phase. Before the middle of the fourteenth century, it was not uncommon for presentment jurors to be reconstituted as a trial jury to try a case that had been set in motion by their earlier presentment.[54] A statute enacted in 1352 gave formal recognition to a defendant's right to challenge a trial juror solely because he had also served on the presentment jury, and the late thirteenth-century law text known as *Britton* states that this was already common practice in his day.[55] Thomas Green has written extensively about the overlap between presentment and trial juries, particularly in the context of "jury nullification," the frequent acquittal of defendants in felony cases by trial jurors who had served on the presentment jury responsible for the indictment.[56]

Presentment jurors may also have been exempt from challenges because they were constituted in a significantly different way than were other jurors. They were ordinarily selected by local notables who were not officially associated with royal administration. The procedure is spelled out particularly well in the eyre courts, but appears to have applied in other courts as well. Bailiffs began the process by nominating two men of high status who were well respected by, and well connected to, the other prominent families of their hundred.[57] These two men were known as "electors" and are often so designated in surviving court records. They were required to choose the other men who would form the jury, on which they also usually served. Originally, bailiffs had even been excluded from nominating the two who would serve as electors; the instructions for the eyre of 1194 stipulated that the county should elect four knights who would then select the two knights from each hundred who would then choose the other presentment jurors.[58] Corruption and cronyism may not have been entirely removed from the presentment process by these precautions, but the more elaborate procedure, which also required special oaths from the bailiffs and electors, probably fostered a sense that presentment jurors operated according to rules different from those applying to other jurors.

Each of the other three main types of jury procedure allowed for challenges and they will be dealt with in turn, starting with inquest juries. Challenges raised against inquest jurors are infrequent in existing documentation, but enough examples can be found to suggest that they were treated as legitimate procedural devices. A particularly revealing illustration of their use is furnished in an inquest held in Devon in 1234–35 to investigate whether a new market founded by Richard son of Stephen in Dartmouth damaged the preexisting market franchise of Eva de Braose in Totnes.[59] The sheriff's inquest originally found in favor of Braose, but when Richard, son of Stephen, complained in the king's court that he was not present when the inquest was taken and that three of his enemies had served on it, the justices agreed to reconvene the inquest in their presence and ordered the sheriff to supply three new jurors to take the place of the three who were alleged to be partisan.

Challenges of inquest jurors also feature prominently in a dispute in Southampton in 1290 that ultimately came before Parliament.[60]

The dispute revolved around the right of appointment to the wardenship of the town's hospital. Three parties had a stake in the dispute: the borough, the bishop of Winchester, and the king. The people of the town claimed that the hospital had been founded by a burgess as an act of charity and that many other burgesses had contributed to its endowment. They based their right of appointment on this tradition of foundation and ongoing material support. The original basis of the bishop's claim is not clearly stated, but he insisted that his right had been established in an earlier court case determined in the court of Common Pleas. This earlier case is still extant and does indeed support the bishop's contention.[61] The king's claim was based on the fact that the previous warden had died while the town's right to self-government was under suspension, meaning that the king exercised direct control over the borough's administration, including its right to appoint a new warden.

Because the dispute involved consideration of royal property rights, the king decided that the matter could best be settled by inquest procedure. Accordingly, he appointed two justices to conduct an inquest and ordered the sheriff of Hampshire to provide them with a jury. Specifically, he ordered his justices to reach a decision based on "the oath of upright and law-worthy men, both from the town of Southampton and from the adjacent districts." These instructions, however, were fiendishly difficult to implement. According to the bishop, the burgesses had been involved in so many acrimonious disputes with him in recent years that it was impossible to find anyone in the town who was not prejudiced against him. When the sheriff received the writ ordering that some of the jurors be chosen from the men of the town, the bishop went to the king to complain. The king agreed to issue another writ, this one instructing the justices to limit the selection to men who were not resident in the town. Thus, when the justices convened in Southampton to take the inquest, they found themselves confronting two conflicting writs—one calling for a jury that included men from the town and the other calling for a jury that excluded them. They decided to proceed according to the terms of the original writ, allowing men from the town to be put on the jury. The bishop's attorney immediately challenged their ruling, but the justices held firm. The bishop's refusal to even consider the presence of townsmen on the jury, they said, was tantamount to a challenge "of the whole community in general and as a group" and as such ran contrary to traditional usage in the king's court, which required that juror challenges be aimed at specific individuals. Forced to accept defeat on this central point, the bishop's bailiff issued challenges against three of the jurors who had been empanelled by the sheriff, indicating that they had been involved in earlier contentions between town and bishop. The justices dismissed the three and then assembled a jury of 12 others who delivered the verdict. But the matter did not end there. Recognizing the contentious nature of the verdict, which was generally balanced but ultimately upheld the king's right of appointment, the justices decided that the whole matter should be discussed in Parliament. When the matter came up for discussion before Parliament the bishop claimed, not surprisingly, that the justices had acted contrary to the custom of the realm by denying his right to challenge. The king inspected the record of the inquest, asked the justices to explain their ruling, and then discussed the matter with his council. After consulting, they announced that the justices had handled the inquest properly, and the bishop was sent home empty-handed.[62]

As this Southampton dispute illustrates, there were situations in which the choice of jurors for royal inquests could be highly contentious. As a rule, however, challenges of assize jurors were much more common than challenges of inquest jurors, because assizes were inherently adversarial. The procedures governing challenges in assizes are first discussed by the author of *Glanvill,* who states that both plaintiffs and defendants could exclude assize jurors for cause and goes on to note that they could exercise their right even when the jurors were first being selected.[63] The law text ascribed to Bracton also went into the matter in some depth and gives a list of justifiable challenges that is both interesting and informative.[64] First on the list came "infamy" by which the author meant someone who had previously been convicted of perjury. Next came "enmity," provided it was deep and enduring. Ties based on close personal bonds are then treated in several different guises, including long-lasting ties of "friendship" and "intimacy," relations based on marriage or blood, and membership in a common household or at a common table. Similarly, people who were beholden to others could be challenged for that reason, as might happen through the exercise of lordship. Any juror who stood to benefit personally from the verdict could also be legitimately excluded, as could jurors who had other legal relationships with one of the parties, such as codefendant in another case. The author went on to note that challenges had to be based on current or recent relationships and not on relationships that had existed long ago, and he ended by saying that his list was intended merely to provide examples rather than to be exhaustive.

Many of the grounds for challenging assize jurors given by Bracton can be confirmed in court records of the thirteenth and fourteenth centuries.[65] One other factor not included in the list also crops up regularly in the court records, namely favoritism shown by the bailiff or sheriff who assembled the jury. The author of the Bracton text probably chose to exclude bias of officials from his list because technically the challenges were directed against the jurors rather than the person who created the panel. In practice, however, those who issued challenges often justified them by referring to the partiality of a bailiff or sheriff. The courts were indeed willing to recognize challenges based on the constitution of entire panels (the "array"), even though they tended to steer litigants toward challenges of individual jurors.[66] Thus, in 1206, a defendant in an assize of mort d'ancestor challenged the entire jury by alleging that the bailiff's daughter was married to his adversary.[67] In an assize of novel disseisin heard in 1359, the defendant challenged the panel because the sheriff who had constituted it wore the livery of a relative of the other party.[68] The justices accepted the challenge and ordered the coroners to constitute a new panel for the case. Upon hearing from the defendant that one of the coroners wore the same livery as the sheriff, they emended their order and excluded the suspect coroner from the process, stipulating that the county's other coroners should take responsibility for the new panel. One of the litigating parties could also challenge a panel simply on the grounds that a bailiff had followed the advice of an adversary when selecting jurors.[69]

A private document related to a case heard c.1293 provides a fascinating glimpse into what sometimes went on behind the scenes in preparation for making a challenge.[70] The document occurs in a cartulary of Lilleshall abbey and concerns a dispute between the abbey and James of Astley over property in the village of Fresley in Warwickshire. One of the central issues to emerge in pleading was the refusal of a certain Richard of Whitacre to acknowledge the validity of a charter that was the foundation of the abbey's claim. The document in the cartulary lists the names of the jurors drafted for the case, and behind each name states simply and directly the justification for challenging. All of the entries refer, directly or indirectly, to relationships between the jurors and Richard of Whitacre, the principal roadblock to the abbey's claim. Thus the first entry runs as follows: "John of Manchester ought not to be [a juror] because he is related to Richard of Whitacre and is sworn to him and bound by faith." Others were challenged for being friends or tenants of Richard or for being in his service. Many involved indirect relationships: William Fundu, for example, was challenged because he was married to one of Richard's friends; Jordan of Eastley because Richard's father was his godfather.

The web of relationships and influences alluded to in the document has remarkably long and intricate strands, and illustrates how difficult it must have been for a bailiff to find jurors who were knowledgeable about the case but not beholden to one of the principals.

A note entered at the end of the list provides even more insight into the abbot's keen interest in exercising his right to challenge. It states that the abbot sent an "expert" to the area where the jurors lived, who was to "diligently inquire about the jurors and seek out their names and persuade them to be favorable and ask who ought to be challenged and who not, and what allegations would be good and true to use against them and to keep track of good jurors if he found any." The abbot's actions were of dubious legality, constituting, or very nearly so, the crime that would come to be known in the fourteenth century as "embracery," the attempt to pressure or influence jurors before the trial to return a favorable verdict.[71] Embracery had yet to be formally designated a crime in the 1290s, but Parliament did enact a measure against the related crime of "conspiracy" in 1293.[72] There is little thirteenth-century case law available to determine the propriety of the "research" undertaken by the abbot's legal expert. Assize litigants could and often did interact with the jurors before a trial was held, and the issue in early cases alleging conspiracy and other forms of tampering was not contact per se but rather contact with the intent of subverting a true verdict.

Juror challenges in criminal cases had many features in common with those in assize cases, but there were also some significant differences.[73] First of all, they appear to have been less common.[74] No statistical data on challenges in medieval trials has ever been compiled so definitive statements about frequency of use are not possible, but it is suggestive that both *Bracton* and *Britton* treat challenges primarily in the context of assize procedure and secondarily in the context of criminal procedure. In fact, the author of Britton devoted an entire chapter of his work to challenges of assize jurors, but only five sentences to challenges of jurors in felony cases.[75] Second, differences in the form of trial procedure also made challenges more likely in assizes than in criminal trials. Assizes were invariably adversarial, meaning not only that challenges were available to two litigating parties (as opposed to one criminal defendant) but also that tampering with juror selection was more likely, because two sides sought to exert pressure on the selection process. Furthermore, since criminal defendants were generally of lower status than civil litigants and often incarcerated before their trial, they were less likely to have any influence over the process of juror selection.

Though less common, they were still an integral part of trial procedure and an important precaution against conviction by a biased jury. The author of *Bracton* described two scenarios in which challenges of criminal jurors would be allowed by the courts.[76] The first involved greed for the property of the accused, as might be found when a lord hoped to eliminate a tenant in order to add his land to his demesne farm. Happily, evidence from court records of such Machiavellian manipulation of trial procedure is hard to come by, although the author may well have had a specific case in mind when he came up with the example. The second scenario involved enmity against the accused, a motive that the author did not develop in any detail but that is borne out in existing court records. In practice, the courts were willing to allow a variety of justifications for challenges in criminal cases, some involving enmity but others based on other grounds that might prejudice a jury against a defendant. Jurors were successfully challenged for being related to the victim, for example, or for being prejudiced against the defendant because they were of higher status.[77]

Somewhat surprisingly, the author of *Bracton* did not discuss peremptory challenges, and the whole tenor of his discussion indicates that the courts expected defendants to justify their challenges.[78] Careful scrutiny of challenges was the norm through most of the fourteenth century. In 1382, for example, a justice noted in passing in a case before the court of Common Pleas that the trying of challenges sometimes took so long that the court could adjourn for the evening without resolving them all.[79] By the middle of the fifteenth century, however, the right to issue peremptory challenges had become well established, at least in felony cases: Sir John Fortescue, writing in the late 1460s, declared that defendants in felony cases could challenge up to 35 jurors without justification, and most modern authorities have accepted his position as normative for earlier periods.[80]

Fortescue portrayed the defendant's right to use peremptory challenges as proof of the inherent fairness of the Common Law system. Many modern jurisdictions allow peremptory challenges for the same reason, although most impose limits well below the number stipulated by Fortescue. The origins of the practice described by Fortescue are, however, hard to uncover. One possibility worth considering is that peremptory challenges developed out of the right to challenge trial jurors solely because they had served on the presentment jury responsible for the indictment, in the manner described by the author of *Britton* in the late thirteenth century.[81] Fortescue praised peremptory challenges because they gave the defendant leverage "in favor of his own life," and it is interesting to note that the author of *Britton* used similar language to explain why the courts allowed challenges justified solely with reference to prior service on the presentment jury: such challenges should be allowed, he wrote "where a man's life is at stake."[82]

Prior to the emergence of peremptory challenges, the courts were unwilling to take a defendant's assertions about juror bias at face value. Their resistance in this regard was probably based on the fear that defendants would use challenges as a pretext for delay, hoping that delay might create an opportunity to avoid trial altogether.[83] Even in assizes, delay was likely to benefit one side more than the other, and so the courts insisted not only that challenges be justified but also that the justifications be verified. The procedure for determining the validity of challenges was known as "trying" and is well described in a case from the later thirteenth or early fourteenth century reported in a Year Book.[84] A presentment jury indicted John de Thornton for burying someone without calling for the coroners and also for retaining a horse that had caused the person's death (the horse should have gone to the king as a "deodand," an object causing death). John denied the allegations and said that he was far away when the deeds ascribed to him occurred. He asked to have a jury's verdict on the truthfulness of his assertion, and the justices consented to his request. When the jurors were brought into court, one of the justices proclaimed: "Behold, here is a good jury of twelve, read their names, and may they stand up to all legitimate challenges." When their names had been read, Thornton challenged several of them, although the text fails to mention his reason for doing so. It does, however, go on to say that the other members of the jury who were not challenged then tried the validity of the challenges and decided that they did not constitute legitimate grounds for rejection. The trial then proceeded with the 12 originally brought into court.

The procedure of trying challenges was common to all forms of jury trial and could be adapted to fit just about any situation. Standard procedure followed the steps taken in John de Thornton's case, with the jurors who had not been challenged serving as the "triers." When a principal challenged an entire panel, as might happen when a sheriff or bailiff had been bribed or otherwise favored one party over the other, the court might appoint other people who were not associated with the case to serve as triers.[85] The justices hearing a property dispute in Northamptonshire in 1329–30 came up with a creative solution to a similar problem.[86] Some of the jurors were challenged by one of the litigating parties and the remaining jurors were challenged by the opposing party. Four of the challenged jurors were then chosen to serve as triers, two of whom were chosen from the jurors rejected by the plaintiff and two from those rejected by the defendant (the text does not indicate who made the choice). The four triers constituted in this fashion then tried the other challenges until they found three jurors whom they judged to have been challenged with insufficient justification, and these three were then drafted to take over the role of triers. The new trio of triers then weighed the challenges against the four original triers, as well as those against the other jurors, and eventually managed to come up with a body of 12 whom they judged competent to hear the case (themselves and nine others). The trial then proceeded.

CONCLUSION

Like many of the procedures described in this chapter, the method employed for trying juror challenges testifies to the great faith people had in the ability of juries to reach fair decisions, in spite of widespread recognition that they were subject to almost relentless pressure from those who stood to gain or lose from their workings. Explaining this faith is not an easy task. Modern historians tend to be cynical about the motives of the people they study, generally preferring to explain human behavior in terms of greed and lust for power or standing rather than in terms of faith or trust or conviction. While it would be naïve to think that medieval jurors were somehow immune from the baser instincts of human nature, it would be equally wrong to dismiss their ideals of fairness and justice, or to suggest that such ideals could never be as influential as their negative counterparts. Medieval people were well aware that bailiffs and other officials could be bribed or otherwise influenced and that personal animosity could be easily camouflaged as a lawsuit or an allegation of criminal misconduct.[87] It was precisely because of their awareness that might could so easily trump right that people committed themselves to the proper working of the jury system, the best defense they knew against the greed and corruption that was so obviously a part of their world.

In many respects, the evidence presented in this chapter serves as a commentary on the concerns medieval people had about the legitimacy of the jury system and the commitment they made to protecting its integrity. That such concerns would arise was almost inevitable, given the wide competency of jury procedure and the rapid growth that characterized its early history. Jury verdicts governed some of the most fundamental issues confronting medieval English society: the preservation of property rights; the maintenance of public order; the taking or sparing of life. Other stakeholders exercised authority over these same areas, but they all accepted that when matters came to a head, the pronouncement of the members of the jury would be decisive. To a great extent, the interests of kings, judges, and other royal officials were actually in sync with those of the broader society. All recognized that a system of governance and law that was organized around the input of jurors operated best when the procedures developed to ensure the fairness and integrity of the jury's work were respected.[88]

Ultimately, the test of the jury's work came after the verdict had been rendered and judgment pronounced. It is natural for the historian whose primary evidence is drawn from court records to treat the verdict and sentence as the conclusion of a story, and, by extension, to consider the process by which the verdict was reached as forming the body of the text. But for the people who were directly involved in the process, and often for society at large, the rendering of a verdict was as much a beginning as an end: Jurors and litigants or defendants ordinarily disappear from the historical record after the delivery of the verdict, but they did not disappear from the village or town where they lived their lives. The jurors who acquitted a defendant in a felony trial could reasonably expect to interact with that person again, in the parish or at a market or in any number of other ways.[89] Even when they convicted and then watched the felon be led away to be hanged, the trial jurors understood that they might well confront the implications of their decision in the world around them as they interacted with the surviving friends and family of the person they had condemned to death. In assizes and civil litigation, the prospects for future interaction were higher still. The stepson whose title was vindicated in an assize of mort d'ancestor joined in the rhythms of the agricultural year with the jurors who decided his fate; the uncle who lost may have sought his fortunes elsewhere, but even he was more likely to carry on where his roots were than to try his fortunes elsewhere. Similarly, when a tenant sought a favorable verdict in an assize of novel disseisin against the lord who had taken possession of his land, the jurors could count on the fact that not only the litigants but also the power relations put in judgment before them would persist when the trial was over.

Viewed from this perspective, the effort taken to create a body of jurors that commanded the assent of the individuals whose fortunes were linked to the verdict makes a good deal of sense. The goal was to create an environment in which the verdict had to be respected, whatever its outcome. A losing party naturally had a strong incentive to impugn the decision and reject its implementation. Since the verdict had already gone against the loser, the obvious point of attack for someone who lost was to challenge the credibility of the jurors or the legitimacy of the process that resulted in the verdict. Had the jury been arbitrarily selected and arbitrarily imposed on the parties, such arguments may well have found sympathetic ears. But when it was clear to everyone that the selection process had been fair and reasonable, and that the losing party had been given due discretion over the jury's constitution, then any attack on the legitimacy of the verdict was unlikely to carry much weight. Basically, the system was designed to accept high front-loaded costs in order to minimize the costs of enforcement down the road.

In many respects, this was simply a concession to the reality of the medieval world. The medieval English state could, with some difficulty, bring jurors into court and conduct trials in an organized and responsible manner that met prevailing standards of justice and fairness, but its influence over what transpired before or after the legal process had run its course was minimal. Or, it is probably better to say that its influence was minimal without the cooperation and support of society, or at least of those elements in society that provided leadership at local and county levels. The bureaucratic apparatus that modern states rely on to implement decisions that originate in a courtroom simply did not exist 700 years ago. Respect for verdicts was, consequently, something worth cultivating generally, since the broader society was the ultimate guarantor that judgments would be implemented according to the terms established by the court system. The jurors themselves were pivotal figures in securing the acceptance and cooperation needed to implement judgment. Even more than the formal court record, the jurors constituted a repository of what had transpired in court, what decisions had been taken, and what actions were necessary as a result. Their ongoing presence and involvement in local society was a fundamental part of the process by which legal decisions acquired legitimacy and social acceptance.

Finally, it is important to recognize that the state itself had a vested interest in cultivating a climate of respect for jury verdicts. The prodigious growth in the power of the monarchy that characterized the period from the middle of the twelfth century to the beginning of the fifteenth century was intimately related to the equally prodigious growth in the business of the king's courts.[90] What drew people into the king's courts was not an intrinsically superior procedure or an ideological preference for justice meted out by a king, but rather the belief that the king was particularly good at enforcing the decisions reached in his courts. Successful enforcement enhanced royal power; unsuccessful enforcement undermined it. Thus, kings were highly motivated to develop a system in which judicial decisions would be implemented in predictable and orderly ways. They lacked the resources to create a body of paid officials capable of carrying out such a huge task in any meaningful way, and so *faute de mieux* they cultivated the good will and support of their subjects. And here, once again, the legitimacy of the decision-making process rose to the fore. Goodwill and support had to be earned. The jury system constituted a kind of currency that could be exchanged between the king and his subjects, but like the kingdom's silver pennies, its value could ebb and flow depending on the care taken of it.

CHAPTER 4

JUROR QUALIFICATIONS

Extraordinary growth in the use of juries brought in its train a burgeoning demand for jury service. Medieval English people had been actively involved in local government and legal administration long before they were regularly asked to serve on juries, in such capacities as suitors to courts, oath-helpers, and witnesses to charters.[1] They had also been drafted to serve on early forms of jury, notably royal inquests. From the second half of the twelfth century, however, the frequency of demands for service grew substantially, as the jury system extended its competency over ever-increasing areas of law and government. Service as a juror typically involved commitments of time and energy well beyond those characterizing earlier forms of governmental service, and the frequency with which such service was called for imposed much heavier demands on a much broader segment of society. Indeed, one of the most notable consequences of the dramatic growth in the use of juries was the involvement of a substantially greater number of people in the governing process. Social groups that had once been on the periphery of power structures were increasingly asked to serve as decision-makers. By making juries so central to the operation of law and government, the Crown gave power and authority to a wide spectrum of medieval society.

Historians have long recognized that the effective operation of the jury system required extensive cooperation and participation on the part of the king's subjects, but they have not always appreciated the full extent of these demands and their social implications. As a result, they have often described jurors as men drawn primarily from the higher ranks of society. The distinguished legal scholar C. T. Flower, for example, once wrote that knights were the dominant group serving as jurors on possessory assizes.[2] More recently, Anthony Musson has stipulated that "jurors in the royal courts in the thirteenth century were expected to be knights or reasonably substantial property owners."[3] Such views seem almost unassailable at first glance. Jurors held positions of power after all, and it is difficult to imagine a hierarchical and deferential society such as the one that existed in medieval England welcoming the exercise of power by nonelites.

On the other hand, the weight of numbers has to be given its due: Elite groups would have been overwhelmed by the demands for jury service had they insisted on monopolizing all positions. Clearly, the system needed to make room for service by people of more humble social background. But how far down the social scale were royal administrators and political elites willing to go? This is the central question that animates this and the following chapter. Chapter 5 will approach the question by presenting a series of case studies exploring the social backgrounds of individuals serving on various juries of the later thirteenth and early fourteenth centuries. The present chapter provides a more global overview of the issue, examining the language used to describe jurors in contemporary documents of practice, the assumptions behind various legislative enactments governing the selection of jurors, and the practice of rejecting jurors who failed to meet judicial expectations of social standing for jury service. Before turning to these subjects, however, it will be useful to look more closely at what other historians have had to say about the matter. Existing literature is characterized by great diversity of opinion and the lack of agreement among scholars who have looked at the issue suggests that a thorough review of the question is well worth undertaking.

RECENT INTERPRETATIONS
OF JURORS' BACKGROUNDS

Over the past two decades, several legal historians have used jury panels and other lists of jurors to evaluate the social dimensions of jury service in medieval England. In 1988, for example, Bernard McLane, J. B. Post, and Edward Powell contributed essays informed by analyses of jury lists to the multiauthored volume *Twelve Good Men and True*, edited by J. S. Cockburn and Thomas A. Green.[4] Though their methods and sources were similar, their conclusions were quite diverse. McLane examined jury lists that were entered on the rolls of special courts of trailbaston, recording the work of both presentment juries and trial juries. He had limited success finding the jurors in other sources but most of those he did find were of relatively high standing, particularly the presentment jurors. He concluded that "local notables," described in the essay as people of "gentry or equivalent status," formed the mainstay of the juries, along with a secondary pool of people who had experience as local or royal officials.[5] Post worked with a selection of 21 jury panels culled from a gaol delivery file amalgamating courts held in several southern counties in the 1370s and '80s. He emphasized the frequency with which jurors failed to appear, and argued that the courts regularly employed "talesmen" to serve in their stead (a "talesman" was someone who was present in court for some other reason and who could be called upon to fill out a jury that lacked the requisite number of members.) Post made little effort to trace the jurors in other sources, but suggested that most jurors were probably appointed because they had other business that required them to attend the court.[6]

Like J. B. Post, Edward Powell worked with panels associated with gaol deliveries in several counties, with a focus on the first decades of the fifteenth century. His contribution to the volume suggests that sheriffs and bailiffs were guided by two main principles when they selected jurors. First of all, they generally favored men who had legal or administrative experience, either through previous service as trial or assize jurors or as tax assessors or local administrators. In this respect, his conclusions mirror those reached by Bernard McLane. But Powell also argued a much different position on the question of social background. He suggested that members of the gentry seldom served as jurors, unless the felon being tried was of relatively high status. In most instances, Powell concluded, the jurors "were presumably yeomen and prosperous husbandmen."[7]

Powell's use of the word "presumably" underscores a fundamental problem affecting not only his contribution to the volume but also those of McLane and Post as well. None of the contributors to the volume enjoyed great success in tracing the jurors outside the courts. To their credit, all three emphasized that their essays were preliminary forays into the subject and that much further research was needed before any definitive conclusions could be presented. It is, however, important to understand why they couched their findings in such tentative language, and also why they differed so much in their conclusions. All three emphasized internal evidence derived from the courts themselves to buttress arguments about the nature of jury service, and as a result all three emphasized the theme of prior experience and service in local administration. This is certainly an important finding, but it does not shed much light on the more general issue of social background. There are two obvious questions worth asking: From what background did those who built up profiles of repeat service and involvement in local administration come? And what was the background of the many jurors who were not repeatedly involved with the court system and local administration? Only McLane made a serious attempt to answer these questions by looking at other types of nonlegal evidence, but he was able to find relevant material only for a minority of the jurors appearing in the panels he examined. His evidence for gentry involvement certainly merits attention, but it does not tell the whole story. McLane decided to focus his analysis on jurors he was able to locate in other documents rather than on the total pool of jurors. The problem with such an approach is that members of the gentry were more likely to leave traces in other sources than members of lower social groups. McLane argued that among the jurors he was able to find, a significant number came from the ranks of the gentry. Such a conclusion was almost inevitable in light of the sample he worked with, since his subset of findable jurors was much more likely to include people of relatively high status.

A few years after these three studies appeared, R. B. Goheen published an important article in the *American Historical Review* that succeeded in overcoming some of their limitations. Goheen focused his research efforts on lists of jurors drawn up for a number of courts held by Justices of the Peace in Gloucestershire in the 1440s and '50s.[8] He cross-referenced the people appearing in the lists with similar lists occurring in various inquests held in the county in those two decades, and also with other sources, such as manorial court records that gave greater insight into the local context from which the jurors were drawn. While he did not furnish many details about his research method, he clearly devoted considerable effort to sifting these other sources for clues about the social background of the jurors appearing in the peace sessions. He concluded that most of the jurors appearing in the peace sessions were peasants, mainly wealthier peasants who were prominent in the affairs of their local villages. Both his method and his conclusions marked a great advance in our understanding of the medieval jury, but they have yet to be fully tested or incorporated into a broader synthesis encompassing wider temporal and geographical horizons. It would certainly be easy to build a case against Goheen's model as normative for earlier periods. The mid-fifteenth century was a period of great social and economic dislocation, with traditional social structures, such as serfdom, undergoing rapid and extensive change.[9] It was also a period of great political turmoil, characterized by ignominious defeat in war and the rule of one of the most hapless kings in all of English history, Henry VI. Traditionally, historians have described the period as "one in which an inert king allowed a group of grasping courtiers to take hold of his government. . . . [and] to manipulate the legal system at will against all those who were not under their protection."[10] Goheen did not address these broader contextual issues, nor did he follow his article with other publications designed to demonstrate the general applicability of the position he advocated.

The failure of Goheen's article to make much of an impact on the study of medieval juries is well illustrated in the work of Anthony Musson, a leading authority on the legal history of the fourteenth century. In his book, *Public Order and Law Enforcement,* published in 1996, Musson discussed the significance of jury panels for understanding the nature of jury service in the period, but failed to cite Goheen's work or incorporate its main arguments into his analysis.[11] Based on his examination of jury panels from the period, Musson suggested that definitive conclusions about the backgrounds of the jurors were seldom possible, and offered several general observations about the subject: Jurors often served on more than one jury; they sometimes included knights; and they more often included people who held other official positions. In an article published the next year dedicated more directly to the composition of juries in the early fourteenth century, Musson again adumbrated the difficulty of finding information about individual jurors, but went on to note that knights can be found as jurors.[12] He then noted again the tendency for some people to be drafted as jurors on different occasions and suggested that the practice made sense if there was a relatively small pool of people from which jurors were drawn, implying that jurors were generally of elevated status.

While some interesting working hypotheses have emerged in the literature of the past two decades, there is clearly still much to be learned about the social history of medieval jurors. These preliminary forays present points of departure for future work rather than definitive end points. For one thing, they embody significantly different points of view on the matter at hand, with some works reinforcing the idea that jury service was dominated by the higher echelons of society but others suggesting that peasants were routinely drafted to serve as jurors. Another issue left unresolved in these works is the social context of jury service in areas other than the criminal law. Assizes and inquests have been left out of the picture in most recent studies, in spite of the fact that these two forms of jury loomed large in the development and operation of the jury system in the period under examination. Finally, even when all of this specialist literature is put together, the sample of available material is still relatively small. Published work exists for only a limited number of courts in a small handful of counties. To be sure, this work provides valuable insights into the practices of the courts in question, but at this juncture it is still too narrow and too limited to underpin broad generalizations. Reliable conclusions have to be based on a broader range of evidence involving a broader range of jury forms. A particularly helpful place to begin the necessary process of broadening is with a careful examination of the language of the writs and administrative documents used to assemble juries in the period.

FREEDOM AND LAWFULNESS

The most common contemporary expression used to describe the people sought as jurors stipulated that they should be drawn from the ranks of "free and lawful men" (*libri et legales homines*), a phrase that recurs countless times in the writs ordering sheriffs and bailiffs to constitute juries. The phrase was clearly formulaic and probably did not cause sheriffs and bailiffs to linger much over its meaning, but it did in fact correspond well with what happened in practice. Both the adjectives and the noun in the phrase were ripe with meaning, and unpacking the assumptions and expectations they conveyed reveals much about the social context of jury service in the period.

The Latin noun *homines* (*homo* in the singular) is the simplest and most straightforward part of the phrase. In traditional usage it could be gender-neutral and can often be translated as meaning "humans" or "people." Medieval philosophers and theologians, for example, often used it to refer to the human species as a whole, as in the famous work by Anselm of Canterbury known as "*Cur deus homo.*" But it could also be used to refer only to the male half of the species—to "men" as opposed to "humankind"—and there is no question that this was the intended meaning of the framers of the writs and the meaning understood by the officials who received them.[13] Jury service was, with two relatively rare exceptions, a male preserve, as were almost all other forms of office-holding in the period.[14] The exclusion of women from jury service was, perhaps, even more thoroughgoing than that found in other areas of administrative service, where one occasionally finds the widow of a sheriff or church warden exercising some of the traditional public authority of their dead husbands.[15]

The two exceptions to the rule are interesting and, since they bear on some of the other general criteria used to determine suitability for jury service in the period, merit some attention here. Both involved situations in which a court's decision had to take account of a woman's physical condition as it impinged on the case. The first situation involved an appeal, or formal accusation, launched by a woman against a man she accused of raping her. If the accused rapist sought to defend himself by claiming that the woman was still a virgin and thus could not have been raped, the courts might constitute a jury of women to examine the accuser to determine whether she had lost her virginity. Such at least is the account given in the Bracton text, which refers to a specific case in which this procedure had been followed.[16] The second and more common situation in which women served as jurors involved cases in which the court needed guidance about the veracity of a female defendant's claim to be pregnant. Such juries were constituted specifically for the purpose of "inspecting the belly" (*de ventre inspiciendo*) of the defendant to determine if she really was pregnant. Historians have referred to these panels as "juries of matrons" or as "juries of the belly," and have demonstrated their ongoing use into the late nineteenth century.[17] The women appointed as jurors were expected to feel the defendant's abdomen and breasts and look for other telltale signs of pregnancy, and then to deliver a formal verdict to the court giving their conclusion about the claimed pregnancy.[18]

The issue of a woman's pregnancy was important in two legal contexts. The first involved women convicted of felony who claimed to be pregnant in order to avoid hanging. Ordinarily, the hanging of a convicted felon followed immediately upon conviction, but for the sake of the unborn child, the courts could delay the hanging of a pregnant woman until after she delivered.[19] For obvious reasons, female felons had a strong incentive to claim pregnancy in these circumstances, and the courts had an equally strong reason not to take their word at face value. Because a physical examination was considered to be the best method of determining the likelihood of the felon's story, a jury made up of women was deemed necessary to handle the situation. The second context in which verifying pregnancy was important resulted from situations in which the birth of a child would affect the inheritance rights of collateral relatives. A case heard in Norfolk in 1221 illustrates the matter very well.[20] A property-holder named William of Melton died, leaving behind a widow named Muriel and a brother named Peter. Peter laid claim to William's land as his heir and successor. Muriel, however, claimed to be pregnant with William's child and sought to retain control of the land in the name of the heir she was carrying. Peter challenged Muriel's claim, and the court sought to have the matter examined by a jury of "lawful women," *per legales feminas,* who were directed to inspect

Muriel and report on her condition. In this instance, the jury proceeded by means of inquest procedure with the sheriff supervising the inquest and then sending a written verdict to the justices. The women of the jury found that Muriel was indeed pregnant and Peter's claim to his brother's land was rejected. In an unusual twist, though, Peter did eventually prevail in the dispute. Muriel failed to deliver a baby in due course, and when the likely due date had come and gone, Peter returned to the court to repeat his claim to the land. The justices this time agreed with him, reasoning that since some 48 weeks had elapsed from the time Muriel had last had contact with her husband, she could not possibly produce an heir.

The antipathy toward having women serve as jurors is readily apparent, though, even in cases involving obstetrical and gynecological examinations. The standardized writ given in the Bracton text to empanel women to examine a claim to pregnancy stipulates that the female jurors were to conduct their examination in the presence of men, who appear to have served either as co-jurors or as a superior jury.[21] Several early cases corroborate that this was common practice.[22] In one unusual case heard in 1206, the court ordered a number of men to go with their wives to examine a woman claiming to be pregnant, and also stipulated that the couples were to report the results of their examination as witnesses rather than as jurors.[23] Similarly, a verdict given by a jury of women constituted to examine the virginity of Amicia le Roer, who filed an appeal of rape in London in 1282, had to be supplemented by a verdict given by a jury of men from the neighborhood.[24] The attitude of the legal establishment is well represented in the Bracton text, in which the author emphasizes that if the women who examined the rape victim swore that she had lost her virginity, the verdict about whether the accused rapist was guilty as alleged by the victim should still be delivered by a jury of men.[25]

To some extent, the evident discomfort with women jurors was simply part of a broader social pattern that restricted women's participation in all areas of public life. It was, however, also connected to the specific conceptualization of what made a person suitable to serve as a juror, particularly as encompassed in the term "lawful," one of the two key adjectives commonly used to describe jurors. Among other things, a lawful person was someone who was not beholden to someone else, someone who had the ability to make an independent judgment about a matter set before them.[26] Society viewed women as being ruled by the men in their lives and therefore lacking in the requisite independence needed to participate fully and effectively in an act of public judgment. Though the women who served as jurors to determine virginity or pregnancy were sometimes referred to as "lawful women," in ordinary circumstances such a phrase was an oxymoron. Elevated wealth and social rank did not change the basic assumption; no matter how wealthy or powerful an individual woman was she was still considered to be under the thumb of her male family members.[27] Even widows and single women, whose independent standing was widely recognized in private law, could not alter the cultural pattern assuming that public judgment ought to be exercised by men.

While lawfulness was gendered male, it does not follow that all men were lawful. It is hard to be dogmatic about who was and was not lawful because the concept itself was flexible and depended on the matter at hand. Official records sometimes demonstrate the relativity of the term by describing some people as more lawful than others.[28] But there were limits to the term's elasticity. The same logic that dictated that women were not ordinarily lawful also dictated that certain other categories of men would not ordinarily be considered lawful. Monks, for example, were ordinarily not lawful, because they were beholden to their order and to their religious superiors. Likewise domestic servants, whose situation made them dependent on the master of the household, and thus akin to minor children. Writing in the 1560s but reflecting on the laws and statutes of earlier centuries, Sir Thomas Smith decided that the best equivalent he could offer to describe what earlier texts meant by "lawful man" was the English word "yeoman," itself an imprecise term that denoted a male independent householder of some substance.[29]

In addition to being independent, a lawful man had to be law abiding. Another sixteenth-century legal commentator, Thomas Marowe, thought that this was the most essential trait characterizing a lawful man.[30] According to Marowe, a man lost his lawful status if he was outlawed, had abjured the realm, or had been convicted of felony or treason. The late thirteenth-century text known as *Britton* implies something similar when describing the treatment of petty thieves, who could be punished by a stint in the pillory and were henceforth to be excluded from serving as jurors or witnesses.[31] Other early sources emphasize the issue of public reputation and credibility. For the twelfth-century author of Glanvill, the key aspect of lawfulness was the ability to bear witness in court, a public standing that could be lost by perjury.[32] Anglo-Saxon law texts take a similar point of view, emphasizing the link between lawfulness and oath-taking.[33] The author of the Bracton text actually broke away from his Latin narrative to give a popular English saying on the matter: "*He nis nocth othesworthe the is ene gilty of othbreche,*" or, in modern English, "He is not oath-worthy who is once guilty of breaking his oath."[34] Since the defining act of jury service involved the taking of an oath, the insistence that jurors should be lawful clearly drew upon well-established traditions that characterized a lawful person as someone who lived within the sphere of the law, and who could therefore be trusted to uphold the law.

This notion of trust was a public attribution rather than a private one. It was closely related to reputation, another complex sentiment that involved issues of personal integrity, honesty, and reliability refracted through the prism of public observation and scrutiny.[35] The relationship between public reputation and lawfulness is well illustrated in the trial of Roger Lelman for theft in 1212.[36] Lelman was accused of breaking into a house in Yorkshire and stealing a cloak and hood. He denied the charge and stated that "he was a lawful man and of good repute," and asked to have his reputation verified by an inquest of the countryside. The court granted his request and constituted a jury to look into the matter. The jurors reported that after conducting a thorough investigation the only thing they had heard about Lelman was that he was indeed a lawful man. On that basis he was acquitted. The case is interesting not only because the acquittal was so explicitly connected to the jury's assessment of the defendant's general reputation, but also because it suggests that the concept of lawfulness was current in society at large, or at least in the minds of the jurors who delivered the verdict.[37] Though hard to define, people of the time apparently knew a lawful man when they saw one.

In addition to being lawful, jurors were also expected to be free (*liber*). Freedom was, however, a complicated matter in medieval England. It was understood principally with reference to the social and juridical category of serfdom: A free person was someone who was not a serf. In some respects, insisting that jurors be free as well as lawful was redundant, since serfs, like most women, lacked the formal independence that was an essential attribute of lawfulness. Serfs, or "villeins" as they are generally called in the context of medieval England, were sometimes described in contemporary sources as a lord's private property, and while such descriptions do not accurately reflect the reality of their situation, it is nonetheless true that their personal and tenurial dependency meant that they were unlikely to be considered lawful, since independence was one of the core elements of lawfulness. And yet the adjective "free" is ubiquitous in the sources and the phrase "free and lawful" looms large in the writs and court documents that describe the qualities sought in jurors. This suggests that the category of lawful men did not simply subsume the category of free men, and the reasons why deserve careful consideration.

The antipathy toward allowing villeins to serve on juries was sometimes quite stark. In the words of Paul Hyams, "The basic rule is clear and stable: villeins were ineligible to serve as jurors in royal courts."[38] If a justice learned that one of the jurors was a villein, he usually dismissed him from the jury on the spot, even if that meant that the other free jurors had to be sent home and resummoned to appear at a later date.[39] Sheriffs and bailiffs were liable to be fined for making such a mistake, partly to ensure that they fulfilled their obligations faithfully in the future and partly to punish them for causing so much inconvenience.[40] Justices apparently took the exclusion of villeins from the juries they supervised as a matter of course. In 1334, several justices reviewed a case that had been tried in a local court and imposed a substantial fine of ten marks on the suitors of the court for having made a false judgment. The justices stipulated, though, that the fine was to be paid only by the free suitors of the court since, as the record states, "a villein cannot give judgment."[41] This was generally not true of local courts at the time, but it illustrates the assumptions royal justices made based on their own experience in royal courts.

In addition to underscoring the antipathy toward villeins as jurors, however, such cases also suggest that it was not always a straightforward matter to implement a policy excluding them. The personal status of a prospective juror was not manifestly self-evident: Villeins could not be distinguished from the free on the basis of physical appearance, or on the basis of wealth, or on the basis of any associated life style; "villein" and "peasant" were not synonyms. This point bears emphasis, particularly for the nonspecialist, because it is easy to assume from popular literature that every peasant was a serf. This was certainly not the case in medieval England. While it is largely true that every villein in England was a peasant, many peasants were not villeins. Villeins were a subset of the peasantry, a juridically defined group within peasant society; villein is to peasant as union member is to working class in modern America, or as adjunct instructor is to the professoriate. The precise relationship between the two groups is uncertain, but most historians believe that free peasants made up at least half of the peasantry, and many believe that the real figure may be closer to two-thirds.[42] Some of these free peasants were wealthy by peasant standards, merging into the ranks of the gentry, but many were poor. Conversely, while some villeins eked out an existence on the edge of starvation, many were substantial householders owning their own plough team and 30 or more acres of land. In other words, a sheriff or bailiff could not simply draft the 12 wealthiest men from a village and assume that he would end up with a jury of freeholders. In some parts of the country this might be true, but in other parts he might end up with a jury made up entirely of villeins.

Wealth alone did not mark a significant boundary between free and villein, but none of the alternatives was significantly better. Indeed, as will be discussed more fully later in this chapter, income levels often were used by the Crown to define eligibility for jury service. Since it was not practicable to use wealth to separate free from villein, however, it must be assumed that sheriffs and bailiffs used other criteria when selecting people for the jury panel. There was, however, no single and universal quality that made someone unfree, and so it is hard to figure out what those criteria might have been. It is, in fact, quite likely that people living at the time found the distinctions between villein peasants and free peasants nearly as perplexing as we do. Villeins were more likely than freeholders to pay their rent in the form of personal work services for their lord than in cash, but freeholders often owed some work services too, so the simple fact of performing work for the lord was not a reliable indicator. Villeins also typically owed special fines and taxes to their lord, including a tax for inheriting land, known as an entry fine or *gersumma,* and a tax for permission to marry, known as merchet.[43] But neither of these was an immediate and obvious feature of a man's status. Entry fines were one-shot events that might have been paid decades before a man was considered for jury service and merchet fines were imposed on women rather than on men. Fathers often paid the merchet fine for their daughters, but even so, not all men had daughters, nor could something as irregular as a marriage fine make a convenient point of reference for a royal official. When the king's courts were called upon in other contexts to decide whether an individual was free or villein, they were interested to know about work services and special payments like entry fines and merchet, but for the most part they sought to solve the case with reference to the status of an individual's parents and relatives.[44] A villein was someone whose parents were villeins, whose siblings were villeins, and, ideally, whose aunts and uncles were also villeins. In some villages, generally those belonging to the church, such purity of ancestry could be found. In most villages, however, the situation was far more complicated. Villein and free peasants routinely intermarried, and the courts had real difficulty deciding what to do in such cases. In practice, they tried to determine if the individual whose status was in question was born while his parents were living under the dominion of the lord who claimed him as a villein.[45] It was a complicated way to reach a decision, and it meant that there was no clear and simple rule of thumb that could be applied to ascertain the status of a child born to parents of mixed status.

Considering that jury service was burdensome and generally viewed as a duty rather than a privilege, it is possible that villeins routinely used their personal status as a shield to ward off a bailiff's effort to recruit them for jury service. Many free men were willing to pay to be exempt from jury service, and, in this respect, villeins were actually in a more enviable position than their free neighbors. But villeins may also have had other reasons for accepting an appointment to a jury and may not have wanted to claim exemption on the basis of their personal status. It is possible, for example, that a villein might have preferred not to make an unequivocal public statement about his personal status, even if doing so meant avoiding jury service. If there was any ambiguity about an individual's status, for example, such as might exist when one of the parents was free, then making a public statement embracing unfree status may not have been a good idea. Such an explanation may help to account for what would otherwise be odd behavior on the part of John Paris of South Witham, Lincolnshire, who, at some point prior to 1298, paid 4 shillings to a bailiff to be exempted from jury service, even though he was a villein.[46] The payment represents more than pocket change and presumably could have been avoided if Paris had been willing to proclaim his villein status.

Another possibility worth considering is that villeins may have been willing to accept appointment to a jury because they saw some tangible benefit in doing so. A dispute between the abbot of Abingdon and his tenants in the village of Winkfield, Berkshire, heard in the king's court in 1225 suggests one such potential benefit, namely that service as a juror created a presumption in favor of freedom.[47] In the case, the abbot claimed that the tenants were villeins and owed him an assortment of servile dues and services, while the tenants claimed that they were free and owed only an annual money payment. The jury called to determine their status could not reach a unanimous verdict, and the justices, departing from their normal practice, allowed the substance of the jurors' dispute to enter the formal record of the case. Ten of the jurors sided with the abbot and told the justices that the tenants owed all of the claimed services. The eleventh juror confessed that he did not know what services they owed but had no reason to disagree with the other jurors. The twelfth juror said that he had never seen the tenants perform the services claimed by the abbot, and went on to say that he had seen some of them swear as assize jurors before royal justices "and therefore thought that they were free." The justices disregarded the contrary testimony of the twelfth juror and ruled in favor of the abbot, but his statement suggests that jury service in a Common Law court was perceived as an indicator of free personal status. Paul Hyams has noted that cases in which jury service was invoked to support a claim to freedom are rare in the thirteenth century, but the author of *Britton*, writing in the late thirteenth or early fourteenth century, thought the matter worthy of discussion in his account of how disputes about personal status were resolved in the king's courts.[48]

The task of finding jurors who met the freedom criterion was further complicated by inconsistent application of the policy itself. Villeins were, in fact, regularly sworn as jurors in manor courts; on some manors, service as a juror in the local court was so dominated by villeins that free men were unwilling to serve for fear that they might jeopardize their free status if they accepted the duty.[49] Technically, manorial courts were venues for private jurisdiction and thus the issue of jury service by villeins did not have a direct bearing on the policies enforced by the Common Law courts. But the situation became murkier when a lord had the right to hold the view of frankpledge on his manor, a development discussed in chapter 2. Frankpledge jurors did have a recognized role in the king's legal machinery, particularly when making presentments of felony.[50] Some manors skirted the problem by empanelling a second jury of freeholders to sit at frankpledge sessions, but many did not have enough freeholders to make this a viable proposition. Freeholders were scarce on most of the Ramsey abbey manors, for example, and it is clear that even in the abbot's frankpledge courts the jurors were drawn overwhelmingly from the ranks of the villein tenants.[51]

If frankpledge sessions conducted in manorial courts had constituted the only point of contact between villein jurors and the Common Law courts, a policy of excluding villeins from Common Law juries may not have posed too great a problem, apart from the issue of correctly diagnosing an individual's personal status. But there were other situations in which villeins were more directly involved as jurors operating in a Common Law environment. The basic problem was one of numbers: While villeins constituted a minority of the population as a whole, in some areas they formed an overwhelming majority of the local inhabitants. Villeinage was regionally concentrated: In the old Danelaw counties of northern and eastern England, villeins were rare and bailiffs had a large pool of freeholders from which to form their jury panels; in some other regions, though, villeins were far more numerous than free peasants, and the small number of freeholders must have created headaches for sheriffs and bailiffs searching for jurors. Freeholders were so scarce in some hundreds that the jury system would have been untenable if villeins had been completely excluded. The situation was put into stark relief in an eyre court held in Berkshire in 1284, when a jury of nine rather than the customary 12 was allowed to make presentments for the hundred of Roeberg. Conventional practice was disregarded in this instance because "there are only nine free tenants in the hundred."[52]

The problem was addressed in a variety of ways, two of which deserve a closer look. The first was to allow villeins to serve as jurors when the procedure did not produce an irrevocable judgment, or a judgment on a matter of great substance. To some extent, this was implicit in the tacit acceptance of villeins as frankpledge jurors just mentioned. It was, however, explicitly formulated as a policy in the Statute of Exeter in 1285.[53] The statute sought to regularize a procedure for investigating the behavior of coroners, many of whom had been either lax or corrupt when performing their duties.[54] It stipulated a procedure requiring jurors to make presentments to royal justices or inquisitors in response to specific articles delivered to them in writing, as was common in other forms of presentment. Of particular note are the provisions the statute made for dealing with towns or villages that did not have enough free men to form a jury. In such cases it was permissible to empanel villeins, though they should be "the best, and most discreet and lawful" available. The statute records the oath that all jurors, presumably including villeins, were to take before serving on "this inquest for the king," and reiterates in the inquisitors' charge to the jury the likelihood of villein participation by enacting that free men who failed to carry out their duties faithfully would suffer the loss of their patrimony and villeins would suffer imprisonment. The different punishments were necessary because the law held that a villein's property belonged to his lord, and thus any attempt to seize it could be construed as an act of disseisin against the lord.

Implicit in the formal acceptance of villeins on presentment juries investigating the deeds of coroners is the possibility that villeins were also regularly conscripted to serve on coroners' inquest juries. Service on a coroner's jury would have been a natural extension of service on a frankpledge jury, and in jurisdictions like Roeberg hundred in Berkshire it is hard to imagine how a coroner could have found 12 local men who could furnish information about a suspicious death without calling on villeins. The problem with staffing coroners' juries was rehearsed in a royal edict of 1305 that decried the fact that the "better people" (*meillures gents*) commonly refused to cooperate with the coroner so that the "poorer people" (*poveres gents*) were the only ones available to make the inquest.[55] Surviving coroners' records are not plentiful and ordinarily do not identify who the jurors were, let alone identify their status, so the presence of villeins cannot be clearly documented. But the plausibility of the argument is vouchsafed by an escheator's inquest held in Yorkshire in 1297.[56] The escheator in question constituted a jury to investigate the suspicious circumstances that led to the seizure of a foreign ship in Hull by the archbishop of York. The jurors convened by the escheator recounted an eventful story that included a group of villeins acting in the guise of a coroner's jury. Their narrative began with an account of a foreign mariner who became so ill while the ship was docked that a local priest had to be summoned to administer last rites. After the administration of the rites, the mariner traveled to Beverley "in search of health"—Beverley had a reputation as a site of miraculous healings—but died on his way back to his ship. A number of mates conveyed his body to the ship, held a wake in his honor, and then carried him back ashore the next day for burial. When their cortege reached the graveyard, however, it was accosted by a group of men representing the archbishop, who seized the body and hauled it away. When they finally laid the body down, they conducted a "view" and pronounced a verdict of death by misadventure, which the archbishop used as a pretext to seize the ship as a deodand. The archbishop's seizure was accompanied by an offer to return the ship to its owners in return for a payment of £20. For present purposes, it is the "view" that is the most interesting part of the story. Although the document does not mention the presence of coroners, the view was clearly intended to serve as a coroner's inquest; what the document does make clear is that it was conducted by the archbishop's villein tenants. It is possible that the villeins were acting out something they had previously watched as spectators only, but it seems far more likely that they were reenacting a scene they knew from direct personal involvement.

In addition to accepting the participation of villeins on certain types of juries, royal administrators also circumvented the dearth of qualified free jurors in some jurisdictions by allowing juries that were a mix of villeins and freeholders. The two policies were similar in that they both involved relatively modest exercises of discretion and responsibility, but the policy of permitting villeins to supplement free jurors went a step further in according a role to the unfree. The early fourteenth-century treatise known as "The Manner of Holding Courts" notes that stewards might constitute juries made up of six villeins and six freeholders to review the presentments made by frankpledge jurors.[57] The reference is not entirely clear, but appears to refer to the higher form of frankpledge jury that was used on some manors to corroborate the presentments of the villein jurors, the form of jury that was ostensibly constituted to give the presentments of manor court jurors legitimacy as an exercise of royal jurisdiction. Mixed juries of villeins and freemen also sometimes conducted inquests ordered by the king, particularly those held to appraise the value of property in which the king had an interest.[58] The sheriff of Oxfordshire, for example, constituted an inquest jury to make a survey of the manor of Headington and the surviving text of the inquest includes a list of 12 free jurors followed by a list of 12 villein jurors.[59] An escheator's inquest in Essex found that the guardian responsible for property in Hanningfield, Essex was guilty of wasting his ward's inheritance and of oppressing the villeins living there, but a second inquest requested by the guardian reversed the original verdict and declared that he had actually improved the property.[60] The second verdict was confirmed by a jury of 12 villeins, presumably sworn on the matter because their treatment was one of the central issues in the dispute. Similarly, a dispute about a substantial villein property that had come into the king's hand after the failed rebellion of Thomas Earl of Lancaster makes mention of an earlier inquest into the tenement that had been conducted by 12 free men and 12 villeins.[61] These references indicate that villeins were sometimes considered to be acceptable as inquest jurors, particularly when the inquest involved matters that they knew about firsthand, and as long as their verdict could be strengthened or corroborated by free jurors.

The limited acceptance of villeins as jurors involved with certain types of inquest and presentment procedures is not entirely surprising when one considers the extent of villein involvement in manorial court juries and other forms of village self-government. Anne and Edwin DeWindt have recently demonstrated extraordinary levels of participation in local government by villeins living in the small market center of Ramsey, home of the great fenland monastery, and their findings echo those of other scholars who have examined power structures at the village level.[62] Within their own communities, villeins, or at least the wealthier villein men, were accustomed to frequent service as jurors and bore the public responsibility associated with local arbitration and decision-making as a matter of course. On privileged manors vested with the right to try and hang thieves captured red-handed (known as the right of *infangentheof*) juries of villeins sometimes exercised discretion over capital offenses, although the Common Law courts viewed the practice with disfavor and eventually rooted it out.[63] Even high-level royal administrators sometimes openly acknowledged that villeins could be "lawful," including, for those who framed the statute of

Exeter, specifically in the context of serving on a jury.[64] Though they always viewed villeins as inferior to free jurors and not competent to participate in the core areas of the law's competency, the king's agents inhabited a world in which juries were so pervasive that it was simply not possible to exclude them entirely.

While the role of villeins in the machinery of royal justice deserves more attention than it has generally received, the larger point to be made by looking at their involvement actually concerns the free peasantry. If it is true that even villeins were formally acknowledged as suitable for some types of juries, then it follows that free peasants were prime candidates for yet more, since their personal status fully conformed to what the law demanded. The same pressure to find jurors that made jury service by villeins legally palatable in certain circumstances inevitably pressed on the free peasantry, only with much greater force. Unlike their villein neighbors, free peasants could not expect sheriffs and bailiffs to ignore them when constituting panels for pending property assizes or gaol deliveries, nor could they use their relationship with a lord as a shield against demands for service on behalf of the king. Free peasants constituted a social group of exceptional variety, ranging all the way from poor or destitute wage laborers to the sort of wealthy farmers that are difficult to distinguish from the lower ranks of the gentry. Those who found themselves on the low end of this spectrum would seldom have met the requirement that they be lawful as well as free, but those on the higher end of the spectrum fit the bill perfectly. Bailiffs were looking for independent male heads of household who enjoyed a measure of prosperity and met public expectations of stability, accountability, and trustworthiness. They found such individuals in all of the more elevated social ranks of the time, but they found them in greatest number among the upper ranks of the free peasantry. As Sir John Fortescue noted in the fifteenth century in his encomium of the Common Law, England was a country in which "no hamlet, however small, can be found in which there is no knight, esquire, or householder of the sort commonly called a franklin, well-off in possessions; nor numerous other free tenants, and many yeomen, sufficient in patrimony to make a jury"[65]

STATUTORY DEFINITIONS

Further insight into the social dynamics of the medieval jury system is provided by a series of royal statutes and decrees that sought to define the basic qualities of potential jurors.[66] Starting in the later thirteenth century and continuing for many centuries thereafter, these enactments provided sheriffs and bailiffs with a more concrete definition of what the king and his justices intended when they issued writs ordering that juries be made up of free and lawful men. Some of these laws were of limited scope or geographical application, but a number of them aimed to provide general guidelines that would govern the system as a whole. An analysis of these broader pieces of legislation reveals a good deal about the social assumptions and expectations of those responsible for administering the jury system and suggests, among other things, that wealthier peasants were perfectly acceptable as jurors in the period.

Two statutes enacted in 1285 and 1293 were particularly important in terms of defining eligibility for jury service. The first was part of the second statute of Westminster, a sweeping enactment that dealt with a wide range of reforms, mostly related to the law.[67] Chapter 38 of the statute addressed problems with the behavior of sheriffs and bailiffs when empanelling juries and set standards for them to observe in the future. It began with a preamble that mentioned two problems that were damaging the integrity of the jury system. First, it noted that sheriffs sometimes included on their panels people who were elderly, infirm, diseased, or who were not resident in the area.[68] Second, it criticized the practice of summoning more jurors than were needed in order to collect bribes from people willing to pay rather than have their names presented to the court. As a result of such official malfeasance, the statue noted, assizes and juries were often staffed by poorer men (*pauperiores*) while wealthy men (*dives*) stayed home. To remedy such abuses, the statute enacted a series of provisions governing what sheriffs and bailiffs could and could not do henceforth. They could summon no more than 24 people. Men above the age of 70 were to be spared jury service, as were those who were sick or resident in another county. The key provision of the statute imposed an income test to determine an individual's suitability for jury service. If the jury on which an individual was chosen to serve delivered its verdict within his home county, then each juror should have lands capable of producing an annual income of 20 shillings. If the jury delivered its verdict elsewhere—the framers of the statute obviously had Westminster in mind here—then the property qualification was set at an annual income of 40 shillings. Men with annual landed incomes below 40 shillings could still be summoned out of the county if they had witnessed a charter or other document that was pivotal to the resolution of the case, but only if they were of sound body.

Eight years later, in 1293, another enactment, known in later statute books as the "Statute of Those Who Ought to be Put on Juries and Assizes," revisited the issue of juror qualifications and made some significant changes.[69] The enactment was a focused piece of legislation that dealt exclusively with juror qualifications. It repeated the criticisms of the second statute of Westminster concerning the propensity of royal officials to accept bribes from wealthier people in return for exemptions from jury service, but stated that this was a problem especially prevalent with respect to summoning jurors who had to travel beyond the boundaries of their home county. The statute sought to resolve the problem by raising the minimum annual income threshold for service outside the county from 40 to 100 shillings. Wealthier men, it seems, were more willing to perform onerous service for the Crown, even though their wealth made it easier to afford the sweeteners needed to fend off a sheriff or bailiff looking for potential jurors. In addition to raising the income expectation for jury service outside the county, the statute also doubled the minimum income threshold for jurors serving within their counties, from 20 to 40 shillings. This new minimum for service within the county was mandated for all forms of juries and inquests except those convened for eyre courts or courts held in towns and cities which could continue to operate according to customary practices. Apart from the increase in the minimum property requirements, the statute stipulated that the other provisions enacted in the second statute of Westminster were still to be observed.

The income limits stipulated in the statute of 1293 remained in force well into the sixteenth century. Fourteenth- and fifteenth-century statutes made numerous changes to the procedures associated with the making and use of jury panels, but they did not alter the basic income qualification. A parliamentary petition presented by the "poor people" of Wirral hundred in Cheshire in 1330, for example, referred to the 40 shilling limit as a benchmark against which demands for jury service should be measured.[70] Similarly, a litigant in 1333 cited a failure to observe the 100 shilling requirement for jurors serving outside their county as grounds to overturn an unfavorable verdict in a land plea litigated in Westminster in the previous year.[71] In 1414, King Henry V assented to a parliamentary petition asking for enforcement of the 40 shilling minimum for service within a county, and a statute passed in the same year reiterated the king's commitment to maintaining the threshold.[72] In the sixteenth century, inflation severely undermined the utility of a limit set centuries earlier, but the basic income qualification was not raised until 1584–85, when the minimum annual income level was doubled.[73] At various points between 1293 and 1585 different income limits were prescribed for new or special forms of juries, but these special directives did not affect the qualifications for service on the standard forms of juries. Thus, the jurors who sat in judgment on suspected Lollards were required to have annual landed incomes of at least 100 shillings, while the minimum annual income of a juror involved with an attaint (a formal process for examining the integrity of assize and trial jurors who had previously delivered a verdict) was set at £20 in 1436–37.[74] The only significant exception to the 40 shilling norm for common types of jury service was an enactment in 1483–84 that required presentment jurors in sheriffs' tourns to have annual landed incomes of at least 20 shillings if they were freeholders and at least 26 shillings 8 pence if they held their land by copyhold.[75] The provision for service by copyholders is worth noting, because copyhold was a successor form of villein tenure and its inclusion in the statute supports the argument that villeins had sometimes played a role as presentment jurors in local courts in earlier periods.

The income levels defined in these statutes were probably meant to serve as general guidelines for sheriffs and bailiffs rather than as strict cutoff points. Calculating annual incomes was not easily done in a society so deeply influenced by harvest fluctuations and having so many other uncertain revenue streams. Nor could royal officials readily refer to standardized documents summarizing the yearly earnings of their constituents. Sheriffs and bailiffs must have had a general sense of the financial resources belonging to the people under their jurisdiction, but they probably understood the statutory income definitions as reference points that had to be brought into conformity with observable social and political attributes and observable modes of consumption and display. It is, however, difficult for modern historians to figure out what such culturally-determined perceptions actually meant on the ground. The only realistic way to do so is to find comparable evidence that illustrates the broader context in which these reference points were established.

The practice of using income levels to differentiate the duties and perquisites of different social groups relative to the state was by no means a new phenomenon in the later thirteenth century, nor was it uncommon in later periods. Perhaps the best known example is the requirement that voters in parliamentary elections be freeholders with annual incomes of at least 40 shillings, a provision first put in place in 1429.[76] The overlap between the income level seen as desirable in a voter and the earlier standard set for eligibility for jury service was clearly more than coincidence. Income qualifications were also regularly used in the thirteenth and fourteenth centuries to determine who would be formally required to assume the status of knight, with figures ranging between £20 and £40 being commonly fixed.[77] A figure of £20 was also prescribed in 1439 for service as a JP.[78] The most ambitious attempt to delineate society on the basis of income levels is provided by the various enactments related to the Assize of Arms in the later twelfth and thirteenth centuries. These enactments are worth looking at in more detail because they help to situate the income qualifications for jurors in a broader social framework.

The Assize of Arms was originally implemented by King Henry II in 1181 to foster greater military preparedness by promoting ownership of weapons and armor.[79] It divided society into a number of different groups using a combination of annual landed income and the value of personal possessions as the basic principle of division. Each group was required to possess a specified array of military equipment. Thus, in Henry's formulation of the assize, a free man with rents and belongings worth 10 marks (£6 13s. 4d.) was expected to have a hauberk, an iron helmet, and a lance; other combinations of arms were prescribed for men of greater or lesser wealth. The assize was updated several times by Henry's successors, including once by Edward I in the statute of Winchester enacted in 1285, and thus contemporary with the two early statutes defining juror qualifications discussed above.[80] The statute of Winchester defined five main groups: those with lands worth £15 or more and personal belongings worth 40 marks; those with lands worth £10–15 and belongings worth 20 marks; those with lands worth £5–10; those with lands worth 40–100 shillings; and those with lands worth less than 40 shillings. For the three lowest levels, only landed incomes are noted; there is no corresponding figure for personal goods. Two residual categories are also described: people with goods worth less than 20 marks but without landed income, and "all others." These additional categories were probably intended to cover people living in towns and market centers whose wealth and social standing was derived from professions and trades.

The assize clearly did not extend to the traditional armigerous classes in society, whose incomes were ordinarily well above the upper limit of £15 and whose possession of arms could be taken for granted. As was just noted, knights were often associated with annual incomes of £20 or more, so it is reasonable to infer that the statute was designed for groups who, at the upper end may have bordered on the knightly classes but who are better described as members of the gentry, a group that is traditionally seen as occupying the social space between peasants and knights. This, in turn, suggests that the 40 shilling division which was so important in terms of jury service ought to be understood as defining a level of society well below that of the gentry. It would not be unreasonable to interpret the three upper categories in the statute as defining three ranks of gentry in the counties, an upper level with landed incomes of £15 who were close to the level of knighthood, a middle level with landed incomes of £10 who probably held lands in more than one village and may have exercised some rights of lordship, and a lower stratum with landed incomes of £5 whose property was likely to be concentrated in a single village, with perhaps a few tenants, and with social pretensions of being better than a peasant villager. At the 40 shilling level, though, any pretensions of gentility must have been hard to sustain, and it is far more likely that the figure refers to a distinction within peasant society between the well-endowed holders of virgates or yardlands (typically endowed with more than 30 acres of land), who formed a peasant elite, and the remainder of the land-holding peasantry. Members of this well-endowed elite would be known in Chaucer's age as franklins and in Shakespeare's age as yeomen, and in our own more analytical age have been labeled as "super-villagers" or "Type A villagers."[81] The terminology is, unfortunately, sometimes awkward and often imprecise, betraying the intrinsic difficulty of defining meaningful boundaries in a social environment that was often fluid and indeterminate but was nonetheless sensitive to matters of social status.

Such an interpretation of the social gradations in the Assize of Arms has the merit of according well with the actual military hardware associated with each group in the assize. The defining trait of those at the top of the spectrum was ownership of an iron breastplate and helmet, a horse, a sword, and a knife; for those a step below, the weapons and armor were similar but a horse was no longer required; for the third-ranking group, a doublet (a reinforced coat designed to prevent puncture wounds) replaced the iron breastplate. The most striking feature of the arms of those in the 40–100 shilling group is their modesty: a sword, bow and arrows, and a knife, with no provision made for any type of armor. Those in the lowest category (below 40 shillings) were expected to have only farm tools and household implements that could do double-duty as weapons: scythes, an axe-like implement known as a *gisarme,* knives, and other undefined small implements. The 40–100 shilling category thus seems to indicate a social group that merges into the bottom tier of parish gentry on the one end and into the ranks of simple peasant farmers on the other.

Another way to come to grips with what it meant to be a 40 shilling freeholder is to look at land values in the period. The rental value of land was frequently recorded in financial documents such as

manorial accounts and surveys, and while the figures given in these
sources must be treated with caution, they indicate in a general way
the plausibility of associating the Crown's definition of desirable
jurors with the upper ranks of the peasantry. The shortcomings of
such an approach merit a few words at the outset. Rents recorded in
manorial surveys and similar types of documents were often fixed by
custom and cannot simply be taken to indicate prevailing market rents
at any given moment in time; the land may have been worth considerably more to its holder than the amount indicated in a document.
Similarly, the rents recorded in many surveys were based on appraisals
and estimates made by ad hoc juries, as in the case of inquisitions *post
mortem,* and local juries were usually inclined to give low valuations
so as to minimize a local landholder's obligations to the Crown or a
superior lord. Rents and land values also varied greatly depending on
the same three factors that determine the value of modern real estate:
location, location, and location. An acre in densely populated Norfolk, for example, was likely to generate a much higher rent than an
acre in Northumberland, even if the intrinsic quality of the land was
comparable. Finally, rents could also fluctuate over time depending
on population levels, commercial opportunities, and monetary influences. Given all these caveats, it is clear that any consideration of
rental values can give only a general sense of magnitude and will not
bear precise statistical analysis.

In the later thirteenth and early fourteenth centuries, when relevant documentation is particularly full, rental values tended to range
from a low of 1 pence per acre, if one excludes land that was described
as worthless because worn out or sterile, to a high of about 3 shillings
per acre.[82] Some of the surviving data are derived from actual renders
of rent, but most come from appraisals of the net value of the land,
representing the differential between the cost of farming the land and
the revenues that could be expected from doing so. Figures at the
extreme ends of the spectrum were relatively rare, and rents between
4 pence per acre and 12 pence per acre are encountered much more
frequently.[83] Rents in this range suggest that a freeholder would have
needed rental income from 120 acres to meet the income qualification for jury service if his land was rented at the low end of the spectrum of common rents (4 pence per acre), or 40 acres if he collected
rents at the high end. This is exactly the territory where historians traditionally situate the upper echelons of peasant society.[84] The standardized peasant holdings known as yardlands or virgates were
generally provided with between 30 and 40 acres of land, and the
holders of such properties tended to be heavily involved in local gov-

ernment and economic life, controlling offices such as reeve and manorial juror. Possession of 120 acres was not common at the village level, and individuals who held property on that scale should probably be conceived of as blending into the lowest ranks of the gentry. It is worth emphasizing, however, that the method of using rental values per acre derived from surveys and account rolls is likely to overstate the quantity of land needed to reach a certain income level. As noted above, the sources conveying information about land values were more likely to understate than overstate the value. Furthermore, the ownership of land generated income beyond the stated rental value, because it provided the owner with a claim to exploit common resources, such as woods, streams, and common pastures. Landlords also frequently benefited from "incidental" payments that renters paid to gain or keep their land, such as entry fines and land transfer fees. The possibility that standard rental values might significantly understate the value of land is suggested by the estate records of Gloucester abbey. In the abbey's main cartulary, a series of manorial surveys document free rents that fall in the common range, with rents of 6 pence per acre appearing with great frequency.[85] Yet a memorandum in one of the abbey's estate manuals noted that a carrucate of land, a unit that comprised approximately 120 acres in most parts of the country, could be expected to generate a profit of £10 per annum, more than three times as much as might be expected on the basis of the rents paid by the abbey's tenants.[86]

An alternate way to conceptualize the social and economic status of a 40 shilling freeholder is to compare the figure with an estimate of likely incomes from farming based on knowledge of productivity and prevailing prices. Christopher Dyer has popularized the method of reconstructing individual household budgets for different groups in society, based on the amount of land a typical member of each group held. His calculation of the budget for a well-endowed peasant possessing a full yardland (assumed in Dyer's reconstruction to comprise 30 acres of land) is particularly relevant to the issue at hand.[87] Using traditional farming practices and assuming typical yields, Dyer calculated that in an average year a yardlander would have been able to feed himself and his family, pay his rent, and still have a surplus that was near the 40 shilling level, slightly below that mark if he employed a conservative two-crop rotation (calculated as producing an annual surplus of 38 shillings) and moderately above it if he employed the more productive three-crop rotation (calculated as producing an annual surplus of 51 shillings). Dyer assumed that the yardlander was a villein, and therefore likely to pay more rent than a freeholder, that his wife and children brought in no outside income, and that he had no other sources of income such as might be had from selling garden produce, poultry, and eggs. On the expenses side, however, he did not make provision for depreciation of capital equipment or wages to hired workers. There is obviously a great deal of guesswork involved with making calculations of this nature, and it would therefore be unwise to put too much weight on them in isolation. But Dyer's model is notably cautious in its assumptions about yields and prices and is a useful complement to the other evidence set out above. What all of these approaches suggest is that a well-endowed peasant was likely to enjoy an income level that would have qualified him for jury service within his own county.

Useless and Impoverished Jurors

Although the Crown regularly sought to ensure that jurors were drawn from the ranks of the most substantial village freeholders, there is good reason to believe that its expectations were often frustrated by realities on the ground. It is worth remembering that the earliest legislation defining income levels appropriate for jury service contained in the statute of Westminster set the figure at 20 shillings rather than 40. This much lower figure may well be closer to common practice at the time; the fact that the 20 shilling figure was itself cast in the guise of reform implies that people of even lower status were being drafted at the time. Similarly, the fact that Parliament felt obliged to petition the king in 1414 to return to the 40 shilling minimum indicates that it was a mandate that was often overlooked or forgotten. The language of the various statutes, with its repeated emphasis on reforming the practice of conscripting poor and insufficient men to serve as jurors, also points in the same direction. While the threshold was officially set to incorporate only the wealthier strata of peasant society, sheriffs and bailiffs often failed to observe it when filling out their panels.

The laments of king and parliament about the selection of people from the ranks of poorer peasants can, in fact, be substantiated from the records of the courts, as well as from several other sources in the period. Royal justices exercised a general supervision over the quality and character of the jurors brought into court, and while they appear not to have probed too deeply into the matter, they sometimes refused to accept some of the people who appeared before them, dismissing them as unfit on account of their mean status. Such jurors were sometimes described as "useless" (*inutilis*), and their dismissal from a case was usually accompanied by a court directive ordering a sheriff to find better men as substitutes. Sometimes entire juries were dismissed as useless, although more commonly a few of the jurors were singled out for dismissal while the other jurors were retained.[88] This must have been a great annoyance to the justices as well as to the litigants, since the dismissal of a few jurors often meant that the case had to be postponed.

In most instances, surviving court records indicate only that certain jurors were removed and fail to indicate what lay behind the decision to remove them.[89] Occasionally, though, a few words of description were appended to the court entry, allowing some insight into the matter. Judging from these brief entries, there appear to have been three principal reasons for characterizing a juror as useless. Some fit that description because they had a vested interest in the outcome of the case, as in the case of eight Sussex jurors who were removed because their lord was one of the principal litigants.[90] Dismissal in these instances was similar to dismissal of jurors who were challenged by one of the parties, and it is possible that the terse statement of uselessness in the court record elides a challenge with the statement of dismissal. Other men were deemed useless because they were empanelled for juries that specifically required men of higher status (such as the procedures associated with the Grand Assize and attaint).[91] All jurors in a Grand Assize were supposed to be knights, for example, but sheriffs sometimes included men who were substantial landowners but who had not been formally knighted.[92] From the court's perspective such men could be described as useless, but only insofar as they failed to conform to the demands of a specific form of procedure.

The third reason for rejecting jurors is the one most germane to the argument of this chapter: They were useless because they did not have sufficient wealth or social standing to be considered lawful. In a few such instances, the court record notes that the dismissed jurors were villeins. In a case from Norfolk in 1225, for example, all but two of the jurors were removed by the justices "because they are villeins and useless."[93] On numerous other occasions in the early thirteenth century villeins were removed from juries after admitting their status in court, although without any direct reference to their "uselessness."[94] These instances indicate the system's commitment to enforcing the exclusion of villeins from jury service, but they also indicate the likelihood of service on the part of peasants who were not villeins: If freeholding peasants were not being empanelled regularly then it would not have been conceivable for sheriffs and bailiffs to nominate their villein counterparts. In a case from Norfolk in 1232, one juror admitted his villein status in court and was removed from the jury, while four others were described simply as "useless" and were likewise removed.[95] In this instance, the term "useless" must have referred to freeholders who lacked sufficient wealth or social standing to be treated as viable jurors. The record of a case from Essex in 1226 explicitly states that a number of jurors were removed because "they are poor and useless" (*pauperes sunt et inutiles*).[96] Justices in Kent in 1202 dismissed an assize jury because all of the jurors were "poor and not suitable" (*pauperes sunt et non idonei*).[97] These cases suggest that even before a formal income qualification was introduced, the courts held that men who were relatively poor were not likely to be treated as lawful. It is important to remember in this context, though, that peasants were not universally poor: Those who were relatively well endowed and who held their land freely were unlikely to be described as useless. Problems emerged only when the jurors were drawn from much lower ranks, as a judge intimated in a Year Book discussion in 1308–9 when he stated that an inquest should be nullified because "all the men on the inquest ought to be landholders, and we tell you that R., M., and S., who were on this inquest, have no land."[98]

The behavior of the sheriffs and bailiffs responsible for sending useless jurors to court is, at first glance, a bit puzzling. Justices sometimes fined them for their mistakes, and in almost every instance in which their choices were rejected they were required to redo the job they had done poorly the first time around. In addition to risking fines and adding to their workload, their bad choices must also have attracted the ill will of the jurors who were retained after the dismissal of the unacceptable jurors, whose burden of service was far greater as a result: When justices dismissed only a few jurors, they ordinarily stipulated that the remaining jurors should reappear with replacement jurors at some future date. The prospect of having to make a second journey to Westminster, or even merely to a county town, because a bailiff had failed to do his job properly must have soured any subsequent interactions with that bailiff. The possible causes of bailiffs' failures in this regard deserve some consideration. Were their errors simply the result of incompetence or insufficient attention to duty? Or were they related to something structural, perhaps an inevitable consequence of the seemingly insatiable demand for jury verdicts in the period? Evidence related to these questions is not plentiful, but a few possible answers can at least be sketched out.

One of the conditioning influences that led sheriffs and bailiffs to lower the bar for juror selection was their propensity to accept bribes to excuse people from serving. The issue is addressed in the statute of

Westminster, the preamble of which specifically associates the need to set a minimum property qualification for jury service with problems stemming from petty bribery. There is no doubt that many bailiffs were willing to pocket a few pennies in return for overlooking someone who would otherwise be likely to find his name on a panel. The Hundred Roll enquiries of the 1270s—based on information supplied by thousands of local inquest juries—provide good evidence of the failings of bailiffs in this regard. In fact, the problem was so prevalent that the articles of enquiry formulated for the inquest included a special article dedicated to sheriffs and bailiffs who accepted bribes to allow people to shirk their obligations to serve as jurors.[99] Some of the returns indicate the potential severity of the problem. A jury in Aswardhurn wapentake in Lincolnshire listed nearly 100 separate bribes paid by different people to persuade bailiffs to leave their names off panels constituted for assizes and inquests.[100] The bribes ranged from 6 pence to the remarkably high figure of 23 shillings. The highest bidder must have desperately wanted to avoid serving, because he threw a sheep appraised at 2 shillings into the deal as well. In a few other jurisdictions, the inquest jurors spoke in more general terms but still indicated a significant problem. A jury in Haverstoe wapentake in Lincolnshire stated that bailiffs had accepted a collective bribe to exempt all of the men from the village of Waltham from jury duty, while a jury from the Norfolk hundred of Freebridge remarked that bribes had been paid by "a large number of free tenants."[101] In the Nottinghamshire wapentake of Bassetlaw, the inquest jurors said that all of the officials responsible for constituting juries had taken bribes to exclude people, and that this had gone on since the battle of Evesham a decade earlier.[102] They went on to name 16 different officials who had accepted bribes.

Behavior akin to that of the bailiffs singled out in the Hundred Rolls can be found in a wide array of sources from the period. Contemporaries were probably resigned to such petty corruption and saw problems only when bailiffs deliberately set out to secure a particular outcome in a specific case. A bailiff accused by a presentment jury in the early fourteenth century of having accepted bribes defended his behavior by telling the justices that he never took anything to remove jurors, but "he accepted things from a few people to spare them and leave them in peace."[103] Bailiffs and sheriffs routinely made up for their desultory or nonexistent wages by collecting small "sweeteners" from the people they interacted with in carrying out their duties. An inquest jury in Holderness in Yorkshire in 1291 noted that the local bailiff made £10 a year by collecting payments from people who wanted to avoid jury service, but pointed out that there were few other sources of income available to him.[104] The high level of tolerance for petty influence-peddling in the constitution of juries is well illustrated in a review of questionable practices conducted in the Cumberland eyre of 1292.[105] The eyre justices were troubled by a number of cases that came before them for review, one of which involved the acquittal of Richard le Bere for harboring a felon. Le Bere's case was first tried at a gaol delivery, but the eyre justices found irregularities in the report of the case and so constituted a new jury to examine the original verdict and the procedure by which it was obtained. This ad hoc review jury told an interesting story about the composition of the original jury. The defendant, they said, was a forester employed by the Countess of Aumale. His trial jury had consisted of 12 men from the town of Cockermouth, six men from villages in the vicinity of the town, and 12 men from the rest of the county. (Such large juries were uncommon but not unprecedented in the period.) The 12 men from the town were all tenants of the countess, as were the six jurors from neighboring villages. The remaining 12 jurors were not personally bound to the countess, but six of them resided in villages near the countess's forest and so were inclined to acquit the forester because he "could be of use to them in giving from his lady's wood." The remaining six jurors were from more distant parts of the county and had no personal stake in the outcome of the trial. For good measure, the review jury also noted that two of the 12 jurors from the town were related to the defendant's wife.

Not surprisingly, the eyre justices were troubled to learn that such a jury had been allowed to determine the forester's guilt. They asked specifically whether the gaol delivery justices had proclaimed at their session that kinsmen and others closely associated with the defendant should recuse themselves. They were told that the gaol delivery justices had not, and furthermore that such pronouncements were not customary. The most revealing part of the whole story, however, is the review jury's conclusion about the validity of the trial. The review jurors recognized that the original jury had been prejudiced in favor of the defendant, but they still maintained that it had been an appropriate body to sit in judgment because it comprised the "stronger and more faithful and best men of the town." The eyre justices were not so sure. They fined the gaol delivery justices for negligence and ordered that the forester be returned to prison. But even they were reluctant to jettison the original verdict and they decided not to conduct a new trial until after they had consulted with the king. The role of the sheriff and bailiffs in constituting the jury never came up for discussion, as far as the record of the case reveals.

It is easy enough to draw a line connecting the behavior of sheriffs and bailiffs with the problem of useless jurors, as contemporaries themselves sometimes did. A popular poem in the early fourteenth century lamented the hardships confronting poor men who could not afford to bribe royal officials, one of which was to be "dragged hither and thither and placed on assizes."[106] If wealthier freeholders were routinely buying their way out of jury service, then the bailiffs would have had no alternative but to look to the ranks of lesser men to fill out their panels. The amounts given as bribes in Aswardhurn wapentake, noted above, do indeed suggest that the relatively well off would not have found it too onerous to avoid jury service. They could take a bribe of 6 pence in stride without suffering any real hardship. While this figure was certainly not out of the reach of peasants—fines in manorial courts were often fixed at that level—it would have imposed real hardship on a laborer who expected to make one or two pennies a day and must have squeezed hard on a middling peasant. Even wealthy peasants would have had a tough choice to make when weighing the benefit afforded by a bribe with the cost of serving. Only more substantial freeholders—the gentry—would have been able to part with 6 pence or more without having to worry too much about their standard of living. And since the pool of gentry in any given jurisdiction was not likely to be overly big to begin with, bailiffs who cut deals with a significant number of them would inevitably have been forced to delve into the ranks of the peasantry to meet the Crown's demands for free and lawful jurors.

The situation was exacerbated by the fact that the Crown itself was willing to issue personal exemptions from jury service. Scott Waugh found that King Henry III sold lifetime exemptions to more than 1,100 people between 1233 and 1272.[107] The period studied is too long to be fairly described as constituting a single generation, but even if treated as encompassing two generations Waugh's figure still suggests that the royal policy of granting exemptions removed a large number of prime candidates from the jury pool. Waugh's research shows that most of the exemptions flowed to people of gentry standing, the very people the Crown otherwise saw as ideally suited to perform jury service. The number is not high enough to suggest that members of the gentry rarely served on juries in the period, but it does lend support to the notion that sheriffs and bailiffs had to look lower in the social hierarchy than prescriptive sources generally imply.

Waugh's research suggests a final reason why sheriffs and bailiffs had difficulty coming up with enough men of high standing to meet the central government's expectations about juror quality. Waugh noted that many of the people who acquired lifetime exemptions from jury duty can be found performing other types of service on behalf of the king, and he argued that most of those who sought exemptions were not angling for a life of leisure but simply preferred to get out of one of the least rewarding forms of service. As Waugh rightly points out, the demands on the gentry and higher-ranking members of county society encompassed much more than juries. The king also recruited many of his officials from this echelon of society, and the demands for administrative service were on a relentless upward trajectory during the thirteenth and fourteenth centuries. The gentry were tapped to be coroners, escheators, tax assessors, purveyors, and justices on ad hoc enquiries; they were also expected to implement many of the directives by which the Crown sought to direct affairs at a local level.[108] Furthermore, the upper gentry's services were required on elevated forms of juries, including those commissioned to perambulate boundaries, to hear appeals of lower jury verdicts, and sometimes even to settle property rights litigated by means of the Grand Assize, members of which were supposed to be knights but which sometimes included upper level gentry when insufficient knights were available. It might also be recalled that jurors who were required to travel beyond the boundaries of their home counties were supposed to be recruited from those with incomes above 100 shillings, or, in other words, from members of the gentry. In short, men of gentry standing had their hands full without monopolizing service on juries, at least not on those juries whose primary concern was the maintenance of local order and local property rights.

The central issue related to the jury service of the gentry class was, however, probably not workload, pure and simple, but rather the social and cultural perceptions that were associated with particular forms of administrative service. By the middle of the thirteenth century, if not earlier, most jury service had become mundane and unrewarding to those whose horizon was the county rather than the village. As some gentry began to find ways to free themselves from regular jury service, either through bribes or through charters of exemption, all those who aspired to membership in gentle society must have revised their expectations and assumptions about their own service in light of what other people of comparable status were doing. If, as this chapter has argued, the inevitable accompaniment to the trend of gentry withdrawal from certain types of jury service was an increasing reliance on jurors from social ranks below the level of the gentry, then the incentive for the gentry to withdraw from the more routine and localized forms of juries—such as coroners' inquests, inquests *ad quod damnum*, trial juries dealing with minor cases of trespass, criminal trial juries, and even many possessory assizes—must have been even stronger. Jury service was not voluntary and members of the gentry never enjoyed full discretion over the forms of service they rendered to the Crown. Still, their attitudes would not have been irrelevant to a sheriff who was likely to come from a similar social background, nor would bailiffs have found it easy to oppose the gentry's sense of where they stood in society and how they ought to be treated. The jury system was, in fact, extensive enough to need a great deal of service from many different social groups. The gentry were certainly one of those groups, but so were other lesser groups of freeholders, including those who in other contexts are commonly described as peasant villagers.

CONCLUSION

The central contention of this chapter has been that demands for jury service penetrated into peasant society and drew wealthier peasants into the routine operation of royal law and government. Some degree of peasant involvement with juries can be found already in the early thirteenth century, as the explicit dismissal of villein jurors from cases heard in the king's central court at the very beginning of the century attests. While peasant involvement as jurors in Common Law procedures was probably limited at this early date, the prospects for their engagement with the system could only have increased over time. Ultimately, their participation was due to the rapid growth of the jury system that characterized the period from Henry II's innovations in the second half of the twelfth century to the emergence of the Justices of the Peace in the second half of the fourteenth century. This growth was in turn predicated on two prominent trends in the development of the Common Law during the period. The first was a widening of the social groups who sought to make use of the king's legal system, a development that stemmed first and foremost from the tremendous success of the possessory assizes. As the demand for judgments based on jury verdicts grew and penetrated deeper and deeper into the social hierarchy, the demand for jurors inevitably followed suit. Whether they wanted to or not, the only realistic way royal officials could meet the burgeoning demand for jury verdicts was to widen the social base from which jurors were drawn. The second crucial development behind the embracing of lower status jurors was the tendency to create and nurture procedures that could be conducted at the local and county level. Once again, the possessory assizes were at the forefront of this development, but it extended to other forms of jury procedure as well. In this respect, the eventual emergence of the Justices of the Peace and the link between their work and the work of the assize justices was a natural, though not inevitable, process of adaptive evolution. Legal historians have an understandable tendency to gravitate to the central courts in Westminster to study the development of the legal system, but in terms of jury procedure what transpired in the central courts was much less important than what occurred in the judicial sessions convened in the counties to hear possessory assizes and conduct trials of prisoners. By committing themselves to procedures that were conducted at the level of hundreds, wapentakes, and counties, English kings made it not only possible but also even likely that social groups below the level of the gentry would be drawn in to serve as partners of the Crown.

The evidence in this chapter has been drawn mainly from writs, statutes, and records of the king's central court. These sources intimate the likelihood that people of relatively modest social standing served as jurors in the period, but they do not fully substantiate it, nor do they facilitate a precise understanding of who was actually called upon to serve in the period. There is, however, another body of evidence relevant to the subject that was referred to above in the discussion of existing secondary literature, namely the jury panels crafted by sheriffs and bailiffs to record the names of jurors called upon to serve in specific cases. Now the time has come to examine these panels in greater depth, sifting them for clues about the social backgrounds of individual jurors. This task will be taken up in the following chapter.

CHAPTER 5

THE PEOPLE OF THE JURY

In chapter 4, a variety of prescriptive sources that shed light on the formal qualifications for jury service in medieval England came in for special scrutiny. It was argued that while the state hoped to recruit jurors from relatively elevated social ranks, its extraordinary reliance on jury verdicts led it to set qualifications that allowed a relatively wide spectrum of the population to be treated as eligible for service. Although the ideal juror was conceived of as someone drawn from the ranks of the gentry or lower nobility, the volume of work assigned to jurors meant that the qualifications could not be set so high as to exclude people of lower social standing, including wealthier peasants. Judging from the language of statutes and parliamentary petitions, those responsible for administering the system often felt compelled to disregard the formal qualifications and search for jurors from even lower social ranks than those formally designated in official documents, and it is clear that there was an ongoing tension between the state's ideals about who should serve and the reality that confronted justices and other officials in their day-to-day work on behalf of the king.

This chapter probes the social backgrounds of medieval jurors by examining the personnel of specific juries assembled in the period. The approach taken here is primarily prosopographical, that is to say, it aims to recover the names of individual jurors and link those individuals to other documentary sources capable of conveying information about wealth and social status. Prosopography is a method that has been used by historians in many different ways in recent decades.[1] Of particular relevance to the approach taken here are the numerous detailed histories of individual towns and villages, studies that have frequently included accounts of the individuals who were active as jurors in local manorial and municipal courts.[2] These studies have been greatly aided by their narrow focus on the records associated with a single place, allowing individuals to be studied in a variety of different settings—as buyers and sellers of land, as debtors and creditors, as officials in local government, and so on—and often even allowing researchers to recreate familial relationships and study sequences of generations within particular families. Such depth of analysis is seldom possible in the case of individual jurors involved with royal administration and the Common Law courts, but the basic method of linking individuals named as jurors in one document with references available in other contemporary sources is sometimes practicable and in some instances can shed valuable light on that individual's standing in their local community.

The goal of this chapter, then, is to furnish concrete information about individuals who can be documented as serving on juries in the period, with an eye toward assessing their relative wealth and social standing. The first section will summarize the types of source material that can be drawn on in such an endeavor, and gives an overview of the basic methods used to find jurors in other sources. Succeeding sections will analyze specific juries from the period, with each section focusing on a particular type of jury. Chronologically, the focus will be on the late thirteenth and early fourteenth centuries, a period that has a number of sources that are particularly well suited to the task of cross-referencing, as well as the earliest substantial body of records documenting who actually served on particular juries.

SOURCES AND METHODS

The frequency with which individual jurors are named in medieval sources can be easily overlooked. Most previous research devoted to the history of the jury has focused on the development of trial juries, and has usually assumed that the best evidence of their behavior is to be found in the records of the courts in which they operated. The plea rolls produced so prodigiously by the Common Law courts, however, ordinarily do not mention the names of jurors serving in the court. A standard entry on a plea roll gives the names of the principals involved in the case, the substance of the criminal act or other dispute, and a jury verdict. Typically, scribes entered jury verdicts on the roll by saying something simple and direct like "the jury says." Sometimes they used variants like "the twelve say" or "the twelve of place X say." There are exceptions, but as a rule the scribes who made the plea rolls recorded the names of jurors only when they failed to appear in court, in which case their names might be written down along with the fines assessed for nonappearance. Since the plea rolls are a rich and uniquely valuable source for legal history, and since they have survived in overwhelming abundance from the period, historians have typically focused their attention on the substantive legal issues documented in the rolls and have seldom found it necessary to search for other sources that could lift the veil of anonymity covering the jurors, who appear in collective guise in the rolls. The plea rolls certainly have plenty to say about how jurors operated in the courts and how they reached decisions, but they have relatively little to say about who the jurors actually were.

Even when the names of jurors are recorded in standard sources, as they generally are in the voluminous series of inquests discussed in chapter 1, earlier generations of editors and historians found them to be of little value. Jurors are routinely named in the series of inquisitions *post mortem*, for example, but one would be hard pressed to know of their presence from the standard edition of the source, which, until fairly recently, simply omitted their names from the text. A similarly revealing example of the earlier lack of interest in identifying jurors is furnished by Hubert Hall's well-known *Formula Book of English Official Historical Documents*.[3] Many of the documents collected in volume two of Hall's work emanate from jury verdicts. Each document is printed as a verbatim Latin transcript, except when jurors are named. Hall transcribed the name of the first juror listed in the document and then broke the flow of his Latin transcript to insert in parentheses a note in English stating that 11 other jurors were also named. After skipping over the list of jurors in this fashion, he then resumed his literal transcription of the documents. The lists of individual jurors apparently struck him as lacking significance compared to the substance of the verdict they rendered. To be fair, one has to recognize that the inclusion of every name of every juror would have added considerably to the length of the volume and the corresponding expense of publication, but the decision to leave them out still betokens a mind-set that found the forms and procedures of law and government more interesting than the people involved.

Fortunately, neither of the problems just outlined—the absence of juror names in original court records and their omission in earlier printed editions—is insurmountable. In the case of the inquests and other administrative sources that have modern editions with excised jurors, the original sources replete with juror names can still be consulted in manuscript form in the National Archives in London, and the earlier calendars are still immensely useful tools for understanding the context of the documents. Since the jurors are almost always listed in the preamble to the verdict, the task of finding and transcribing juror names is relatively straightforward. In the case of jurors who delivered verdicts in court, the research process is slightly more complicated, but still manageable. Lists of jurors associated with particular cases were routinely drawn up in the period, typically in the form of jury panels crafted by sheriffs and bailiffs and submitted to court officials. Indeed, the omission of juror names from the formal court record can probably be attributed to the existence of these other documents: Scribes did not need to record juror names on the court roll because they were already written down on the jury panel. The panels essentially liberated the scribes from the tedious task of entering each juror's name with every new case, allowing them to concentrate on the principals involved in the litigation and the arguments they made in court. The rolls on which the pleadings and verdict were written were naturally treated as the essential record of court proceedings, meaning that care was taken to preserve them, while the multitude of jury panels tended to be treated as ancillary appendages whose utility waned over time, meaning that they were generally not preserved.

Although the vast majority of jury panels from the period have perished, many have survived. A considerable number can be found in the archival class of the National Archives dedicated to gaol deliveries. Most gaol delivery documents are standard plea rolls that record the outcomes of trials without identifying the jurors. But there are also several dozen "files" in the series that contain the documents that were created to prepare for the court session, typically the writs directing the sheriff to bring the prisoners and juries before the justices and the jury panels created by the sheriff in advance of the session.[4] Criminal trial juries were usually constituted for each hundred rather than for each individual case, and so the panels usually appear as lists of names written below the name of the hundred from which they were drawn; the guiding principle was that a single jury drawn from a particular hundred would be competent to hear all of the cases arising in that hundred.[5] Other jury panels have survived among the ancillary records of the eyre courts, and generally relate to property assizes and other civil suits. Michael Clanchy edited the panels associated with the Berkshire eyre of 1248 and drew attention to other files of jury panels related to other eyre sessions.[6] These eyre panels have not survived in numbers comparable to the gaol delivery panels, but they are plentiful enough to facilitate meaningful analysis, as will be demonstrated below. Finally, the names of jurors were occasionally entered on some plea rolls, for reasons that are difficult to determine. The practice was generally limited to courts convened in the counties rather than in Westminster. Even outside Westminster the practice was far from routine, but seems to be more characteristic of courts dedicated to prosecuting lawlessness and violence than in those dealing with civil law. A number of the records drawn up in association with sessions convened by JPs furnish lists of jurors, for example, as do some of the records created in conjunction with trailbaston sessions (trailbaston courts were convened for a limited time in the early fourteenth century to expedite criminal presentments and trials).[7] When these occasional appendages to formal court records are added to the juror lists provided by extant jury panels and inquest records, a surprisingly large body of material documenting individual jurors can be assembled.

Somewhat surprisingly, then, the central problem with using jury panels for prosopographical analysis is not the survival of panels but rather the availability of suitable evidence for cross-referencing. Previous attempts to use jury panels for social analysis, such as those discussed in chapter 4, have not paid adequate heed to this methodological conundrum: Most scholars have assumed that the panels themselves were the scarce resource, and that one had to be either remarkably diligent or remarkably lucky to find the listed jurors in other sources. The problem is, however, best approached the other way around, with the working assumption that lists of jurors are relatively common and that the scarce resource is suitable material for tracing jurors in other contexts. The problem of scarce contextual material needs careful consideration. The problem is not a general dearth of other records from the period; compared to other premodern societies, medieval England is blessed with an abundance of documentation, particularly from the middle of the thirteenth century on. The problem is more specific to prosopography: The sources seldom provide the dense coverage needed to contextualize the social position of 12 or more individuals hailing from multiple locations. Single villages sometimes have an impressive run of records that are well suited to recovering intimate details about their history, but such villages were typically surrounded by dozens of others for which only scraps of evidence survive. To be effective, a contextualizing source needs to be fairly comprehensive, covering a wide spectrum of society and a large geographical area, such as an entire hundred or county. It also needs to correspond well with the date of the jury panel; the shorter the interval between the source and the date of the panel, the more likely it is that the jurors will appear in the source.

A model for analyzing legal sources using the methods of prosopography can be found in the work of Anne and Edwin DeWindt,
who reconstructed the social backgrounds of the individuals involved
in the eyre court that met in Huntingdonshire in 1286.[8] The
DeWindts were surprisingly successful in their endeavor, finding
meaningful information for more than half of the nearly 3,000 participants in the eyre.[9] On the basis of their prosopographical research,
they were able to divide the participants into different social categories and establish that villagers and inhabitants of small towns
played a crucial role in the court, sometimes not only as defendants in
criminal cases but also frequently in more active roles, such as accus-
ers, pledges, and litigants in property disputes and trespass cases. In a
wide-ranging introduction to their edition of the eyre record, the
DeWindts presented their conclusions about the participation of different social groups active in the court, and they furnished the evidence on which their conclusions were based in an accompanying
volume containing an alphabetized "biographical register." There
were, unfortunately, no surviving jury panels from the eyre, although
the presentment jurors were named in the text. Lacking information
about the trial jurors and confronted with an abundance of evidence
about the litigants, the DeWindts did not undertake an extended
analysis of the presentment jurors, although the evidence they provided does allow for some insight into the topic and will be considered more fully below.

It would be easy to ascribe the DeWindts's success to a fortuitous
concatenation of divergent source material in Huntingdonshire in the
1270s and 1280s, and thus to accept that their method would be difficult to apply in other places and periods. To some extent this is true,
but it is important to note that their success was due less to the diversity of their source material than to the existence of a few key sources
that could serve as anchors for the entire project. Two sources were
particularly important in this regard, the Hundred Rolls of 1279 and
the lay subsidy rolls. While both of these sources have tight geographical and chronological constrictions, neither is uniquely identified
with Huntingdonshire, and both offer potential for prosopographical
cross-referencing with jury panels that have not hitherto been
exploited. Since both these sources will be used extensively in what
follows, it will be helpful to give some account here of their general
form before plunging into detailed analysis.

As noted in chapter 1, the Hundred Rolls of 1279 were compiled
as part of a royal enquiry that sought, among other things, to identify
and record the names of all of the kingdom's landholders. It is not

entirely clear what the king intended to do with this information.[10]
There were many precedents for surveying major property-holders,
but none, with the exception of Domesday Book, required a complete inventory of all property-holders, regardless of their tenurial
relationship with the king. The most striking feature of the surveys
compiled during the Hundred Rolls enquiry is their remarkable level
of detail. In some counties, the conveners of the enquiry were able to
assemble comprehensive village by village inventories of the names
of individual property-holders, the amount of property they held,
and usually the terms on which they held the property, including the
amount of rent they paid. While these comprehensive surveys have
survived only for a handful of counties, within those counties the coverage is remarkably thorough, often giving the names of people who
held mere cottages or who were subtenants of tenants. It is not
uncommon to find the names of several hundred individual property-
holders recorded for a single village, ranging all the way from the lord
of the manor to a poor widow clinging to a garden plot. The surveys
are, to be sure, not fully inclusive. Even in counties that are well represented, some villages cannot be found, either because they were not
surveyed or, as is more often the case, because some parts of the survey have been damaged or lost. There are also some obvious omissions in the surveys. The names of villein tenants, for example, are
often left out; frequently, the number of villeins holding standard ten-
ements was noted but not the name of each individual possessor. The
surveys also frequently include women who held property in their
own name, but most women were treated as members of a household
and thus subsumed under the name of a husband or father. And, of
course, the surveys manifest little concern with people who did not
hold property, such as servants, lodgers, live-in relatives and so on.
The Hundred Rolls are, in short, a register of free men who owned
property rather than a census of local populations. Since jurors were
generally drawn from the ranks of free men who held property, however, the Hundred Rolls are particularly well suited for tracing individual jurors, even though their omissions might pose problems for
other types of prosopographical research.

The other source that is particularly well suited to shed light on the
social backgrounds of jurors is provided by the tax records known as
lay subsidies. The most common type of subsidy record is a bare-bones
list of names with a sum of money entered beside each name indicating
the amount of tax owed. These lists appear to have been drawn up by
county taxers in order to assist them in collecting the tax. The lists
were often drawn up in duplicate, with one copy being retained by the

collectors at the county level to assist their collection effort while the duplicate copy was sent to the Exchequer.[11] Many of the Exchequer copies have survived, particularly for the first several decades of the fourteenth century. There is no discernible rhyme or reason to the pattern of preservation; records exist for some counties for some subsidies but the Exchequer did not have a policy of routinely preserving every list it received, nor would the listings have been of much use once the collection process was complete. Whatever the reason, Exchequer clerks occasionally chose to file some of the county listings with the accounts of the revenues generated by the subsidy, and in so doing ensured their preservation into the present. Because of their obvious value to genealogists, many county record societies in the last century have edited and printed the returns, making them not only more accessible but also more useful, since most editions included alphabetical indices delineating the people occurring in the documents.

Like the Hundred Rolls, the lay subsidy lists do not provide a comprehensive register of all inhabitants in a town or village. The lists privileged male heads of household and ordinarily included women only when they were not part of a male's household. They are not even a complete register of all male heads of household, however, since many male householders were too poor to owe any tax. Subsidy assessors were instructed to exempt anyone whose property was worth less than a defined minimum; the minimum varied from tax to tax but usually meant that cottagers, servants, and laborers did not have to contribute to the subsidy. The first stage of the assessment was conducted by local assessors, and there is good reason to believe that they too tended to overlook people of modest means, excluding people who were technically wealthy enough to contribute but still relatively poor. In other words, the lists of taxpayers are essentially registers of male heads of household, who were at least moderately well-off at the time the assessment was made. As with the Hundred Rolls, these limitations pose serious problems for certain types of research, but they are not particularly problematic in the case of tracing jurors, since jurors were ordinarily drawn from social ranks that were expected to contribute to the subsidies.

My use of lay subsidy documents in this chapter relies heavily on the relative size of individual assessments recorded in the lists, and assumes that they give a reasonably accurate reflection of actual wealth at the time the list was made. In the assessment of a village, for example, I assume that the person with the highest assessment was probably a lord or at the very least a well-endowed member of the gentry, and, conversely, I assume that the person with the lowest assessment was a peasant of small means. I also assume that most of the taxpayers who contributed to the subsidy were peasants, and that only the wealthiest people in any given village should be considered as belonging to a higher social class. It seems unlikely that more than 10 percent of the people recorded in a village tax list could have come from ranks above the peasantry, and so I have used the criterion of having a tax assessment in the top 10 percent of all village taxpayers as presumptive of a status above the level of the peasantry. As a second analytical benchmark, I have distinguished between taxpayers assessed in the upper and lower halves of the village on the assumption that the upper half of a village's taxpayers (minus the top 10 percent of higher rank) would be likely to include all of the high-status peasants who can be variously described as kulak peasants or as upper-rank peasants, while the bottom half would be likely to include peasants who were not members of the peasant elite within the village. In other words, I assume that taxpayers assessed in the fiftieth to nineti-eth percentile consisted of wealthy peasants, individuals who appear in other contexts as the holders of virgates of 30 acres or even larger amounts of land and who often appear in local records as office-holders (reeves, aletasters, manorial court jurors, and so on) while the bottom half was made up of peasants who worked less than a virgate and who infrequently appeared in any official capacity.

Since the pivotal assumption I make in this chapter is that only the top 10 percent of taxpayers in a village were likely to belong to social ranks above the level of the peasantry, a few further words of justifica-tion are warranted here. The number of individuals who appear as taxpayers in surviving subsidy rolls varies widely from one village to the next, depending on the population of the village and the assiduity of the assessors, among other things. In general, the numbers taxed tended to fluctuate between about 15 and 75 individuals. Smaller and larger lists can be found, but they are not common. As an order of magnitude, then, the assumption that the top 10 percent did not belong to the peasantry would anticipate that in a small village with only 15 householders designated as owing tax there would be only one family who could reasonably be described as belonging to the county gentry, while in a large village with 75 taxpayers there might be seven such families. Another way to visualize the implications of my assumption is to consider the absolute number of taxpayers occur-ring in a county's lists. In the small county of Huntingdonshire, for example, approximately 3,400 individuals appear in the lists of con-tributors to the subsidy of 1327, a number that would imply that the county might have had somewhere around 340 families that were of gentry or higher status. By way of comparison, Michael J. Bennett suggested that Lancashire, a much larger county, had around 40 knightly families and 240 gentry families in the later fourteenth century.[12] A list of Huntingdonshire's principal landholders compiled for a special tax on lands collected in 1412 records the names of 64 people with holdings worth more than five marks; suggesting that, if anything, the assumptions made here overstate the ranks of gentle society.[13] Writing about Chaucer's franklin, Nigel Saul suggested that relatively few villages had more than a single individual whom contemporaries would be wont to describe as a franklin, even though the status conveyed by the label was intermediate between peasantry and gentry.[14] More direct evidence about the predominance of peasants in the subsidy lists also supports the contention that at least 90 percent of the taxpayers listed in subsidy records can be characterized as peasants. J. A. Raftis and M. Patricia Hogan examined the taxpayers in six villages in Huntingdonshire with good series of manorial court records, and found that of the 521 taxpayers documented in the subsidy, 481 (92 percent) could be traced in the manor courts of the six villages.[15] Similarly, A. T. Gaydon's careful examination of the taxpayers in three Bedfordshire hundreds in 1297 found that of 1,128 taxpayers recorded in the subsidy only 77 (or approximately 7 percent) can be found in other sources with holdings that could be described as manors; Gaydon thought that the remaining 1,051 contributors to the subsidy could fairly be described as peasants.[16] It is not self-evident that every individual above the ranks of the peasantry was necessarily the holder of a manor, but since Gaydon treated a number of quite small holdings as manors, including four that comprised only 80 acres of land, his findings are probably not far off the mark. For present purposes, then, the assumption that ranks above the level of the peasantry constitute 10 percent seems reasonable; it maintains the sense that we are dealing with probabilities rather than true statistical precision, and it is likely to err on the side of caution in defining the role of peasants as jurors.

The combination of the subsidy rolls and the Hundred Rolls provides a surprisingly rich body of material with which to search for evidence about the social backgrounds of individual jurors. In fact, the main problem these sources present is diametrically opposed to the one that is often assumed to preclude prosopographical analysis of jurors: Far from a dearth of source material there is actually so much available that the quantity can almost seem overwhelming. To make the project manageable, I have limited my analysis to five counties that are particularly well served by the available sources: Cambridgeshire,

Huntingdonshire, and Oxfordshire, which are particularly well documented in the Hundred Rolls, and Bedfordshire and Hertfordshire, which are well served by lay subsidy rolls. The counties are all located in England's midland belt, an area of nucleated villages and open-field agriculture featuring intensive cereal cultivation with a secondary emphasis on the rearing of sheep and other pastoral pursuits. They are, in short, representative of a broad swathe of England, although they do not do full justice to all parts of the country, particularly the north and the southwest, where population was sparser and more dispersed and pastoralism tended to be a more central part of the economy. The results of my analysis will be presented in the remaining sections of this chapter, which will be organized according to the principal types of jury in the period, with information about each type drawn from whichever county provides the best evidence.

THE PERSONNEL OF INQUEST JURIES

Inquest juries were assembled to deal with an extraordinarily wide range of issues, and their composition tended to reflect the broad diversity of their responsibilities. As a general rule of thumb, inquests that dealt with matters of great importance to the Crown or with the rights and obligations of powerful individuals in county society were staffed by men of gentry rank or higher, while inquests that dealt with more mundane or more local business tended to involve people lower down the social scale, including many individuals drawn from the ranks of peasant villagers. But the distinction should not be drawn too starkly, because many inquest juries included members drawn from diverse social backgrounds and it was not uncommon for a jury made up mostly of peasants to include one or several members of higher standing, or, conversely, for a jury made up mostly of men of high status to include one or several peasants.

A good example of a high status jury assembled to deal with a weighty political matter is the body assembled in Huntingdonshire in 1276–77 in response to a writ from Edward I regarding disturbances in the county during the Barons' Revolt.[17] Edward was specifically interested in knowing who had interfered with the sheriff's management of the county in the aftermath of the revolt, when neighboring Cambridgeshire, administered by the same sheriff, became one of the last centers of baronial resistance. The inquest jury gave its verdict in the county court and pointed to eight individuals, who, along with unnamed accomplices, had prevented the sheriff from conducting his tourn and collecting traditional revenues. Judging from the care the jury took to stipulate the financial consequences of the affair and the fact that the written verdict was sent to the Exchequer, it was clear that the principal intent of the inquisition was fiscal rather than political, but the gravity of the original acts and the high standing of some of the identified culprits suggests that the coroners, who took the verdict in the county court, thought it wise to create a jury that incorporated a good deal of political muscle.

Of the 12 jurors named in the inquest verdict, nine can be securely identified in the Hundred Rolls. William de Broughton appears as lord of the village of Offord Daneys, and three of the other jurors—Richard de Catworth, William le Moigne of Great Staughton, and William, son of Gregory—held property that included portions of knight's fees. All four can be treated as belonging to the upper crust of county society.[18] Four others—John de Aylington (Elton), Richard de Hotot, Ralph de Washingley, and William, son of Ranulf—held a hide or more of land, holdings that in Huntingdonshire usually comprised somewhere between 100 and 120 acres and were characteristic of the gentry. The ninth identifiable juror, Roger Thurstan of Stanground, was of lower status than the others, appearing in the Hundred Rolls as the possessor of a single virgate in Stanground, the holding of a prosperous peasant. Even more striking than the relative modesty of Roger Thurstan's own holding is the fact that a William Thurston also appears in the Hundred Rolls as the holder of a half-virgate of villein land in the village of Sawtry. Thurstan was not a common surname and it is likely that the two men were related to each other. It is hard to explain why a jury with so many high-ranking members included someone from a lower social background; whatever the reason, his inclusion did not seriously alter the overall composition of the jury, which was clearly set up to constitute a body of men who represented the higher ranks of county society.

An inquest *ad quod damnum* held in Huntingdonshire in 1329 exemplifies the workings of a less elevated jury dealing with a matter that was more pedestrian.[19] As discussed in chapter 1, inquests to evaluate potential damages resulting from a change in the status quo formed a significant part of the explosion of inquest procedure that characterized the later thirteenth and fourteenth centuries. In this particular case, the abbot of Ramsey had applied for a license of exemption from the statute of mortmain to allow him to acquire numerous parcels of land in the county. As was standard procedure in such cases, the king ordered a local inquest jury to investigate the circumstances of the proposed property transfers, paying particular heed to their effect on the donors or vendors. Would the donors and sellers, the king wanted to know, retain sufficient land to perform customary obligations in the county if he granted the requested license to the abbot? The jury convened in St. Ives, gave a general statement of the value of the lands involved, summarized the circumstances of the donors, and concluded that the proposed grants would not seriously diminish their ability to fulfill their customary obligations.

Of the 12 jurors who gathered in St. Ives, eight appear in the county's lay subsidy roll of 1332, and a ninth can be found in the subsidy roll of 1327.[20] The nine jurors who can be traced in the subsidy rolls occupy all three of the wealth categories outlined above. Three (John le Clerk of Broughton, John de Earith, and Thomas de la Sale) had assessed wealth that put them in the top 10 percent of all taxpayers in their respective home communities; two others (John de Deen and Ralph Vernoun) had assessable wealth that ranked them in the top half of their home communities, and four (Henry Barker, Benedict Chamberlain, John Porter, and Ralph Clervaux) ranked in the bottom 50 percent of their home communities. The personnel of this jury is particularly interesting because most of the jurors resided on manors belonging to Ramsey and several can be traced in the abbey's manorial records. John le Clerk of Broughton served as a reeve, beadle, aletaster, and pledge for example, and members of his family served as jurors in the local manorial court.[21] Similarly, John de Earith served as a juror and pledge in the manor court of St. Ives and he was also active in the small town's fair court.[22] These other roles suggest that both men are better described as prosperous peasant villagers than as members of the gentry, and the opportunity to observe them in these other contexts suggests that the method of treating the upper 10 percent of taxpayers in the subsidies as presumptive members of higher social ranks is likely to err on the side of ascribing gentry status to too many people rather than too few. Ramsey's records also shed light on one of the lesser figures who served on the inquest: John Porter, who had assessable wealth in the bottom half of his village, appears frequently as a pledge in the manor court of Houghton, where he also served at least once as a juror, and once paid a fine for failing to perform a customary work service in the required manner.[23] His father, John was similarly involved in the local court.[24] Finally, one of the inquest jurors can be linked to a holding documented in the Hundred Rolls compiled 50 years earlier. Ralph Vernoun, who appears in the subsidy as a prosperous individual in the upper half of taxpayers in Hemingford in 1332, also appears in the Hundred Roll survey of the village as a freeholder with a messuage, a virgate, and an additional holding of 31 acres, for which he owed suit to the sheriff's view of frankpledge and the hundred court, among other things.[25] Given the gap between the two records, it seems likely that the juror Ralph Vernoun was a son or grandson of the Ralph Vernoun whose property was described in the Hundred Rolls, but if so he undoubtedly held the same property as his ancestor. Both his property ownership and his tax assessment portray him as a wealthy peasant, prosperous by the standards of other peasants but certainly not someone who could have entertained reasonable pretensions to gentility. In this regard, he was cut from the same cloth as the other members of the jury.

A jury intermediate between the two examples just given can be reconstructed for an inquest in Oxfordshire in 1277.[26] In that year, the king ordered his sheriff to investigate the circumstances surrounding the conveyance several decades earlier of a sizeable property in the village of Lea to the bishop of Salisbury. The ultimate purpose of the inquest is not clear, but its provenance in the Exchequer records suggests that the information was needed to clarify the fiscal liabilities attached to the land. In addition to the names of the jurors the written verdict also notes their villages of residence, simplifying the task of finding the jurors in the Hundred Rolls. Nine of the 12 jurors can be found in the villages with which they are identified in the inquest.[27] Their possessions range from a single virgate, which, in Oxfordshire, usually comprised around 25 acres, to four virgates, or approximately 100 acres.[28] Of the nine findable jurors, two held a single virgate (Roger le Freman of Wykham and Hugh Dene of Shutford), one held a virgate and a mill (Henry Miller of Wykham), three held two virgates (Thomas Hunfrey of Swalcliffe, Robert Pyman (or Fiman) of Swalcliffe, and Stephen, son of Elena of Shutford), one held two and one-half virgates (Gilbert de Walcot of Little Bourton), and one held four virgates (Thomas de Fraxino of Shutford). It would be hard to view the two holders of single virgates as anything other than members of the peasantry. With his four virgates, however, Thomas de Fraxino probably saw himself as having more in common with other parish gentry in the county than with the villagers of Shutford. Those who fell in between these two poles are harder to situate, although it is worth noting that Stephen, son of Elena owed suit to his lord's court as part of the services for his two virgates in Shutford.

Which of the three examples just given should be viewed as typical of inquest juries in the period? The best answer is none, or rather all three. As discussed in chapter 1, inquests were so common that all three of the types described here had plenty of work to do. In the twelfth and early thirteenth centuries, juries comprised of men of higher status were probably the norm, because inquests were generally reserved for weightier and more difficult matters, or for matters that directly affected the interests of society's upper ranks. The jury that investigated disturbances in Huntingdonshire's administration following the Barons' Revolt can be seen as a direct successor of the inquest juries that Henry II used to investigate the behavior of sheriffs in 1170. Throughout the period treated in this book, major governmental initiatives continued to emphasize the involvement of the higher ranks of county society in the management of the kingdom, and so one finds knights and gentry in the later thirteenth century frequently serving on inquests in which the king's rights were centrally concerned, such as the Hundred Roll enquiries and numerous other inquests related to knighthood, lordship, tenure, or the management of royal government. But as the central government began to arbitrate and adjudicate matters at a more local level and endeavored to establish a more direct relationship with society's base—one of the great governmental projects of the thirteenth and fourteenth centuries—it inevitably found itself turning to jurors drawn from more humble backgrounds. Well connected and powerful members of county society continued to serve on major inquests, but wealthier peasants had to be drawn in for verdicts involving more quotidian affairs: The dramatic expansion of inquests over the course of the thirteenth century inevitably brought in its train an increasing reliance on peasants as jurors. Consequently, it is likely that by the century's end peasants predominated as inquest jurors, because the number of local inquests dealing with routine matters was so much greater than the number that dealt with more elevated affairs. Far more inquests *ad quod damnum* were held in the reign of Edward I, for example, than sweeping inquests of national significance in the entire medieval period. But such a sharp distinction between the two levels of inquest ultimately cannot be sustained. Inquests *ad quod damnum*, like inquests *post mortem* and other types of inquest, regularly involved the political and economic interests of men of high standing, and so even when the procedure was localized and routine it could still have major implications for both the reality and the display of power among the higher ranks of society. The routinizing of inquest procedure did not preclude the participation of local notables; enlisting peasants was a necessity rather than a virtue. When the stakes were high enough, inquest juries could still be dominated by members of the gentry. Conversely, while the great national inquests, such as the one that produced the Hundred Rolls, typically record the names of lords and prominent regional landholders as jurors for entire hundreds or entire counties, the information they presented was often first assembled by local juries that reported to them before they made their formal statement to the king's officials.[29] Inquest juries were, in short, flexible enough to draw on the knowledge of a broad spectrum of society, including peasants, and it is this very flexibility that made them such central features of English government.

THE PERSONNEL OF PRESENTMENT JURIES

A similar diversity of social background can be found among individuals who served as presentment jurors. Presentment jurors bore a heavy responsibility, not only for sifting charges related to felonies but also for providing sensitive information about local affairs to royal officials. The Crown naturally preferred to have men of high standing, and may have originally managed to limit service to the higher ranks of local society. But as the use of presentment grew over the course of the thirteenth and early fourteenth centuries, the social base from which jurors were drawn inevitably had to be expanded. Several related developments drove this expansion. First of all, the number of large-scale royal inquests featuring presentment increased over the course of the thirteenth century. While many of these inquests were administrative rather than judicial exercises, the obligations and responsibilities of the jurors drafted to serve on them were comparable to those borne in more strictly judicial settings. Second, within the legal system itself, presentment became more widespread during the thirteenth and fourteenth centuries. The extension of presentment to manorial courts meant that many peasant villagers developed firsthand experience working on or with a presentment jury. One might argue for a sharp distinction between presentment as practiced in a manor court and presentment as practiced in a royal court, but the difference was not as stark as is sometimes portrayed: Peasants on manors that had frankpledge privileges bore responsibilities that merged into those borne by presentment jurors in the king's own hundred courts and formal distinctions between the two venues were far from clear-cut at the time. In a similar vein, the introduction of the office of coroner at the end of the twelfth century brought with it a new mandate for presentments by juries convened by coroners. Contemporaries complained frequently about rising levels of violence, particularly in the later thirteenth and early fourteenth centuries, and even if some allowance is made for exaggeration in the tales of woe, it does seem likely that the work of coroners, and therefore of coroners' presentment juries, grew through the period. Perhaps the most significant extension of presentment occurred with the creation of the courts convened first by the Keepers and then by the Justices of the Peace. Peace sessions were originally conceived as venues for hearing presentments and even when they were given competency for conducting trials, the hearing of presentments continued to be central to their function. To some extent, the peace sessions took over some of the presentment work that had earlier been conducted in other venues, particularly in the eyres. But the notion that from their inception peace sessions competed with all other venues in a Darwinian struggle is misguided. The presentments heard at peace sessions were designed to supplement rather than compete with those made in other legal venues and only toward the end of the period covered in this book is it possible to talk about them as crowding out the older forms of presentment. It is true that eyre courts fell into abeyance in the late thirteenth century and that much of their work subsequently fell to the JPs, but other venues, notably the sheriffs' tourn, continued to thrive well into the fifteenth century. But even if the later eyres are used as the basis of comparison, it is obvious that the use of presentment advanced rather than declined in the later thirteenth and early fourteenth centuries, because eyres were held so infrequently.

Two quantitative examples can help to illustrate the widening use of presentment and give some indication of what it meant on the ground. The first is drawn from the Hundred Roll enquiry conducted in London in 1275.[30] As elsewhere in the country, the city's presentment jurors were required to answer a series of specific questions designed to elicit information about aberrant officials and others who had abused or ignored their responsibilities to the king. Many of the presentments made in London came in response to a question about individuals who had contravened the king's recent embargo on wool exports to Flanders, an issue that was particularly sensitive in the nation's commercial capital. What is important in the present context, though, is not the substance of the presentments but rather the procedure and format of the enquiry. Rather than rely on a single jury for the entire city, the justices who conducted the inquest constituted a separate presentment jury for each ward. A list of jurors serving in the wards was drawn up as part of the process and gives the names of approximately 340 individuals who served on the inquest.[31] London's population at the time was probably over 40,000, so statistically speaking the jurors can be said to have included only a small fraction of the total population, although they obviously represented a much larger proportion of the male heads of household in the city. But the jurors appear not to have constituted a who's who of the city's mercantile elite. This is suggested most directly by the occurrence of numerous name forms associated with relatively modest trades, such as Baudechon the butcher (*Baudechon le Bocher*), Gilbert the potter (*Gilbert le Poter*), and Thomas the carpenter (*Thomas le Carpenter*). Several of the presentments also suggest that the juries included men who were not exclusively from the city's upper crust. The jury for the ward of Coleman Street, for example, presented several elite citizens because they refused to contribute to common tallages "which ought to be common and borne equally by all and to which all ought to contribute," and went on to point out that the entire burden consequently fell on "the poor and middling sorts" (*pauperes et medioc- res*).[32] The jurors ended their presentment with the declaration that such behavior was leading to "the utter destruction" of the city and that the king would suffer as a result. This is clearly not language that can be ascribed to a body of wealthy oligarchs.

A second quantitative example is provided by the gathering of pre- sentment juries before the king's Keepers of the Peace in Kent in 1316–17.[33] As was standard in early peace sessions, the Keepers were authorized only to hear presentments and not to conduct trials related to the presentments; the trials were held at a later court ses- sion by royal justices commissioned to deliver the county's gaols. The Kent peace sessions are particularly interesting because records for some of the subsequent gaol deliveries have survived, allowing nu- merous cases to be followed through from the original jury present- ment made before the Keepers to the concluding jury trial conducted before royal justices.[34] The trials were held about two weeks after the presentments were made, making for an unusually speedy process. For present purposes, it is the work of the presentment juries rather than the trial juries that calls for special scrutiny, although it is worth bearing in mind that the work done by the presentment juries was only part of the overall workload of jurors involved with keeping the peace in the county.

As in the case of the London presentments made in the Hundred Roll enquiry in 1275, the file of documents associated with the Kent peace sessions includes a list of the jurors who participated in the ses- sions. It includes the names of 505 jurors altogether, organized into separate juries representing the county's separate administrative dis- tricts, known as lasts, and a small number of towns.[35] (Kent's lasts were similar to the hundreds and wapentakes of other counties.) It would be hazardous even to suggest a ballpark figure for Kent's pop- ulation in the early fourteenth century, but the 505 jurors clearly accounted for only a minute fraction of the total population. And yet the number is sufficiently large to suggest that the jurors could not have been drawn only from the county notables. Bertha Putnam, who edited the records, noted the inclusion of many people from humble social backgrounds among those listed as jurors. While her main interest in the records lay in other areas, she paused long enough over the jury lists to note that "there is evidently a wide range in the status of the jurors; some are apparently of humble occupation, and others belong to the official class, that is, to the group of men responsible for the local government of the shire."[36]

A direct prosopographical analysis of the individuals serving as presentment jurors in London and Kent would be difficult to undertake given the nature of surviving documentation, but similar lists from two other counties permit a fuller investigation of the matter. One of these counties is Huntingdonshire, where lists of presentment jurors serving in the eyre of 1286 can be cross-referenced with the detailed lists of property-holders recorded in the Hundred Rolls in 1279 and a rich assortment of other records. The task of making these links is relatively straightforward, thanks to the extensive biographical register of individuals appearing in the eyre compiled by Anne and Edwin DeWindt.[37] A few prefatory remarks will help to contextualize the analysis. Though a small county, Huntingdonshire had relatively large hundreds. As a general rule, bailiffs in counties with large hundreds could afford to be more selective when empanelling juries than their counterparts in counties, like Kent, that had relatively small hundreds or equivalent administrative districts. It is also worth noting that the eyre was the most august judicial institution operating in the period, and so one would expect the jurors it convened to be worthy of its elevated status as a legal tribunal.

The task of making presentments in the eyre fell to 62 men, 14 representing the town of Huntingdon and 48 the county's four hundreds.[38] The jury constituted for Hurstingstone hundred provides the best opportunity for prosopographical analysis because the hundred had a high concentration of villages that were part of the well-documented Ramsey Abbey estate.[39] Of the 12 men sworn to make Hurstingstone's presentments, three cannot be positively identified in other sources: One was the hundred bailiff Laurence de Rede, whose inclusion on the jury can be ascribed to his administrative role rather than his personal wealth or social position; two others had the surname "Clerk," which was common enough in the county at the time to preclude positive identification with similarly named Clerks in other sources. The nine remaining jurors can all be traced with some degree of confidence in other sources. One (John de Deen) is documented in the Hundred Rolls as possessing an entire knight's fee in Stukeley.

Throughout his life he received an assortment of high-level commissions from the king, appointing him as a commissioner of array, a county tax assessor, and a local justice. He also represented the county in Parliament. His high status undoubtedly explains why the eyre justices asked him to choose the other members of the presentment jury, a duty he fulfilled in conjunction with the bailiff of the hundred. He was clearly a member of the county elite and a natural choice to head up a presentment jury at the eyre. Two of the remaining eight jurors clearly belonged to the county gentry: Ralph de Hinton, who held one-quarter of a knight's fee in Bluntisham that included lordship over 22 villeins; and Ivo de Hirst, who held a carrucate (roughly 120 acres) in Old Hurst and owed suit to the abbot of Ramsey's honor court in Broughton. Two others can be ascribed to the gentry on the basis of family and service rather than property. Richard le Fraunceys married the widow of a wealthy and well-documented member of the gentry, and William Bygeney represented Huntingdon borough in Parliament several times in the early fourteenth century, suggesting that he too was a man of substance in the county.[40] Thus, it is possible to conclude that five of the nine identifiable jurors in Hurstingstone came from relatively elevated social backgrounds.

The four remaining jurors, however, were clearly men of lower social status, drawn from the ranks of elite villagers below the level of the gentry. John Aspelon, identified in the Hurstingstone jury list as living in St. Ives, appears in the Hundred Rolls as the holder of a single virgate in St. Ives, with a separate holding of four acres of meadow land and a messuage in Slepe, the rural hamlet attached to St. Ives. He does not occur in the manorial court rolls for St. Ives, but others with the same surname, presumably family members, were fined for brewing infractions, and a William Aspelon was active in the manor court between 1306 and 1332, including service as a juror.[41] John Goscelyn, identified in the jury list as hailing from Broughton, occurs in the Hundred Rolls as the tenant of a messuage and virgate in Broughton, and is well documented in other local records.[42] He served numerous times as a capital pledge and juror in Broughton's manor court, for example, and his wife Beatrice was fined at least once for brewing ale against the assize.[43] William de London, identified as residing in Warboys, held a messuage and 24 acres of land in Warboys and a second holding of a messuage and 12 acres of land in nearby Broughton. Like John Goscelyn, he was active in his local manor court, serving as a pledge and juror. His wife was a brewster and his descendants continued to be prominently involved in local affairs for several generations, constituting one of the village's leading families.

The fourth lower-status juror, Roger de Grendal, identified as living in Fenton, can only be traced in the Hundred Rolls as a tenant of the bishop of Ely holding two virgates and 20 acres of land, or about 80 acres altogether, but he cannot be found in other sources.[44] His landed holdings would have made him very wealthy by peasant standards, but probably would not have sufficed to raise him into the ranks of the parish gentry. The appropriateness of including him with the three other peasant jurors is further suggested by a piece of evidence internal to the juror list itself. Each of the three other better documented peasant jurors appears in the list with his full name followed by a scribal entry noting his village of residence. The five higher status jurors, though, are recorded only by name, without any reference to their place of residence; their "name recognition" apparently obviated the need to use geographical delimiters to identify who they were. Thus "John de Dene" was sufficient on its own, but "John Goscelyn" was not; the scribe felt it necessary to write "John Goscelyn of Broughton." This practice is worth noting not only in the case of Roger de Grendal, but also with respect to the two jurors in the list named "Clerk," who also occur with geographical delimiters: Alexander Clerk of Stukeley and Reginard Clerk of Houghton. If these two are treated as socially comparable to the other peasant jurors, then it would be possible to conclude that at least half of the men serving on Hurstingstone's presentment jury in the 1286 eyre were peasants. Even if a more conservative position is adopted, it is clear that at least one-third of Hurstingstone's presentment jurors in 1286 were drawn from social levels below the rank of gentry.

The second good opportunity to link presentment jurors to other sources indicating social standing comes from Bedfordshire. Included in a file of documents recording the presentments heard by Keepers of the Peace there in 1314 is a list of the jurors serving in each hundred and town.[45] For each of the county's nine hundreds and two towns (Bedford and Leighton Buzzard) 12 jurors are named and a special jury of "triers" (*triatores*) reviewed and supplemented the presentments made by the local districts.[46] Thus, the peace sessions required the services of 144 men in total. As with the Kentish peace sessions discussed above, the sessions held in Bedfordshire were entirely devoted to taking presentments, with trials based on the presentments taking place at a later date before justices of gaol delivery. For the purposes of identifying the social background of the jurors, the most relevant source is a lay subsidy roll documenting taxes paid in 1309.[47] How did the taxable wealth of the men selected as jurors compare to the wealth of the rest of the taxpaying population? As discussed in section one of this chapter, the basic assumption made here is that members of the gentry and higher social groups were assessed with taxable property ranking them among the top 10 percent of all assessed taxpayers in their place of residence, while those with lower assessments are assumed to belong to lower social groups, chiefly the peasantry.

The hundred of Biggleswade can stand as an example for the rest. As was customary, the subsidy roll of 1309 required local assessors to examine and evaluate their neighbors' movable property to determine how much each person should pay. Earmarked for the king's war in Scotland, the final tax burden assigned to each individual represented one twenty-fifth of the assessed value of their property, with exemptions granted to people with property worth less than a fixed threshold, which appears to have been set at 10 shillings. In the Bedfordshire account of the assessment, the names of individuals are recorded under the name of their principal village of residence, with each name accompanied by the amount of tax owed. The roll names 436 taxpayers in the hundred who contributed a total of just over £53 to the king's coffers, yielding an average (mean) of approximately 2 shillings 6 pence per taxpayer. Alice Latimer made the highest tax payment in the hundred, contributing nearly 27 shillings for her property in the village of Sutton. The Latimers were a prominent Bedfordshire family who exercised lordship in Sutton and provided at least one member of Parliament for the county, so Alice's prominence in the subsidy comes as no surprise.[48] At the bottom end of the scale, three individuals made payments of 5 pence and nine others made payments of 6 pence Presumably, as in other subsidies, many people were not required to pay tax in 1309 because they owned taxable property below the minimum threshold defined for the assessment, meaning that those who paid 5 pence or 6 pence should be understood to represent households of slender means rather than individuals who were nearly destitute.

Of the 12 jurors for Biggleswade hundred, 11 occur in the subsidy roll. Two served as local assessors and were recorded in a separate section of the subsidy roll listing the tax liabilities of assessors, without any indication of village of residence.[49] Neither appears to have been particularly wealthy: Richard of Colchester contributed 2 shillings 8 pence to the assessment and Robert le Rede contributed 2 shillings 5 pence Both men were, in other words, assessed on property valued near the mean of the hundred as a whole. It is possible, of course, that their power as assessors led to an undervaluing of their personal wealth, but even when they are compared to the other assessors in the hundred, who presumably enjoyed the same benefit of office, their wealth is best described as middling: Richard of Colchester ranked eighth of 28 assessors in the hundred and Robert le Rede ranked ninth. Both were assessed well below the level of their fellow assessor Milo of Drayton whose tax assessment was fixed at the sum of 7 shillings 9 pence.

Of the nine jurors who can be traced as taxpayers in specific villages, three had taxable wealth that placed them in the top 10 percent of their native village. Simon of Astwick, for example, paid over 8 shillings in Astwick, making him the wealthiest individual assessed in the village. Similarly, William Everard ranked second of 49 taxpayers in Tempsford while William Torold ranked third in the same village. Everard and Torold cannot be found in other standard sources suggestive of high standing, but Simon of Astwick was a figure of some note in the county, having a share in the lordship of Astwick.[50] The six other jurors were men of lesser substance: Representative of the upper end of the group was John le Blund who paid 5 shillings in Biggleswade village, ranking him sixth of 37 taxpayers; representing the lower end was John Whytbred, who contributed 1 shilling 4 pence in Stratton, placing him eleventh of 21 taxpayers in that village. Whytbred was the only juror whose tax assessment was below the mean for the hundred, but one other was at the mean and three others were only a few pennies above it.

Thus, like their counterparts in Hurstingstone hundred in 1286, the presentment jurors for Biggleswade hundred were drawn from several different social levels. On one end of the continuum were men who had resources that were consistent with gentry status and who probably expected to be treated with deference by the other members of their local community. On the other end were well-endowed peasants, men who were rooted in the soil of their native village and who were probably accustomed to holding positions of authority in local governance. In between were men who had one foot planted in a local village and the other in the county. A good representative of this intermediate group is John le Blund whose property holdings can be traced in an inquistion *post mortem*. In 1304, about a decade before he served as a presentment juror for Biggleswade hundred, John le Blund inherited his father's lands, some of which were held directly from the king.[51] The inquest found that his father held property in two places: a messuage and 40 acres in Wardon and a second messuage with 20 acres in Biggleswade. The holding in Wardon is described in the inquisition as being one-twentieth of a knight's fee. Assigning a social status to him on this evidence is not easy: Historians generally consider someone who held only 60 acres of land to have been a wealthy peasant, but such a label seems inappropriate for someone who had property in two different villages, was a direct tenant of the king, and descended from a family that, many generations earlier, had possessed a knight's fee. In the 1309 subsidy roll, le Blund appears only in Biggleswade village, where his 5 shilling assessment ranked him sixth of 37 taxpayers, as mentioned above. The amount paid as tax is relatively high; only three other jurors paid more and they have all been ascribed gentry status using the analytical framework employed in this chapter. His ranking within his own village, though, suggests a lower social status, although it also suggests that he was one of the most prosperous of the non-gentry jurors: All of the other non-gentry jurors were assessed with property that required tax payments of less than 3 shillings, and all but one of them had a lower relative ranking within their home village. If le Blund, with his two messuages and 60 acres, can be taken to represent a high end "yeoman" juror, then it is reasonable to suggest that most of the other non-gentry jurors, who were considerably less wealthy than le Blund, are best described as peasants. It would, of course, be unwise to draw any categorical conclusions about the Biggleswade jurors on the basis of a single tax assessment, but the weight of evidence suggests that royal administrators viewed peasant villages as fertile soil for the recruitment of presentment jurors.

THE PERSONNEL OF ASSIZE JURIES

Juries that were involved in the property assizes show affinities to those involved with inquests and presentments, but they tended on the whole to draw on the services of a wider swathe of society. Although they were formally constituted as a royal procedure, the assizes were less directly connected to the exercise of state power, and so the impetus from central government to empanel men of "quality" was not quite as compelling as it was in the case of presentment and at least higher-level inquests. The key issue governing the selection of assize jurors was the requirement that the parties involved in the litigation accept a bailiff's choice of jurors for the case. In most instances, the parties wanted to have jurors who were responsible and trustworthy, but they often defined these qualities in the context of localized disputes, meaning that an experienced village leader was often a more natural choice than a lord. From the perspective of the center, assize juries could also be treated as a less elevated form of jury service because their decisions were limited to matters of property rather than life and limb. This is not to say, however, that service on an assize jury was undertaken lightly or deemed too trivial to merit attention. Verdicts awarding property to one party over another frequently had serious ramifications for the social and economic well-being of the contending principals, and often therefore also for their local communities; assize juries often determined who would continue to wield political and social clout in their village or hundred as well as who would enjoy the benefits of owning a piece of land. Their verdicts were, consequently, of interest to many who did not have a direct stake in the property under dispute. The dictum that "all politics is local" was coined in recent memory but applies almost equally well to medieval England.

Thanks to an extraordinary file of jury panels associated with the property assizes conducted at the Cambridgeshire eyre in 1272, it is possible to investigate the social backgrounds of assize jurors at a single point in time in exceptional detail.[52] The file has 215 separate jury panels, written on small slips of parchment with brief annotations indicating the principals and the nature of the property in dispute. Many of the cases related to the jury panels can be found in the surviving record of the eyre proceedings, providing insights into the disputes that the juries were called upon to adjudicate.[53] The overlap is far from complete, since many of the cases were terminated before a trial was held and parts of the eyre record and some of the jury panels have sustained damage, but dozens of panels can be linked to a corresponding case. This material is even more valuable than might appear at first glance, because Cambridgeshire is also unusually well documented in the Hundred Rolls, compiled within seven years of the eyre session. The Cambridgeshire assize panels are, in other words, particularly well suited to prosopographical analysis as well as to internal analysis based on the formal court record.

Four of the panels will be examined here. Each is in good physical shape and can be associated with a case record on the eyre roll. The four are unusual in that the scribe who composed them wrote the village of residence on the panel beside the name of each juror, but are otherwise typical of the other panels in the file. Having a place of residence to work with as well as a name makes the task of locating the jurors in the sprawling Hundred Roll surveys much easier and increases the likelihood that a positive identification can be made.

The first panel was assembled for a case of novel disseisin in which Guido Mortimer alleged that Richard de Frivill and his bailiff had disseised him of 25 acres of land in the village of Caldecote in Longstowe hundred. Both principals were men of relatively high status. De Frivill was lord of the manors of Caxton and Little Shelford and his family had once held one-fourth of a knight's fee in Caldecote.[54] Guido was not prominent in his own right, but he was probably related to William Mortimer, who exercised lordship in the neighboring village of Kingston.[55] The Hundred Rolls reveal that de Frivill's portion of a knight's fee in Caldecote had been parceled out to several tenants, including William Mortimer who held 42 acres from Richard de Frivill.[56] Presumably, Guido Mortimer's land as noted in the suit of novel disseisin in 1272 formed part of this holding.

Though ostensibly about land, the record of the case on the eyre roll indicates that the central dispute between de Frivill and Mortimer was principally about jurisdictional rights.[57] The jurors' verdict notes that the main issue was de Frivill's demand that Mortimer attend his court in Caxton. It does not specify the type of court, but the Hundred Rolls indicate that de Frivill held a view of frankpledge in Caxton. The verdict notes that de Frivill, acting on the advice of his court, had distrained (that is to say, impounded) one of Mortimer's animals as a way of forcing him to attend. When Mortimer continued to hold out, de Frivill seized a second animal, and then upped the ante by impounding four oxen from his plough team. The last distraint appears to have motivated Mortimer to launch his suit of novel disseisin; being deprived of a plough team was tantamount to being deprived of the land. As the jurors were narrating these details, a justice asked if Mortimer had any other animals that could have been distrained in place of his plough oxen. They answered that he did not. The record of the case ends abruptly after their response without giving a final determination. A note on the back of the jury panel, however, indicates that Mortimer was awarded damages of two marks, suggesting that his refusal to attend de Frivill's court was ultimately vindicated.

The jury panel drafted for the case comprised 22 men, 12 of whom are noted as having sworn.[58] All but three of the names on the panel are accompanied by a village of residence, all situated in the hundred of Longstowe. One of the jurors lived in Caxton, where de Frivill's court met, and two lived in Caldecote. The others hailed from eight other villages. There are no significant differences between the men who swore and those who did not; so, for the sake of simplicity, only the 12 who swore will be discussed here. Eight of the 12 can be found in the Hundred Rolls and in each case they appear in the villages indicated on the panel. Three were of at least moderately elevated status, with holdings described as portions of knight's fees. The largest belonged to Robert Miles of Bourne, comprising one-half of a knight's fee, of which 30 acres were held in demesne with the remainder parceled out to tenants.[59] The two others were Elias de Bledsoe, who held one-third of a knight's fee in Hatley St. George, and John Carpenter, who held one-fourth of a knight's fee in Caldecote.[60] These three probably sufficed to give de Frivill confidence that his outlook on tenant relations would be well represented in the jury's deliberations. The five other identifiable jurors were, however, of lower standing. None held more than 35 acres. The most substantial of the five was Henry Peverel of Toft, who appears in the Hundred Rolls with a messuage and 31 acres of land in Toft and an additional three acres in the neighboring village of Eversden.[61] The poorest juror was Richard Passevant of Bourne, who held only three acres at the time of the Hundred Roll survey.[62] Other Passevants are named as landholders in Bourne, so it is possible that Richard had once held a larger property, but even when all the Passevant holdings are combined they do not surpass 30 acres. Analysis of the jurors can be extended even further in this instance because the property interests of the four jurors who do not appear directly in the Hundred Rolls can also be reconstructed. A holding of 35 acres in Longstowe is described in the Hundred Rolls as "formerly belonging to W. Albert" and this must have been the main holding of the William Alberd of Longstowe who served as a juror in the assize. Similarly, Simon Elys is recorded as holding 30 acres in Bourne, which he may well have inherited from the Robert Elys of Bourne who served as a juror in 1272. Thomas son of William Smith held five messuages and 26 acres in Caxton; William Smith of Caxton served as a juror in 1272. Finally, it is likely that the juror William Campiun of Longstowe held the messuage and approximately 20 acres in Longstowe that were attributed to Hugh Campiun in the Hundred Roll survey.[63] Accepting these four attributions as valid leads to the conclusion that the assize jury convened before the eyre justices in Cambridge in 1272 consisted of three men of gentry status and nine men who held land commensurate with peasant status. Of the nine probable peasants, four held roughly 30 acres of land, which would have conveyed high status by peasant standards, while five held lesser amounts.

Litigants of high status were also involved in a case yielding a second jury panel that can be explored in detail. In this case, the prior of the Hospitallers prosecuted a suit of novel disseisin against John de Burgh, escalating a dispute that began in the village of Harston. John de Burgh exercised lordship in several different villages in Cambridgeshire and was a member of the county's upper crust; the prominence of a prior of the Hospitaller order is self-evident.[64] As in the previous assize, the dispute was ostensibly about property but was actually more about jurisdiction.⁶⁵ It began when the prior and some of his men dug into a meadow belonging to de Burgh; the reason for their excavation is not given. De Burgh's bailiff treated this as a "trespass" (*transgressio*) and summoned the prior to his lord's manor court to answer for the deed, taking two sluice gates from the prior's water mill in the village as distraint. The prior proceeded to build new sluice gates and put the mill back in business; the bailiff then seized the new sluice gates; the prior again installed new ones. Rather than continue this dance, de Burgh's bailiff tried another tack. When the prior sent a horse with a sack to take the multure from the mill, the bailiff seized both the horse and the sack full of multure. The situation was further exacerbated when the bailiff began to harass people who wanted to use the mill, so that people avoided using it. Contending that the seizure and ongoing harassment damaged his property rights in the mill, the prior sued de Burgh and his officials for an act of disseisin. A justice asked the jurors who were narrating the details of the case if John de Burgh was present at the alleged disseisin. They said that he was not and mentioned that the prior had talked to him privately about the earlier distraints and trespasses, hoping that he would intervene directly to settle the matter. Informal conversations like this were probably more important mechanisms for dispute resolution in the period than formal court proceedings, but in this instance de Burgh chose not to negotiate, and so the problem lingered. The justices, though, appear to have held out hope that the two parties would be able to settle their differences amicably, leaving the case unfinished at the eyre. The jurors ended their account before the justices by saying that the prior would be able to mill again if he made amends to John for the original trespass. A note on the back of the jury panel states that damages to the prior, "if there are any," would be set at 50 shillings.⁶⁶

The front of this same jury panel gives the names of 19 men drafted as potential jurors, of whom 12 took the oath. Three of those who swore cannot be securely identified in the Hundred Rolls or other standard sources. Of the nine who can be identified, six held property commensurate with gentry or higher status, ranging from William Bretun, who held an entire knight's fee in Barton, to William Sterne, who possessed three messuages, approximately 90 acres of land, and had at least three tenants in the village of Haslingfield.⁶⁷ The remaining three held land commensurate with peasant status: Ralph le Eyre of Grantchester held a virgate, Roger Clerk of Haslingfield held the equivalent of a virgate (about 30 acres), and Robert

Marshall of Thriplow, the poorest of the lot, held a messuage and 16 acres.[68] The weight of the jury was clearly on the wealthy end of the spectrum, but it is interesting to note that even on a jury so clearly made up of men of substance a few lesser lights were also called upon to serve.

The third panel of jurors from the Cambridgeshire eyre that merits careful scrutiny also involves an assize of novel disseisin, but with a plaintiff of much lower social standing than Guido Mortimer or the Hospitaller prior. Alan Osmund brought two suits of novel disseisin against Roger Russell and several others for preventing him from pasturing his animals in West Wickham and for obstructing a path that gave access to land he worked in the village of Wilbraham. Osmund can be found in the Hundred Rolls with a holding of only 15 acres, corroborating the contextual evidence of the assize that he was a peasant of relatively small means.[69] His main opponent Roger Russell does not appear in the Hundred Rolls, although an Alice Russell is recorded in West Wickham with over 50 acres of land and it is likely that this property was in Roger's hand at the time of the assize.[70] The two assizes were combined into one case determined by a single set of jurors.[71] They sided with Osmund on both counts. With regard to the pasture, they noted that Osmund had four acres of arable land in West Wickham on which he was accustomed to pasture his animals when the village's fields were thrown open for common pasture (in other words, after the grain had been harvested). With regard to the second dispute, they corroborated Osmund's story that Russell's construction of a wall in Wilbraham obstructed a path Osmund had long used with his cart and plough team when cultivating his land. In addition to finding for Osmund on both matters, the jury also awarded him damages.

Of the 18 names that appear on the jury panel, 12 are marked as swearing an oath.[72] Only one of the 18 men on the panel was of any real substance: Walter Burree of Shudy Camps, who held one-half of a knight's fee and had numerous tenants in the village.[73] Interestingly, he was fined for failing to appear in court, and it is tempting to see his dereliction as related to the petty nature of the assize. Nine of the 12 who swore can be traced in the Hundred Rolls and they were all men of limited substance. The best endowed member of the group was William Marshal of Horseheath, who held 36 acres of land.[74] The least prosperous was Robert de Stowe, also of Horseheath, who held a messuage and only three acres of land. The remaining jurors tended more to Robert de Stowe's side of the ledger than William Marshal's; none held more than 20 acres and two held less than ten acres. A tenth juror, Nicholas le Newman of Horseheath, probably held at the time of the eyre the 30 acre holding ascribed to Richard le Newman in the Hundred Roll entry for Horseheath.[75] Newman's inclusion, though, does not change the composition of the assize jury in any significant way; it was basically a body made up of peasants, most of whom were not wealthy even by peasant standards.

The fourth sample panel from the Cambridgeshire eyre that is particularly well suited to identifying jurors stems from a case of mort d'ancestor, a form of assize that was procedurally similar to novel disseisin but dealt specifically with disputed inheritances. The case pitted William Panyer against Ralph the Cooper and his wife Edith.[76] William claimed that his mother, also named Edith, had possessed a messuage in the village of Whittlesford that ought to have descended to him when she died. The jurors disagreed with his version of the facts and reached a verdict in favor of the Coopers. They explained the descent of the messuage as follows: It was true that Edith Panyer had once possessed the messuage, but long before she died she transferred her title to her daughter when her daughter married Ralph; in other words, she conveyed the cottage to Edith as a marriage portion. Thus, seisin passed out of Edith Panyer's hands and into the hands of Ralph and her daughter Edith. In bringing his suit for mort d'ancestor, William Panyer was essentially contesting the validity of his mother's wedding gift to Ralph and Edith. Presumably Edith was William's sister, although the jurors were silent on this point. They concluded that since Edith Panyer no longer had seisin of the messuage on the day she died, it could not pass to her nearest heir, and so William's claim was invalid.

Even more than in Osmund v Russell, the circumstances described by the jurors suggest that the principals involved in litigation came from the ranks of the lesser peasantry. Edith Panyer is the only one who can be found in the Hundred Roll entry for Whittlesford, where she is shown renting out half an acre of land.[77] There is also reference to a Matilda Penir who held a messuage in the village, and it is just possible that this was the same messuage that was disputed in the Cambridgeshire eyre.[78] More to the point, however, no Coopers or Panyers appear with any other holdings in the village, supporting the circumstantial evidence of the assize suggesting that the litigants were of humble background.

Unlike Osmund v Russell, though, the jury included several men of gentry or higher status.[79] Of the 12 men who swore in the case—selected from 19 who were on the panel—three could claim to have some standing beyond their village: John le Blund held one-fourth of a knight's fee in Babraham and other lesser properties; Robert Safrey had a similar holding in Pampisford ; and Robert Tristram held one-tenth of a knight's fee in Wicken.[80] Seven of the nine other jurors can also be traced in the Hundred Rolls. One (Henry Bernard of Sawston) held approximately 45 acres of land and might be described as a kulak peasant.[81] Another (William Adam of Ickleton) held a messuage and 22 acres, a holding that might have sustained aspirations for a position among the peasant elite of Ickleton but little else.[82] The five other findable jurors all held less than 20 acres of land; three held less than ten acres. William Kenteys of Sawston is a particularly interesting member of this group of smallholders. In the Sawston survey in the Hundred Rolls, he is documented as having sole possession of a patchwork of four small plots of land: two messuages, a plot of three acres, and a plot of two acres. He is also documented as having a one-third stake in a fifth holding, which is particularly revealing of his status: It was a ten-acre parcel of villein land, for which Kenteys and his partners owed work services.[83]

THE PERSONNEL OF TRIAL JURIES

The final type of jury worth examining by means of prosopography is the trial jury. Trial juries involved with criminal cases are better documented than other kinds of trial jury, so the following analysis will be limited to jury panels associated with gaol deliveries. For much of the period treated in this book, sheriffs and bailiffs were eligible to appoint members of the presentment jury to serve on the subsequent trial jury, so *a priori* one might assume that any findings based on trial juries would simply replicate the findings based on presentment juries, at least prior to the statute of 1352 that gave defendants the right to challenge jurors solely on the grounds that they had served on the presentment jury.[84] In reality, though, the overlap between presentment and trial jury was not necessarily absolute. It is probably true that presentment jurors often did serve on the trial jury; the statute of 1352 presupposes that this was relatively common. But it is far from clear that the entire presentment jury was ordinarily reconvened as a trial jury. It certainly was not a fixed principle of law or administration that the two juries should have the same members. When they did occur, overlaps must often have reflected administrative convenience as much as anything else: Bailiffs must often have found it easier to assign people they had worked with in the past and royal justices must also have seen advantages to working with trial jurors who had prior experience with a case. But since the extent of overlap in practice is still an open question, a separate investigation of trial jurors will not be out of place here, even if it risks repeating the evidence presented above with respect to presentment jurors.

An unusual opportunity to compare personnel on presentment and trial juries comes from three cases that began as presentments at the Huntingdonshire eyre held in the fall of 1286 and ended in trials held before justices of gaol delivery in April, 1287.[85] In the first case, Johanna Buleheved of Stilton was presented at the eyre for being a thief and for other transgressions. She fled before arrest, though, and thus could not be tried at the eyre. Instead, proceedings were set in motion for her to be outlawed. While the outlawry proceedings were underway—a process that ordinarily took several months to complete— she had a change of heart and decided to return to stand trial. Her trial was held at the next gaol delivery session, where she was found not guilty. A similar series of events unfolded in the case of Roger Mowyn of Catworth: accusation in the eyre for numerous alleged thefts; flight; outlawry; trial at the following gaol delivery session; acquittal. The third case involving Robert Rode paralleled the other two cases, except that Rode was accused of murder rather than theft.

Jurors in both eyre and gaol delivery were appointed to represent their hundred before the justices. Because each of the suspects resided in a different hundred, they were presented and then tried by separate juries drawn from their hundred of residence. Thus, Johanna Buleheved was presented in the eyre by a jury representing Normancross hundred and tried by a jury drawn from the same hundred; Roger Mowyn was presented and tried by juries from Leightonstone; and Robert Rode by juries from Toseland. Of interest here is the relationship between the two juries drawn from each hundred. How many of the presentment jurors also served on the trial juries? The answer is about half: The trial juries included nine of the presentment jurors in the case of Johanna Buleheved, and five each in the cases of Roger Mowyn and Robert Rode. Even more interesting, though, is how the social composition of the juries changed in each case. The jurors who dropped out were almost uniformly men of gentry or higher status: 12 of the 17 men who were on the presentment juries but not on the trial juries can be identified in other sources, and only one of the 12 was a peasant; the 11 others were all of gentry or higher status.[86] They were replaced by jurors of equivalent status in a few instances, but were more likely to be replaced by jurors of lower status: Of the 17 trial jurors who had not served on a presentment jury at the eyre, seven were peasants, three were of gentry status, and seven cannot be identified in other sources. The two juries involved in the prosecution of Robert Rode provide a good example. William Gregory was probably the least substantial member of the group who served on the presentment jury but not on the trial jury. His property consisted of a windmill, two virgates, and one-sixth of a knight's fee, along with various smaller parcels. All told, he probably possessed somewhere in the vicinity of 150 acres of land. Among the jurors who served only on the trial jury, the least substantial who can be identified is Roger Smart of Paxton, who held a messuage and a half-virgate (about 15 acres) in Great Paxton and a second messuage in Toseland. The contrast is striking and illustrates an important finding, namely that presentment jurors tended to be drawn from higher ranks of society than trial jurors.

Jury panels occur with some frequency in the surviving gaol delivery rolls, but only occasionally is it possible to find other contemporary documents that permit thorough prosopographical analysis of the individuals entered on the panels. Examples from two counties will be considered here. In both cases, the individuals entered on the panel can be traced in tax records drawn up within a decade of the date of the panel. The first case study involves the county of Hertfordshire, which has several surviving panels from gaol deliveries conducted at Royston in 1313 and 1316 that can be cross-referenced with a record of taxpayers in 1307, recently edited by Janice Brooker and Susan Flood.[87] The tax of 1307 was a subsidy earmarked to defray the expenses of Edward II's coronation, with a fractional assessment rate of one-twentieth of the value of each taxpayer's appraised property.

The panel constituted for Braughing hundred in 1313 provides a good starting point for analysis.[88] It gives the names of 14 men, of whom 13 are marked as having sworn; the odd number of jurors is probably due to a scribal error. Of the 13, 12 marked as taking the oath can be found in the 1307 subsidy. Only one, John le Marshal of Standon, ranked in the top 10 percent of the taxpayers in his village. Eight others ranked in the top half of the taxpayers in their village, while three ranked in the bottom half. One of the jurors was surprisingly poor: John de Bredon paid only 9 pence in Hunsdon; only one other person in Hunsdon paid less tax than he did. The one member of the panel who did not swear with the others was also quite poor according to the evidence of the subsidy: Ralph Giffard paid 15 pence in Gilston, ranking him twelfth of 19 taxpayers there.

Similar results are encountered using a jury panel constituted for Odsey hundred in 1316.[89] The panel names 24 potential jurors, of whom 12 took the oath. In addition to naming the potential jurors, the panel also names two pledges for each one, spreading the web of responsibility for conducting the hundred's trials to 72 men. In spite of the bailiff's precautions, nine members of the panel failed to appear in court when needed; their dereliction is noted by marginal crosses entered beside their name, but fines usually meted out to non-appearing jurors are not indicated. The size of the panel and the resort to pledging suggest that the bailiff expected to have trouble producing a jury in court, but the added precautions appear to have paid off, as 12 men did take the oath. Eight of the 12 can be traced in the subsidy rolls. None of these eight occurred among the wealthiest 10 percent of taxpayers in their village and only five of the eight were among the wealthiest 50 percent of the taxpayers in their village. John West paid the most in tax in 1307, contributing 3 shillings 4 pence on his property in the village of Sandon, a contribution that ranked him eighth of 65 taxpayers. John de Codicote, also of Sandon, paid the least: His 9 pence payment ranked him forty-fifth in the village. This evidence from Odsey hundred in 1316 is consistent with that derived from Braughing hundred in 1313. In both Hertfordshire examples, it is hard to escape the conclusion that trial jurors were drawn primarily from the ranks of the peasantry, indeed often from the middle ranks of the peasantry.

A second good opportunity to analyze the personnel of trial juries is provided by a series of panels drafted for a gaol delivery in Bedfordshire in 1312. In this case, the tax record that was used above to study the county's presentment jurors in 1314—the twenty-fifth of 1309—can once again be called upon to evaluate the relative wealth and social standing of the jurors. The fact that the jury panels were drawn up within three years of the tax assessment means that an unusually high proportion of the jurors can be found as taxpayers. Indeed, the biggest difficulty in correlating the two sources stems from the fact that many of the jurors served as assessors in the subsidy and thus do not appear as taxpayers in their village of residence. As was done in the analysis of presentment jurors, though, two surrogate pieces of data can supplement the data based on rankings within a given village, standing relative to the mean of all taxpayers in the hundred and standing relative to the other assessors.

The gaol delivery file consists of seven panels, of which three yield excellent results when cross-referenced with the 1309 subsidy. In general, the Bedfordshire jurors were of somewhat higher status than those in Hertfordshire, but there were many similarities between the two groups. The panel assembled for Wixamtree hundred provides a good starting point.[90] It records the names of 14 potential jurors, of whom 12 swore. (Interestingly, one of the two who did not swear has a line drawn through his name with a marginal note stating that he was ill.) All 12 of the oath-taking jurors occur in the subsidy roll, seven in association with their home village and five in the separate list of assessors for the hundred. Of the seven jurors who can be associated with a village, two ranked in the top 10 percent of the taxpayers in their village and the five others ranked in the top 50 percent. The case for high status for the two wealthy jurors is strong: John le Child had the highest assessment in Stanford and also had assessable property in another hundred, while Roger of Gostwyk ranked second in Willington.[91] Both men contributed approximately 6 shillings to the king's coffers, or roughly three times the mean for the hundred. Of the five others, a case can be made for treating Roger Blundel as high status. Like Child and Gostwyk, his assessment was close to the 6 shilling mark, but ranked him only tenth of 55 taxpayers in Flitton.[92] The four others, though, were certainly not in the same league: Two had assessments that were below the mean for the hundred and two were only marginally above the mean. Nor did any of the five assessors possess great means, at least not as far as the subsidy reveals. Three paid less than the mean for the hundred and two paid only slightly more than the mean. They ranked sixth, seventh, twelfth, eighteenth, and twenty-first among the hundred's 27 assessors. Their profiles are those of wealthy peasant villagers, not members of the gentry or knightly classes. The composition of the trial jury assembled in Wixamtree hundred in 1312 thus appears to be mixed: two or possibly three of the jurors probably belonged to the gentry while nine or possibly ten belonged to the ranks of the peasantry.

Redbornstoke hundred provides a similarly enlightening opportunity to examine the composition of a Bedfordshire trial jury in 1312. Its panel lists 12 men drafted for the jury, of whom six are marked as having sworn and six are marked as failing to appear in court.[93] The panel does not give any clues about how the court put this short-staffed jury to work. One possibility is that "talesmen" were used to make up the deficiency (talesmen, bystanders pressed into jury service on short notice, are discussed in chapter 3). Another is that the six jurors from Redbornstoke were combined with six jurors from another hundred to make a single jury responsible for both hundreds; though not common, such joining of hundreds was not unprecedented.[94] All of the men on the panel can be found in the subsidy roll. There does not appear to be any significant difference between those who appeared and those who failed to appear, so all members of the panel will be analyzed collectively here. Of the nine who were not assessors, four ranked in the top 10 percent of their village and the five others ranked in the top 50 percent of their village. Richard de Merston was the wealthiest juror. He contributed more than 10 shillings to the subsidy and ranked second of 59 taxpayers in the village of Elstow.[95] On the other end of the spectrum was Henry Mille, also of Elstow, whose payment of 15 pence ranked him twenty-fifth in the village. The three assessors who were drafted for the jury were not particularly wealthy. All three had assessments below the mean for the hundred, and among the 29 assessors their payments ranked sixth, eighth, and ninth. They are best grouped with the five jurors who were not among the elite members of their village, suggesting that four of the Redbornstoke jurors were conceivably drawn from the gentry while eight were likely to have been drawn from peasant ranks.

The panel assembled for Biggleswade hundred provides a third exceptional opportunity for analysis.[96] It had 14 members, of whom 12 swore. The name of one of the 12 is partially obliterated on the jury panel and thus cannot be included in the analysis. Nine of the remaining 11 can be traced in the subsidy, of whom six served as assessors. Two of the three who were not assessors ranked in the top half of their village but not in the top 10 percent and one ranked in the bottom half of his village. Three of the six assessors paid more than the mean for the hundred, but none was of great substance. The wealthiest of the assessors was Richard Embleynes, who paid a little over 3 shillings and ranked fourth among the 28 assessors for the hundred.[97] In other words, while their responsibility as assessors would lead one to expect that they were men of standing within their local villages, none paid tax at a level that is suggestive of gentry status. If this line of reasoning is accepted, then it follows that the Biggleswade jurors were drawn entirely from the ranks of the peasantry. It is possible in the case of three of these Biggleswade jurors to probe a little bit further into their stature. The juror Nicholas Batayle, who was not an assessor, paid 2 shillings 8 pence to the subsidy in 1309, ranking him eleventh of 48 taxpayers in the village of Sandy. He occupied the middle position of the three jurors who were not assessors, both in terms of his absolute contribution to the subsidy and in terms of his ranking within his village. His absolute contribution was equivalent to that paid by Richard of Colchester, who ranked third of the six assessors on the jury in terms of tax paid. Thus, Nicholas Batayle can be taken to represent a juror of average or middling status for the hundred. This same Nicholas Batayle can also be found as a taxpayer in Sandy in a subsidy collected in 1297.[98] Unlike the subsidy roll of 1309 that of 1297 also inventories the property on which tax was levied, giving some inkling of the nature of his wealth. His portfolio of holdings in 1297 comprised one mare, one bullock, one cow, three kinds of grain (amounting to 17 bushels all told), and a small quantity of hay. The nature and quantity of his property is entirely consistent with that of a reasonably prosperous peasant.

Bedfordshire is not blessed with an abundance of local or manorial records in the thirteenth and fourteenth centuries, making it difficult to corroborate the status ascriptions made here by referring to other sources. In one instance, though, one of the trial jurors serving in 1312 can be traced in a series of manorial court records, and the record of his involvement with his local court is worth exploring in detail. The juror in question is Walter Goman, who was a member of the panel put together for Manshead hundred. Technically he was not a juror: He, like all of the other members of the Manshead panel, failed to show up before the justices in 1312. But as was noted above, there were few noticeable differences between the kinds of men who made up the pool of jurors on the panel and the 12 who were selected from the pool to take the oath. The shirking of jury service in this instance was clearly a group decision rather than a series of individual decisions and implies nothing about personal standing or worthiness to serve. The bailiff who put his name on the panel must have thought of him as having the right stuff to be a juror, and there is no reason to question the propriety of the bailiff's judgment.

Goman was assessed on property in the village of Chalgrave, giving rise to a subsidy contribution of roughly 3 shillings.[99] Within Chalgrave, he ranked ninth of 40 taxpayers, in the upper 50 percent of his village but not the top 10 percent; in other words, in a position similar to that occupied by most of the Bedfordshire jurors discussed in this chapter. In the fourteenth century, the manor of Chalgrave was in the hands of the Loring family, represented in the early fourteenth century by Peter Loring. Befitting his dominant position in the village, Loring's tax assessment in 1309 was nearly 16 shillings, making him by far the wealthiest man in the village. Next in line came John Peyvere, whose liability for the subsidy was 6 shillings 8 pence. Several other people had assessments higher than 5 shillings. Goman was thus not only of much lesser substance than the lord of the village, but he was also much less wealthy than the small cohort of Chalgrave residents who were nearest to the lord in terms of taxable wealth. And yet by the standards of the hundred as a whole he more than held his own. In addition to being in the top quartile of Chalgrave's taxpayers, Goman's contribution to the subsidy was high enough above the mean for the hundred as a whole (2 shillings 6 pence) to be significant. In terms of the other men on the jury panel, he was also relatively prosperous. Of the 18 men on the panel, 13 can be found in the subsidy and only one paid more tax than Goman. In short, it is possible to situate Goman within the ranks of the peasant jurors who have featured so prominently in this chapter, but it is also important to note that he should be situated on the high end of the peasant spectrum rather than the low end.

Chalgrave's manor court generated a good but incomplete series of records between 1278 and 1313.[100] The Loring lords of the manor had the right to hold a view of frankpledge in conjunction with their manor court, and as was often the case, the distinction between courts exercising frankpledge jurisdiction and those exercising purely manorial jurisdiction was blurred. As a freeholder, Goman would probably have been subject to his lord's frankpledge jurisdiction, but his obligation to participate in the regular manor court would have been more open-ended. On some manors free peasants did participate regularly in their local manorial courts, but on other manors they avoided them, preferring to make use of the hundred courts for lesser matters and the assize courts for matters pertaining to their real property. Goman, however, appears to have had few misgivings about participating in his lord's court. He first appeared there in 1295, registering an exchange of two small plots of land with Peter Loring, described as the son of the lord of the village and probably the same Peter Loring who appeared in the subsidy list of 1309.

Goman did not appear again in the court until 1303, when he served as a pledge for a fellow villager and accused John Fox of defaming him, an accusation that was upheld by the jurors of the court. From then until the series of court rolls ends in 1313, Goman was actively involved in the court. In a court held in May, 1304, he appeared three times: once for digging a ditch that harmed the property of one of his neighbors, for which deed the court issued an order for distraint; once for failing to bring someone to court for whom he had earlier pledged, earning him a fine; and once for "contradicting the tithingmen in full court," again earning a small fine. This last entry is particularly interesting. While the record does not say explicitly that he contradicted his own tithingman, it does imply that he belonged to a tithing in the village, that is to say, that he was obliged to be in a frankpledge group. Membership in a tithing, or frankpledge group, was a sure sign of peasant status in the period; members of higher social orders were their own surety for good behavior. In December of the same year he was fined for an unspecified default and for leading some of his neighbors out of the village to find good ale.[101] He still had not fixed the problem caused by his ditch, so he was fined for that as well.

In the years between 1304 and 1313 (the date of the last surviving court roll), Goman appears a handful of times in the Chalgrave manor court, mostly as a pledge for fellow villagers. In one entry, he acknowledged an obligation to satisfy his lord for arrears in rents and services owed from land he inherited from Andrew Goman, but unfortunately the entry does not furnish details about the property. His role in a court held in 1306 is particularly interesting and may help to explain why a bailiff tapped him for jury service in the gaol delivery of 1312. Walter de la Hurne found himself in a heap of trouble with Robert Hamund in 1306 and managed to extricate himself only by agreeing to pay Hamund £5 for his "trespass" (the nature of which is not specified) and a further 13 shillings 4 pence to gain Hamund's pardon.[102] The agreement was brokered by Walter Goman, who is described in the entry as Hurne's "attorney" (*attornatus*). Goman also stood as a pledge for Hurne, and even agreed to pay the 13 shillings 4 pence composition on Hurne's behalf if he defaulted. The word "attorney" in this instance should probably be understood more in the sense of "delegated agent" than "professional legal representative," but is nonetheless revealing about Goman's standing in the village.[103] He was a villager who could negotiate a settlement in what must have been a serious affair, judging by the size of the fine. He was well enough respected to arbitrate between and, in effect, to reconcile, two erstwhile enemies. He was, in short, a village leader recognized for his skill, judgment, and perhaps also his knowledge and experience of legal affairs. His background in Chalgrave was undoubtedly the reason for his appointment as a decision-maker for Manshead hundred in 1312. Similar local records are unavailable to study the backgrounds of the other jurors active in the royal courts in Bedfordshire in this period, but it seems reasonable to suggest that what is distinctive about Goman is the fortuitous survival of his village's court rolls rather than anything exceptional or extraordinary in his personal background or standing. Most of the jurors serving in the gaol delivery in 1312 were probably cut from the same cloth.

Conclusion

The evidence presented in this chapter gives rise to two major conclusions about jury composition in the thirteenth and fourteenth centuries. The first is that medieval juries were usually socially integrated bodies. To be sure, they were not democratic: Jurors were exclusively male freeholders of some substance. But in the context of their own period and place, their level of social inclusiveness is quite striking, in that they drew together peasant villagers, members of the gentry, and sometimes even knights and higher lords to cooperate in a common pursuit of justice. The most common form of jury encountered in this chapter is one that called on the services of a few members of the lower gentry complemented by differing mixtures of wealthy free-holders straddling the boundaries between gentry and peasantry and peasant villagers, pure and simple. Juries drawn exclusively from one level of the social hierarchy were actually unusual, at least in the common forms of jury service dealt with in this chapter. Many questions about how this mixing of social levels actually worked in practice remain to be answered. Were the peasants on the jury expected to follow the lead of their social superiors in reaching a verdict? Did the higher-ranking members of the jury treat the others condescendingly, or did they view them in a more positive light as valuable conduits through which local information and values could flow? Perhaps such questions are unanswerable, although surviving source material is plentiful enough to give hope that they are as yet simply unanswered.

The second feature that stands out in the material presented in this chapter is the extent to which ordinary peasant villagers were involved in the jury system, including in some instances even peasants of only middling wealth. Naturally, the level of peasant participation varied depending on the level of responsibility assigned to a particular jury. When an inquest dealt with a matter of great political weight and sensitivity peasants were likely to be outnumbered by jurors chosen from higher social ranks, or sometimes even excluded entirely. In a similar vein, presentment juries, with their overtones of political supervision, were more likely to draw on the services of men above the rank of peasant than trial juries, the responsibilities of which were more narrowly circumscribed. Peasants were also less likely to sit in judgment on assizes that pitted eminent figures as litigants, with manors or other vehicles of lordly status as the prizes being fought over. But though these limitations or exclusions were important in their own right, they do not tell the whole story. The secret of the Common Law's success in the period treated in this book was its ability to penetrate deeply into society, so that inquests, assizes, and even presentments became affairs that involved or affected a wide swathe of society, including the peasantry. Jury verdicts were popular at all levels of society, or at least at all levels of society vested with rights of property. The popularity of jury procedures created a booming demand for jurors, a demand that could be met only by widening the social nexus from which jurors were drawn. Those responsible for choosing jurors had to engage with a wide segment of society when searching for likely candidates to serve; the system simply would not have worked if peasants had been excluded. Thus, when detailed prosopographical analysis of juror backgrounds is first possible in the later thirteenth century, men from peasant backgrounds can be found serving on most forms of jury and often formed a majority of jury membership. In other words, peasant jurors were more than just common; by the later thirteenth century they were normal.

CONCLUSION

While writing this book, I have had numerous conversations with friends, students, and colleagues about their experiences with jury service in modern America. Two issues ordinarily rise to the fore. The first is a pervasive sense that jury service is a great burden. The world I inhabit—admittedly defined by a professional and middle-class life—is full of overcommitted people scrambling to find ways to "squeeze" family, friends, work, school, and multiple other community groups into the fixed number of hours in a day and days in a year. Personal circumstances are never quite the same and yet the results seldom differ: overcommitted workers; overcommitted bosses; overcommitted parents; overcommitted kids. A summons to jury duty, raising the possibility of untold days spent away from life's other demands, is thus typically greeted with dismay, sometimes even resentment. The instructions about how to defer or dodge the requested service are without doubt the most avidly read part of the summons.

And yet there is an equally pervasive sense that jury service is important and potentially worthwhile. Recognition of the value of jury service typically forms the second theme of my conversations with friends. It is a theme that resonates particularly strongly with friends who have actually served on a jury. Many modern courts actively inculcate in prospective jurors a sense both of the history of the jury system and the ongoing role that jury service plays in promoting the values of justice and democracy. But far more important in forming attitudes toward jury service is the experience itself: participation in the formal procedures of a trial; distinguishing between truths, half-truths, and lies; debating with other members of the jury; and ultimately seeing justice done at firsthand. Service on a jury tends to inculcate respect for the judicial system as a whole and sometimes even leads people to consider how trial by jury, with its inherent form of collective decision-making, might be related to the ideals of liberty and participatory government cultivated by the Anglo-American political traditions.

While the experience of jurors in the period treated in this book cannot be directly equated with either of these modern responses, they do have a surprising amount in common. At the outset it must be admitted that questions about how medieval people felt about jury service can be answered indirectly at best and even then only with difficulty: The feelings and inner beliefs of people who lived many hundreds of years ago, particularly those of the nonelite, are rarely accessible to historians. But when evidence about public behavior is reasonably plentiful, as it is in the period's legal records, it is sometimes possible to infer underlying attitudes and perceptions. While recognizing that our knowledge is mostly circumstantial and inferential, it is still possible to say something meaningful about both the burdens of jury service and the political calculus that accompanied it in the medieval world.

That medieval people saw jury service as a burden and even a hardship cannot be doubted. Chapter 2 described how bailiffs were wont to create much larger jury pools than were necessary because they knew that many of the people they named would be willing to offer bribes to be struck from the jury panel. It also noted that jurors commonly failed to appear when summoned, even though they knew they would be fined as a result, and recounted the woes of the talesman Ralph of Ditton, who was pressed into service on a jury that was short a member and as a result found himself in prison for participating in a false verdict. Chapter 4 offered similar evidence when discussing the willingness of people of higher social standing to purchase formal exemptions from jury service. Indeed, as Chapter 4 demonstrated, the legislation governing jury service in the thirteenth and fourteenth centuries makes sense only in a world in which sheriffs and bailiffs had ongoing difficulties constituting juries. The urge to avoid jury service is not a modern phenomenon; it is evident almost from the very moment the jury system began its great expansion in the twelfth and thirteenth centuries. It has been part of the system ever since.

But there are also important historical differences that distinguish how people have perceived the burden in different eras. Our modern sense is conditioned mainly by our perception of time as a scarce commodity, a feeling that is manifest in an often acute awareness of the myriad demands that compete with civic duty. It is intimately bound up with the social and economic realities of modern life, such as single parenthood, job insecurity, lengthy work weeks, and long commutes between work and home. Our daily activities are governed by the clock and we constantly make choices between activities based on close calculations of what our daily or weekly schedules will allow. Allocating time to duties beyond those associated with work, home, and family often seems possible only by making sacrifices in some other important area of our lives.

Medieval people did not lack awareness that time spent on local government and public duty was time taken away from work and farm. In modern idiom, one could say that they recognized the opportunity cost of time even if they did not define it in the abstract terms we do. While in general they led less frenetic lives than we do, there were periods of the year in which every waking hour was highly valued. Representatives from Cornwall petitioned Parliament in 1315, for example, to ask that assize justices be assigned to their county at more suitable times of year than early spring and August, because those were periods of peak labor demand in the agrarian calendar when people ought to be "making their livelihood."[1] A commons petition in 1343 similarly asked that justices not be assigned during haymaking season.[2] These are the familiar concerns of farming communities the world over: Bringing in the harvest trumps all other obligations and responsibilities. Medieval people probably did find it easier to make time for civic participation than we do, but that does not mean that their lives were untroubled by competing demands for their time, nor that they failed to reckon the temporal cost of participating in legal and political affairs.

Finding time for civic duty may have been easier in a society that was predominantly agrarian, but it should also be borne in mind that the temporal costs associated with medieval jury service were often greater than our own. Medieval trials were typically much shorter than their modern equivalents, but the time jurors spent traveling to and from court greatly outweighed the time spent in court. The medieval transportation system was more developed and more efficient than is commonly thought, but traveling long distances by horse was still a slow and laborious affair. It is, in fact, astonishing that English kings and royal administrators ever entertained the idea that they could construct a legal system that presupposed the availability of 12 men from Northumberland or Cornwall whenever needed in Westminster. The same petition from Cornwall in 1315 mentioned above also addresses this issue of travel time. It asked the king to assign justices to the county more frequently than had hitherto been the case, so that it would not be necessary for principals and jurors to travel to the central courts to determine cases.[3] They asked for this royal favor "because the county is so distant that people on the inquisitions have ruined themselves coming to the court, and therefore they are as happy to be ruined and stay at home as to struggle to court and be ruined." We saw in Chapter 4 that royal statutes set the income qualification for prospective jurors at a higher level when they were asked to serve outside their home county than within, indirectly recognizing the hardships that confronted a juror required to travel from his home to Westminster. And as discussed in Chapter 2, the system of itinerant justices authorized to hear possessory assizes, gaol deliveries, and *nisi prius* verdicts in the counties was a real boon in reducing the number of long journeys jurors had to undertake. The situation castigated by Cornwall's representatives in 1315 was thus the exception rather than the rule, but it was not so exceptional that lengthy journeys to Westminster to perform jury service could ever be described as possible only in theory.

Even when cases unfolded in the counties, as was the norm from very early on, traveling to court could still require substantial commitments of time and energy. In most counties, the assizes were held in the county town, with perhaps one or two other towns in the county serving as satellite venues. This was a sensible policy from an administrative point of view. The principal gaols were typically situated in the county towns; the offices of the sheriff and his staff were similarly located; and the county towns were also generously endowed with hostels, alehouses, and eateries. But though it was certainly easier for jurors to congregate in a county town than in Westminster, travel time was still an issue. In the county of Wiltshire, for example, the assizes were ordinarily convened in the town of Salisbury. If one assumes that a good rider with a good horse could cover perhaps 30 miles in a hard day of riding, then about half the county was conceivably close enough to allow jurors participating in the assizes to ride back and forth in a single day, assuming good weather and a propitious court schedule that did not detain them too long before the justices. Jurors from more distant parts of the county could not possibly have made the journey in a single day. Even those who lived within 15 miles of Salisbury must often have found it difficult to fulfill their obligations in a single day. It is really no wonder that the courts had chronic problems caused by jurors who failed to appear when required.

On a practical level, then, finding time for jury service may have been easier in the medieval world than it is today, but the situation was not nearly as one-sided as might appear at first glance. But framing the question as a matter of time management fails to tell the whole story. It leaves out of view something that no longer poses much trouble for modern jurors but formed a major part of the burden of jury service in the Middle Ages, namely the fact that medieval jurors had to function within a web of local relationships rather than simply as anonymous and disinterested agents involved in the dispensing of justice. As discussed on numerous occasions in this book, medieval jurors tended to be drawn from the geographic area where a case or accusation originated, typically the hundred. They often knew the principals involved in the case, if not at a personal level than at least at a social level as a member of the same hundred. In some types of procedure, such as the possessory assizes, the link between prior familiarity with a principal and selection to a jury was a fundamental aspect of the whole legal process. Medieval jurors regularly sat in judgment on people with whom they were familiar, people whose property and sometimes whose very life depended on what they decided in the jury room. Sitting in judgment is a heavy responsibility even when the individual being judged is a stranger; it is even heavier without the benefit of anonymity. The burden of judgment in a medieval trial must have been particularly acute in felony cases, when jurors knew that their guilty verdict would lead almost immediately to a defendant's death.

In addition to imposing unknowable psychological burdens on jurors who had to pass judgment on known or familiar people, medieval jury service also had major implications for a juror's life outside the courtroom. Matters that were contentious enough to require litigation were wont to spill over into other aspects of public life. Christine Carpenter's account of local politics in fifteenth-century Warwickshire makes clear that political tampering with jury selection could be a major problem for royal administration, and while earlier periods did not experience the political factionalism that characterized the period of the Wars of the Roses, there can be little doubt that jurors frequently had to navigate contentious political situations in the course of their service.[4] Chapter 3 described the efforts that the abbot of Lilleshall made to learn who was on the jury deciding a case involving property in which he had an interest; such detective work, frequently shading into lobbying for a particular verdict, was not uncommon at the time. Jurors serving on a possessory assize could expect to be cajoled if not intimidated by one or both parties before the trial was held and they could expect their behavior before the trial to come in for scrutiny when the parties issued their challenges.

A juror's experience in the court room could also have unpleasant consequences. Daniel Seipp has characterized medieval jurors as "prisoners of the court once they were sworn," because after their oath they were required to stay together as a body under supervision until they were ready to deliver their verdict.[5] The justices were more interested in resolving cases than in the well-being of jurors, sometimes even refusing them food and drink until they resolved their differences of opinion and returned a verdict. Reprisals against jurors were also possible. The process of attaint allowed a litigant to appeal an unfavorable verdict by alleging partisanship or corruption of the jury, and if the allegation was upheld, the jurors were heavily fined and could also be imprisoned.[6] Reprisals beyond the law were also possible. At an eyre held in Kent in 1255, a group of jurors sought the court's protection against the family of a man they had just convicted of theft.[7] Two members of a presentment jury in Norfolk found themselves in prison in 1276 shortly after their jury service, falsely accused of murder by someone they had previously indicted for harboring thieves.[8] Retaliation against jurors had become so common by 1353 that the king authorized a series of enquiries to deal with the problem. The first article assigned to the jurors participating in the inquest dealt with "those who hire wrongdoers to beat the men of the court and jurors of inquests;" the third with "those who come forcibly into the king's court against the assizes and so disturb the peace that the jurors dare not tell the truth."[9]

Contemporaries sometimes commented directly on the hardships associated with jury service. The "Song on the Venality of the Judges" composed in the reign of Edward I (1272–1307) includes a verse castigating sheriffs who persecuted the poor. To exemplify such persecution, the poet cites the treatment of jurors, who are "dragged hither and thither and put on assizes" and forced to swear against their will.[10] An inquest jury in the reign of the same king condemned a royal official for fining 20 members of a jury pool in Lincolnshire for their failure to appear in court; the fines were unreasonable, the inquest jury declared, because a great storm had prevented the jurors from keeping their assigned court date.[11] A similar sentiment pervades a parliamentary petition submitted by John of Garston, also in the reign of Edward I.[12] Garston had served in the household of Edward's father, who had rewarded him with a lifetime exemption from service on inquests, juries, and assizes. Recently, however, "by the procurement of his enemies" he had been called to serve on a jury. He refused citing his charter of exemption, but to no avail; the justices fined him £10 for failing to serve. King Edward, perhaps moved by Garston's claim to be in ill health, had a modicum of pity for his father's old servant: He reduced the fine to £5 and agreed that Garston could pay it in installments.

There can be little doubt that medieval people saw jury service as difficult, burdensome, and even potentially dangerous. The eagerness with which exemptions from jury service were sought is easy to understand, as is the willingness of people to bribe bailiffs and sheriffs to remove their names from jury lists. Equally understandable is the propensity of jurors to stay home when summoned, even though they knew they would be fined for doing so. Medieval courts routinely had to postpone cases because jurors had not come to deliver a verdict. Frequently, the entire jury failed to appear at the appointed time, but there were also many occasions when some but not all of the jurors appeared. These situations often led the courts to use talesmen such as Ralph of Ditton, who lacked the local knowledge and contextual familiarity normally expected of a juror but had the great virtue of being available at the required time. Fines for nonappearance were generally not exorbitant, and considering the difficulties of the job, many of the jurors who stayed away must have seen them as utterly fair trade-offs for shirking the job they were summoned to do.

While the travails and tribulations of medieval jurors were neither trivial nor incidental, they do not necessarily sum up the experience of every juror in every situation, perhaps not even most jurors in most situations. The jury system as a whole was extremely popular. As discussed repeatedly in this book, the demand for jury verdicts grew enormously over the period. It is possible to treat the growing reliance on jury verdicts observable from the later twelfth century as centrally dictated and controlled, a direct consequence of assertive state power. But the weight of evidence lies on the other side of the ledger, suggesting that the growth was fuelled above all by popular demand for jury verdicts. It was this relentless demand that really accounts for the success of the jury as a legal institution. Or perhaps a better way to formulate the idea is to say that the jury rose to the fore because it so effectively married the widespread popular sentiment that juries were fair and reliable with the interest of kings and royal administrators in gaining access to local power structures. It is certainly possible to argue that the jury system was forced on people— the early history of presentment, as discussed in Chapter 2, would certainly bear this interpretation—but it is hard to make this argument in the case of civil procedures like the posssssory assizes. Even in the realm of criminal procedure, it is unlikely that juries would have become so central if they had operated in an atmosphere of widespread hostility and resistance. It would greatly overestimate the power and resources of a premodern state to think that such a complex system could operate effectively through compulsion and coercion. The jury system worked because it was seen as a legitimate exercise of royal authority; its success depended on the willingness of people—lots of people including peasants—to cooperate with the king's demands for service.

Favorable sentiments about the jury system are clearly visible in contemporary accounts of legal practice. The twelfth-century text ascribed to Glanvill praised jury procedure because, among other things, he thought that a decision made by many was more likely to be just than a decision made by a few.[13] In the fifteenth century, John Fortescue made the same argument, and his encomium of the Common Law includes an extensive treatment of how jury procedure promotes civil liberty and the rule of law more effectively than the Roman law procedures used in other European countries.[14] The authors of these texts were judges rather than jurors, but they were vocalizing ideas that had general currency when they wrote. Two concrete examples can be offered here to illustrate this.

The first involves a squabble in fourteenth-century London between certain fishmongers and fishermen. A delegation of fishmongers met with the mayor to protest the type of net that some fishermen were using in the Thames.[15] They explained to the mayor that the city had a regulation stipulating that the mesh of nets used for fishing in the Thames ought to have a minimum width of two inches. Some fishermen were disregarding the regulation, however, using nets that had much smaller mesh, so that even very small fish had trouble passing through. The protesting fishmongers were worried that the Thames would be fished out as a result. To support their allegations, they brought eight nets with them to the Guildhall, which they had confiscated from eight named fishermen. They demanded that the mayor check the city's ordinances to verify their claim about mesh size and then take appropriate measures against the offending fishermen. In response to the fishmongers' demands, the mayor took several interesting steps. He first of all had the city's records searched to find the relevant ordinance. When it was retrieved, he announced that the city did indeed have a regulation requiring a minimum mesh width of two inches. But then, even though the law was clear and he had the physical evidence—the eight offending nets—before him, he did not make a ruling or take any action on the spot. It would have been a fairly simple thing for him to measure the mesh himself, or at least have someone on his staff do the measuring. But instead, he ordered that a jury of fishmongers be summoned to the Guildhall on the following Saturday. The jury was to be charged with examining the nets to determine their legality: Those nets that the jury found to have the requisite mesh size could be returned to their owners, but the nets that failed the examination were to be burned. The jury appeared on the appointed day, examined the nets, and found that four were acceptable, while four deserved to be burned.

This vignette illustrates how deeply the jury had penetrated the English sense of fairness and due process by the fourteenth century. The mayor was not obliged to resolve the problem by constituting a jury; in many respects calling a jury was an awkward and inefficient way to deal with the problem he confronted. But the jury was deeply embedded in the mayor's conception of justice. He may have thought that a jury would give a fairer and better judgment than he could himself. More importantly, though, he must have thought that a jury made up specifically of fishmongers—the "more discreet fishmongers of the City" according to the language of the document—was the best way to handle the problem. His thinking reflects the fundamental underlying principle of the medieval jury system that local people with background knowledge of the context of a dispute were the ones best suited to judge the relative merits of a case, a principle that has been noted several times in the course of this book.

The mayor's decision reflects another major feature of the jury system that must account for its popularity and success. Chapter 3 raised the issue of how jury verdicts were perceived after they were delivered and suggested that they were particularly effective tools for enforcing law and maintaining social order in the aftermath of judgment. The jury of London fishmongers provides a good illustration of this social dynamic. By bringing respected fishmongers into the adjudication process, the mayor increased the likelihood that the offending fishermen would accept the legitimacy of the ruling. More importantly, he increased the likelihood that other fishermen who did not have a direct stake in the matter would treat the decision as legitimate; the destruction of a fellow fisherman's means of livelihood was less likely to be perceived as a capricious imposition, if it was the result of this particular form of decision-making. By including fishmongers in the judgment process the mayor reduced the threat of opposition to the ruling, or at least restricted the ideological grounds on which opposition could be mounted. And finally, the jury of fishmongers also provided a concrete benefit in the aftermath of the verdict. The jurors had an ongoing stake in the enforcement of the decision and an ongoing stake in upholding the regulation on which the decision was based. In effect, they became partners in maintaining order; they were drawn into an alliance with the mayor and they came to share his interest in promoting social peace.

The second example illustrating contemporary perceptions of the jury system deals with a matter of broader historical scope than the mesh size of fishing nets in London. It involves one of the measures King Edward I took in his bid to assert English rule over Wales, a process that ultimately led to the conquest of Wales in 1282–83 and the end of Welsh political independence. Edward's military campaigning in Wales began in 1277, at which point he thought it was possible to establish English authority without mounting an all-out war of conquest. He was willing to work with traditional Welsh power structures but at the same time sought to draw the area more directly under his dominion. Edward was an active lawmaker and he was keen to use law as a tool of English sovereignty in Wales. To that end, he appointed a commission in 1281 of three trusted royal officials charged with finding out how traditional Welsh law functioned. It is not clear if he simply wanted to codify and regularize Welsh law—an act that would display his sovereignty—or whether he was intent on laying the groundwork for a major overhaul that would bring it into closer conformity with English law. Whatever his intent, he provided the three justices with a list of 14 questions designed to elicit information from people familiar with traditional Welsh law. Witnesses were to be both Welsh and English.

The ensuing inquest produced a long and complex document. Sworn testimony was given by more than 170 people, including knights, judges, merchants, abbots, clerics, and numerous smaller freeholders. Many witnesses said that they knew nothing about legal procedure; one of the merchants, for example, said that he had no familiarity with any of the legal procedures being investigated because he was always away on trading ventures. A large number of witnesses simply stated that they agreed with what one of the other witnesses had said and had nothing else to add. None of the witnesses addressed all of the questions posed in the enquiry. But a large number made brief statements on the issues that were most directly relevant to them. One of the issues that rose to the fore throughout the testimony was the nature of decision-making in disputes about possession of land, more specifically the role jury verdicts and inquest procedure had played in earlier disputes judged according to Welsh law. An overwhelming majority of those who offered testimony on this particular point asserted that jury verdicts had, in fact, been used in the past.

The most interesting feature of the testimony is the high regard in which procedure by jury was held by the witnesses. A number of witnesses referred to sworn inquests as a procedure designed to elicit "the truth of the matter;" in fact, several used the phrase "the truth of the matter" as a synonym for a jury verdict. They sometimes contrasted it with a procedure referred to as "Keverith" which is never fully described but which, according to one of the witnesses, had some similarities with the English procedure of trial by battle. Asked about procedure in land pleas, one of the Welsh witnesses, Rerich ab Jorveth, stated that "the whole country desires more that pleadings should be according to the truth of the matter than according to the law of Keverith." Interestingly, there is a marginal notation in the manuscript at this point, probably inserted by a Chancery official, drawing attention to Rerich ab Jorveth's statement emphasizing that jury procedure was "the desire of the land" (*desiderium patrie*). Numerous other witnesses expressed similar sentiments. One reiterated Rerich ab Jorveth's declaration that the whole country preferred inquest procedure to Keverith; a second said that jury verdicts were "more pleasing to God" than Keverith; another declared that "if he were king, all should be proceeded with according to the truth of the matter [i.e. by jury verdict]." The only direct comment made by any of the witnesses that did not express support for jury verdicts came from a Welsh judge named Griffin ap Jorverth, who noted that "the country" preferred jury verdicts but only if the verdict could be given by "trustworthy men."

There is some inconsistency in the witnesses' accounts of how "the truth of the matter" had operated prior to King Edward's inquest, but in general the details provided by the witnesses suggest a system that was similar to English practice. Juries ordinarily comprised 12 jurors, but 24 could be used for more important or more difficult cases. Jurors were usually chosen from among local people and neighbors who knew the particulars of the dispute. They were elected to serve on the jury with the consent of the parties, and any who were found to be partial to one of the sides could be challenged and removed. Flawed verdicts could be overturned by a process similar to attaint. Jurors were sworn to give a true verdict, although one witness stated somewhat ambiguously that inquisitors sometimes delivered their verdicts "sworn without an oath." One witness even noted that he knew from his ancestors of a case that had been determined by a mixed jury made up of Welsh and English jurors.

The expression used by so many of the Welsh witnesses, equating a jury verdict with "the truth of the matter," was a commonplace in English legal records of the time. The royal writs ordering sheriffs to assemble juries routinely reminded sheriffs to find jurors who best knew the truth of the matter under dispute. A writ sent to the sheriff of Berkshire in 1247, for example, instructed him to conduct an inquest into a royal tenant's land with jurors "by whom the truth can best be known."[16] The justices delegated to hear felonies and trespasses in Northamptonshire in 1314 were similarly ordered to hear presentments from jurors who "are best able to know and ascertain the truth of the matter."[17] The term also had currency in the formal records of the courts, as, for example, when a plaintiff in the King's Court in 1200 asked to have his property claim vindicated by a jury of people who "best knew the truth of the matter."[18] Given the ubiquity of the term in the working documents of the courts, it comes as no surprise to find the authors of prescriptive texts making frequent use of the same language. The author of the Bracton text, for example, wrote about "the truth of the matter" on more than a dozen occasions, always with reference to the functions of jurors.[19]

When this insistence on the honesty and fairness of jury verdicts is placed alongside the evidence about the burdensome nature of jury service, it suggests that medieval people viewed the jury system in ways that we can find familiar. They found jury service personally onerous and as a result they were often eager to find ways to avoid it. But they also had considerable faith in the jury's ability to solve problems fairly and they believed that juries promoted justice in legal and political relations. How they weighed these two perspectives against each other is hard to know. Like us, they probably held a variety of opinions on the matter, depending on their economic standing, their social and family background, their direct experiences of law and order, and their personal views about public duty. On the whole, they must have thought that the trade-off between burden and benefit was often worth making. The jury system succeeded because it persuaded people to cooperate with royal government in the management of local affairs. The benefits the system brought to a royal government intent on centralization are much easier for historians to discern, but the benefits brought to the jurors themselves and their friends, families, and neighbors need to be part of the story. The people who cooperated with the king's demands for service must have felt that they were getting something back in return. Perhaps they saw themselves as gaining power by being given a share in the state's authority. Perhaps they believed they were gaining status through their association with the king and his representatives. By serving as jurors they were certainly getting a taste of a bigger world, one they were helping to shape. They were also being given an opportunity to function as local opinion makers. Or rather, they were the local opinion makers, whose opinions now counted before the king as well as before their neighbors.

More than anything else, this book has sought to demonstrate the wide scope of jury procedure in medieval England. This scope needs to be understood first of all in terms of the variety of procedures designed to make use of jury verdicts, ranging all the way from the reports on minor local problems delivered by inquest juries to fundamental decisions about life and death made by jurors participating in criminal trials. It also needs to be understood in terms of the latitude given to jurors to determine how laws would be enforced and how individual cases would unfold. But most of all, it needs to be understood in terms of social participation. Jury procedures permeated to the very base of society, relying on the courage, wisdom, and intelligence of peasants as well as more privileged individuals. In fostering the jury system, England's rulers gave the village an active stake in the affairs of the kingdom. They charted a course defined by inclusiveness rather than exclusiveness, emphasizing participation rather than exclusion. It was a policy with many fateful consequences, some of which are still unfolding in the world today.

NOTES

INTRODUCTION

1. Thomas Ertman, *Birth of the Leviathon. Building States and Regimes in Medieval and Early Modern Europe* (Cambridge, 1997). The seventh and last volume to appear in the European Science Foundation Series was *War and Competition between States,* ed. Philippe Contamine (Oxford, 2000). It lists earlier works in the series.
2. *Resistance, Representation, and Community,* ed. Peter Blickle (Oxford, 1997).
3. Discontent with taxation is well illustrated in J. R. Maddicott, *The English Peasantry and the Demands of the Crown.* Past & Present Supplement, no. 1 (Oxford, 1975).
4. Kathryn L. Reyerson, "Commerce and Communications" in *The New Cambridge Medieval History,* ed. David Abulafia (Cambridge, 1999), vol. 5, c.1198-c.1300, pp. 50–70; Peter Spufford, *Power and Profit. The Merchant in Medieval Europe* (London, 2002); John Langdon and James Masschaele, "Commercial Activity and Population Growth in Medieval England," *Past & Present* 190 (2006): 35–81; James Masschaele, "Economic Takeoff and the Rise of Markets," in *Blackwell Companion to the Middle Ages,* ed. Edward D. English and Carol L. Lansing (Oxford, forthcoming 2008).
5. Michael Clanchy, *From Memory to Written Record: England 1066–1307,* 2nd ed. (Oxford, 1993); *Pragmatic Literacy East and West, 1200–1330,* ed. Richard Britnell (Woodbridge, Suffolk, 1997).
6. James Scott, *Weapons of the Weak: Everyday Forms of Peasant Resistance* (New Haven, 1987).
7. Susan Reynolds, *Kingdoms and Communities in Western Europe, 900–1300* (Oxford, 1984); Alan Harding, *Medieval Law and the Foundations of the State* (Oxford, 2002).
8. Alfred B.White, *Self-Government at the King's Command* (Minneapolis, 1933).
9. Thomas Andrew Green, *Verdict According to Conscience: Perspectives on the Criminal Trial Jury 1200–1800* (Chicago, 1985).
10. Some of Green's arguments were anticipated in Naomi Hurnard's analysis of the role juries played in the system of royal pardoning for excusable homicide. See Hurnard, *The King's Pardon for Homicide before AD 1307* (Oxford, 1969), particularly chap. 10.
11. Edward Powell, *Kingship, Law, and Society: Criminal Justice in the*

Reign of Henry V (Oxford, 1989); J. G. Bellamy, *The Criminal Trial in Later Medieval England* (Toronto, 1998); Anthony Musson, *Public Order and Law Enforcement: The Local Administration of Criminal Justice, 1294–1350* (Woodbridge, Suffolk, 1996); idem, *Medieval Law in Context: The Growth of Legal Consciousness from Magna Carta to the Peasants' Revolt* (Manchester, 2001).

12. W. L. Warren, *Henry II* (Berkeley, 1973), chap. 9; Robert Bartlett, *England under the Norman and Angevin Kings 1075–1225* (Oxford, 2000); David Carpenter, *The Struggle for Mastery: The Penguin History of Britain 1066–1284* (London, 2004).
13. Reynolds, *Kingdoms and Communities* (Oxford, 1984).
14. Peter Coss, *The Origins of the English Gentry* (Cambridge, 2003); Christine Carpenter, *Locality and Polity: A Study of Warwickshire Landed Society, 1401–1499* (Cambridge, 1992).
15. John Marshall Mitnick, "From Neighbor-Witness to Judge of Proofs: The Transformation of the English Civil Juror," *American Journal of Legal History* 32 (1988): 201–35; Daniel Klerman, "Was the Jury Ever Self-Informing?" in *The Trial in History*, vol. 1, *Judicial Tribunals in England and Europe, 1200–1700,* ed. Maureen Mulholland, Brian Pullan, and Anne Pullan (Manchester, 2003), pp. 58–80.
16. Morris S. Arnold, "Law and Fact in the Medieval Jury Trial: Out of Sight, Out of Mind," *American Journal of Legal History* 18 (1974): 267–80; Anthony Musson, "The Role of Amateur and Professional Judges in the Royal Courts of Late Medieval England," in *The Trial in History*, vol. 1, *Judicial Tribunals in England and Europe,* ed. Mulholland, Pullan, and Pullan, pp. 37–57.
17. Thomas Lindkvist, "Law and the Making of the State in Medieval Sweden," in *Legislation and Justice,* ed. Antonio Padoa-Schioppa (Oxford, 1997), pp. 224–25; Joseph Strayer, "The Writ of Novel Disseisin in Normandy at the End of the Thirteenth Century," in *Medieval Statecraft and the Perspectives of History* (Princeton, 1971), pp. 3–13; R. C. Van Caenegem, *The Birth of the English Common Law,* 2nd ed. (Cambridge, 1988), p. 71.
18. Ian Douglas Willock, *The Origins and Development of the Jury in Scotland,* Stair Society, vol. 23 (Edinburgh, 1966).

Chapter 1

1. *Calendar of Inquisitions Miscellaneous (Chancery) Preserved in the Public Record Office,* (London, 1937), vol. 3, no. 425, pp. 154–55.
2. Ibid.
3. Francis Palgrave, *The Rise and Progress of the English Commonwealth,* 2 vols. (London, 1832), vol. 1, pp. 239–77.
4. Heinrich Brunner, *Die entstehung der schwurgerichte* (Berlin, 1871).
5. Frederick Pollock and Frederic William Maitland, *The History of English Law before the Time of Edward I,* 2nd ed., 2 vols. (Cambridge, 1898), vol.

1, pp. 138–44; William Stubbs, *The Constitutional History of England*, 3rd ed., 3 vols. (Oxford, 1880), vol. 1, pp. 608–22.

6. Charles Homer Haskins, *Norman Institutions* (Cambridge, MA, 1918), chap. 6.

7. R. C. Van Caenegem, *Royal Writs in England from the Conquest to Glanvill*, Selden Society, vol. 77 (London, 1959).

8. Doris M. Stenton, *English Justice between the Norman Conquest and the Great Charter, 1066–1215*. The Jayne Lectures for 1963 (London, 1965), pp. 13–21.

9. E.g., W. L. Warren, "The Myth of Norman Administrative Efficiency," *Transactions of the Royal Historical Society*, 5th ser., 34 (1984): 123–32; James Campbell, *The Anglo-Saxon State* (London, 2000).

10. Mike Macnair "Vicinage and the Antecedents of the Jury," *Law and History Review* 17 (1999): 537–90.

11. David Roffe, *Domesday. The Inquest and the Book* (Oxford, 2000), pp. 64–66, 251.

12. Patrick Wormald, *The Making of English Law: King Alfred to the Twelfth Century* (Oxford, 1999).

13. On Anglo-Saxon influences on later Common Law forms, see Wormald, *Making of English Law*, and Paul R. Hyams, *Rancor and Reconciliation in Medieval England* (Ithaca, 2003). On early Anglo-Norman influences, see John Hudson, *Land, Law, and Lordship in Anglo-Norman England* (Oxford, 1994). Bloch's admonition is in *The Historian's Craft*, trans. Peter Putnam (Manchester, 1992), pt. 1, sec. 4.

14. C. P. Lewis, "The Domesday Jurors," *Haskins Society Journal* 5 (1993): 17–44; Robin Fleming, *Domesday Book and the Law: Society and Legal Custom in Early Medieval England* (Cambridge, 1998); Roffe, *Domesday*, chap. 3.

15. Jurors are documented more consistently in the Domesday satellites than in *Domesday Book* itself. Lewis, "Domesday Jurors," pp. 18–19; Roffe, *Domesday*, pp. 122–23, 186–87.

16. The close association between juries and royal power is discussed in Paul Brand, "The Formation of the English Legal System, 1150–1400," in *Legislation and Justice*, ed. Antonio Padoa-Schioppa (Oxford, 1997), p. 107.

17. C.A.F. Meekings, *The 1235 Surrey Eyre*, 2 vols., Surrey Record Society, vols. 31–32 (Guildford, 1979–83), vol. 1, p. 33.

18. *Curia Regis Rolls*, ed. C. T. Flower and Paul Brand, 19 vols. (London, 1922-), vol. 13, no. 237. A similar procedure can be found in ibid., vol. 7, p. 245.

19. On litigation related to dower rights, see Janet Senderowitz Loengard, " 'Of the Gift of Her Husband': English Dower and Its Consequences in the Year 1200," in *Women of the Medieval World. Essays in Honor of John H. Mundy*, ed. Julius Kirshner and Suzanne F. Wemple (Oxford, 1985): 215–55; Joseph Biancalana, "Widows at Common Law: The

Development of Common Law Dower," *Irish Jurist,* n.s., 23 (1988): 255–329. Also enlightening are the essays by Loengard and Sue Sheridan Walker in *Wife and Widow in Medieval England,* ed. Sue Sheridan Walker (Ann Arbor, 1993).

20. Examples include *Curia Regis Rolls,* ed. Flower and Brand, vol. 2, pp. 265, 278; vol. 13, no. 1081; vol. 15, no. 1352. This became such a common procedure that scribes often used an "etc." to refer to it in later rolls.

21. *Curia Regis Rolls,* ed. Flower and Brand, vol. 6, pp. 242–43.

22. Ibid., vol. 1, p. 18.

23. For other examples of inquests settling land disputes, see *Curia Regis Rolls,* ed. Flower and Brand, vol. 1, pp. 375–76; ibid., vol. 16, no. 2484.

24. E.g., *Curia Regis Rolls,* ed. Flower and Brand, vol. 15, no. 1291. Van Caenegem, *Royal Writs,* p. 77, discusses the antiquity of these forest perambulations and their connection to other forms of jury procedure. Mike Macnair has made the cogent argument that inquest procedure was particularly common in disputes involving ongoing boundaries and customs: Macnair "Vicinage," pp. 560–71.

25. *Curia Regis Rolls,* ed. Flower and Brand, vol. 15, nos. 1888, 1972B, and 1981.

26. Ibid., vol. 15, no. 1180.

27. Naomi Hurnard, *The King's Pardon for Homicide before AD 1307* (Oxford, 1969), chap. 3.

28. Ibid., pp. 78–79.

29. *Calendar of Inquisitions Miscellaneous,* vol. 1, no. 2101, p. 563.

30. *Calendar of Patent Rolls, 1258–1266,* p. 11.

31. Hurnard, *King's Pardon for Homicide,* pp. 339–74; Roger D. Groot, "Teaching Each Other: Judges, Clerks, Jurors and Malefactors Define the Guilt/Innocence Jury," in *Learning the Law. Teaching and the Transmission of English Law, 1150–1900,* ed. Jonathan A. Bush and Alain Wijffels (London, 1999), pp. 17–32; Hyams, *Rancor and Reconciliation,* pp. 175–84; Susanne Jenks, "Das writ und die exceptio de odio et atia," *Tijdschrift voor Rechtsgeschiedenis* 68 (2000): 455–77.

32. National Archives, Public Record Office, C144/16, no. 46.

33. National Archives, Public Record Office, C144/17, no. 38.

34. National Archives, Public Record Office, C144/29, no. 15.

35. Hurnard, *King's Pardon for Homicide,* p. 364.

36. Ibid., pp. 342–43.

37. *Year Books of the Reign of Edward II,* vol. 12, 5 Edward 11, ed. William C. Bolland, Selden Society, vol. 33 (London, 1916), pp. 46–47.

38. Albert B. White, *Self-Government at the King's Command* (Minneapolis, 1933).

39. *Red Book of the Exchequer,* ed. Hubert Hall, Rerum Britannicarum Medii Aevi Scriptores no. 99 (London, 1897), pp. cclxvii-cclxxxi; William Stubbs, *Select Charters from the Beginning to 1307,* 9th ed., ed. H.W.C. Davis (Oxford, 1913), pp. 175–78; W. L. Warren, *Henry II* (Berkeley, 1973), pp. 287–91.

40. *Red Book of the Exchequer,* nos. 55, 56, p. cclxxx.
41. *Rotuli hundredorum,* ed. W. Illingworth and J. Caley, 2 vols., Record Commission (London, 1812–18); Helen Cam, *The Hundred and the Hundred Rolls* (London, 1930); David Roffe, "The Hundred Rolls and their Antecedents: Some Thoughts on the Inquisition in Thirteenth-Century England," *Haskins Society Journal* 7 (1995): 179–87. Similar enquiries were undertaken both before and after the 1274–75 inquest but are not as well documented. Professor Roffe heads a team of scholars at the University of Sheffield that aims to bring out a new edition of the Hundred Roll enquires of 1274–75 along with other related inquests.
42. Most of the surviving returns are printed in vol. 2 of *Rotuli hundredorum,* ed. Illingworth and Caley. See also *The Warwickshire Hundred Rolls of 1279–1280,* ed. Trevor John, Records of Social and Economic History, n.s. 19 (Oxford, 1992). A good account of the survey can be found in Sandra Raban, *A Second Domesday? The Hundred Rolls of 1279–1280* (Oxford, 2004). Useful comments about the procedure used to compile information can also be found in E. A. Kosminsky, *Studies in the Agrarian History of England in the Thirteenth Century,* trans. Ruth Kisch (Oxford, 1956).
43. *Domesday-Book seu liber censualis willelmi primi regis angliae,* ed. Abraham Farley, Record Commission (London, 1783), fol. 203v; *Rotuli hundredorum,* ed. Illingworth and Caley, vol. 2, pp. 610–14.
44. *Chronica magistri rogeri de hovedene,* ed. William Stubbs, Rerum Britannicarum Medii Aevi Scriptores no. 51(London, 1869), vol. 2, pp. 261–63; National Archives, Public Record Office, C47/1/4; British Library Harley Charter 58.E.40, 41; *Nonarum inquisitiones in curia scaccarii temp. regis edwardi III,* ed. G. Vanderzee (London, 1807).
45. *Calendar of Inquisitions Miscellaneous,* vols. 1, 5, 6, and 7.
46. Kosminsky, *Studies in Agrarian History,* pp. 46–67; Joel Rosenthal, *Telling Tales: Sources and Narration in Late Medieval England* (University Park, PA, 2003). A concise description of the source is also provided on the Web site of the National Archives using "C 132" as a search term in the catalogue.
47. Examples can be found in Hubert Hall, *A Formula Book of English Official Historical Documents* (Cambridge, 1908–09), pt. 2, pp. 68–74.
48. Ibid., p. 71.
49. R. C. Fowler, "Legal Proofs of Age," *English Historical Review* 22 (1907): 101–3; M. T. Martin, "Legal Proofs of Age," *English Historical Review* 22 (1907): 526–27; A. E. Stamp, "Legal Proofs of Age," *English Historical Review* 29 (1914): 323–24; Kosminsky, *Studies in Agrarian History,* pp. 57–63. For a recent discussion of the proofs of age, a form of inquest related to the standard inquisition *post mortem* but held solely to determine an heir's age, see Rosenthal, *Telling Tales.*
50. Under Christine Carpenter's guidance, juror names have finally been included in the recent volumes dealing with inquisitions held in the reign of Henry VI.

51. An example of the tendency to undervalue the jury's work is the chapter by E. R. Stevenson, dealing with the duties of escheators in *The English Government at Work, 1327–1336,* vol. 2, Fiscal Administration, ed. William A. Morris and Joseph Strayer (Cambridge, MA, 1947), pp. 109–67. In the article's 58 pages, which deal extensively with the formal procedures associated with inquisitions *post mortem,* only a single paragraph is devoted to the role of jurors.

52. A brief description of these inquisitions is given in *List of Inquisitions Ad Quod Damnum Preserved in the Public Record Office,* List and Index Society, no. 17 (London, 1904), pp. iii-vii.

53. A specimen writ can be found in Ibid., pp. iv-v.

54. National Archives, Public Record Office, C143/5, no. 11.

55. National Archives, Public Record Office, C143/4, no. 11.

56. National Archives, Public Record Office, C143/38, nos. 1, 2, 4.

57. *Calendar of Inquisitions Miscellaneous,* vol. 1, pp. vii-xiii; vol. 4, pp. vii-viii. The inquisitions *de odio et athia* were treated as a separate series by the author of the preface to vol. 4.

58. *Calendar of Inquisitions Miscellaneous,* vol. 2, p. 513; *Calendar of Close Rolls, 1346–1349,* p. 272; *Calendar of Patent Rolls, 1345–1349,* pp. 321–22, 377–78.

59. *Curia Regis Rolls,* ed. Flower and Brand, vol. 6, p. 169.

60. Women's participation in jury service is discussed in greater depth in chapter 4.

61. *Calendar of Inquisitions Miscellaneous,* vol. 6, no. 85, pp. 40–41.

62. Ibid., vol. 1, no. 1230, pp. 362–63.

63. *Calendar of Patent Rolls, 1272–1281,* p. 464.

64. *Calendar of Inquisitions Miscellaneous,* vol. 1, no. 1578, pp. 443–45.

65. Ibid., vol. 6, no. 306, pp. 164–69. The circumstances of the seizure are discussed in Nigel Saul, *Richard II* (New Haven, 1997), pp. 366–404.

66. Ibid., no. 282, pp. 138–39.

67. Calculated from *Calendar of Inquisitions Miscellaneous,* vol. 2, pp. 232–374; *List of Inquisitions Ad Quod Damnum,* pp. 265–349; *Calendar of Inquisitions Post Mortem and Other Analogous Documents Preserved in the Public Record Office,* vols. 7 (London, 1909) and 9 (London, 1913). I counted 635 miscellaneous inquests, 1,115 inquests *ad quod* damnum, and 1,606 inquests *post mortem* in the calendars. The total includes all forms of inquest calendared in these volumes, including inquests *de etate probanda.* Many of the documents treated as separate inquisitions in the calendars incorporate multiple inquests held in different locations by different juries. This is particularly common in the calendar of inquisitions *post mortem* because many tenants-in-chief held land in several different counties; in these circumstances, separate juries were struck for each county. Multiple juries were sometimes also employed for separate properties within a single county. My tally treats every inquisition as a separate procedure. Thus, when Henry de Thrippelowe died in 1333, two inquests were held in Cambridgeshire and

one was held in Hertfordshire. The calendar, following the practice of the National Archives, treats these as a single inquisition, but my tally treats them as three separate inquisitions. Multiple inquests in response to a single writ also occur in the inquisitions miscellaneous, though on a lesser scale. I treated each of these as a separate inquest as well.

68. In 1249, for example, a writ enrolled on the *Close Rolls* refers to an inquest held by the sheriff of Worcestershire as the basis of a royal grant, but the inquisition itself is no longer extant. *Calendar of Close Rolls, 1247–1251*, p. 136. Similarly, an earlier inquisition referred to in a later inquest held in 1376 no longer exists: *Calendar of Inquisitions Miscellaneous*, vol. 3, no. 1019, p. 395. Losses to the series of miscellaneous inquisitions are noted in *Calendar of Inquisitions Miscellaneous*, vol. 4, p. vii-viii.

69. Inquests commissioned by the Exchequer, for example, can be found scattered among the file of sheriffs' accounts in the National Archives (E199), as well as the file of extents of alien priories (E106), the file of extents of forfeited properties (E142), the file of seizures from Crown debtors (E143), and the file of forest proceedings (E146).

70. R. F. Hunnisett, *The Medieval Coroner*, Cambridge Studies in English Legal History (Cambridge, 1961), pp. 9–36.

71. Counting the three Yorkshire ridings as separate counties and not including Cheshire and Durham.

72. London itself was a common locus for inquests; in one instance, the king even ordered an inquest to be held to determine who was obliged to clean Fetter Lane. *Calendar of Inquisitions Miscellaneous*, vol. 3, no. 521, pp. 191–92.

73. *Calendar of Inquisitions Post Mortem and Other Analogous Documents Preserved in the Public Record Office*, vol. 1, Henry III (London, 1904), pp. vii-ix. Inquests were sometimes used to keep track of escheated property in eyres held in the later twelfth century. The office of escheator was formally instituted in 1232. See Stevenson, "The Escheator," pp. 113–16; Scott L. Waugh, "The Origins and Development of the Articles of the Escheator," *Thirteenth Century England*, ed. P. R. Coss and S. D. Lloyd (Woodbridge, Suffolk, 1995), vol. 5, pp. 89–113.

74. *List of Inquisitions Ad Quod Damnum*, pp. 1–96. The primary explanation for this dramatic growth was Edward's decision to extend the procedure to cases involving grants in mortmain.

75. *Calendar of Inquisitions Miscellaneous*, vol. 1, pp. 1–99.

76. Ibid., pp. 186–288.

77. White, *Self-Government*, pp. 76–125.

78. *Chronica magistri rogeri de hovedene*, p. 262.

79. *Rotuli de dominabus et pueris et puellis de XII comitatibus* [*1185*], ed. John H. Round, The Publications of the Pipe Roll Society, vol. 35 (London, 1913); *Records of the Templars in England in the Twelfth Century*, ed. Beatrice Lees, Records of the Social and Economic History of England and Wales, vol. 9 (London, 1935). The evidence for the use of

inquest juries in the latter source is ambiguous. References to oaths and jurors do occur in the text, but not consistently.

80. *Chronica magistri rogeri de hovedene,* pp. 335–36.

81. Stubbs, *Select Charters,* pp. 254–55 (article 23).

82. *Liber Feodorum. The Book of Fees Commonly Called Testa de Nevill, Part One, AD 1198–1242,* n. a. (London, 1920), pp. 4–10.

83. White, *Self-Government,* pp. 98–125.

84. Van Caenegem, *Royal Writs,* pp. 61–68.

85. *Regesta regum anglo-normannorum 1066–1154,* ed. H.W.C. Davis, Charles Johnson, and R. J. Whitwell, 4 vols. (Oxford, 1913–68), vol. 2, no. 1511 pp. 210–11.

86. Ibid., no. 1561, p. 220.

87. Ibid., nos. 957 (p. 95); 1166 (p. 139); 1192 (p. 144); 1341 (pp. 175–76); 1487 (p. 206); 1505 (p. 209).

88. This subject will be addressed more fully in chapter 2. My argument here runs contrary to Van Caenegem's proposal that administrative verdicts be treated as distinct from judicial verdicts. Even in later periods when the role of the judicial system was much more clearly defined, inquest verdicts were often a species of jury verdict rather than a distinct genus.

89. White, *Self-Government,* p. 99.

90. *Regesta regum anglo-normannorum,* vol. 2, no. 1438a, p. 196.

91. Ibid., no. 1606, p. 231. The writ also empowered the archbishop to compel those who were not his tenants to perform their customary service in the castle.

92. Ibid., no. 1660, pp. 241–42.

93. Ibid., no. 1116, p. 130.

94. Michael Clanchy, *From Memory to Written Record. England 1066–1307,* 2nd ed. (Oxford, 1993), pp. 32–35.

95. Judith Green, *The Government of England under Henry I* (Cambridge, 1986), pp. 108–10.

96. These requests for exemption gave rise to inquests *ad quod damnum.*

97. On the relationship between petitions and legal procedure, see Alan Harding, "Plaints and Bills in the History of English Law, Mainly in the Period 1250–1350," in *Legal History Studies 1972* (Cardiff, 1975); idem, *Medieval Law and the Foundations of the State* (Oxford, 2002), chap. 6.

98. Paul Brand, *The Making of the Common Law* (London, 1992), especially chaps. 4 and 7; idem, "The Formation of the English Legal System," pp. 103–22.

CHAPTER 2

1. Michael Clanchy, *From Memory to Written Record. England 1066–1307,* 2nd ed. (Oxford, 1993), pp. 67–69. On Henry's personal commitment to legal reform, see Paul Brand, "Henry II and the Creation of the English Common Law," *Haskins Society Journal* 11 (1990): 197–222.

2. Much has been written about the role of presentment in criminal law. Major contributions include: Frederick Pollock and Frederic William Maitland, *The History of English Law Before the Time of Edward I*, 2nd ed., 2 vols. (Cambridge, 1898), vol. 1, pp. 151–53, vol. 2, pp. 641–48; Naomi Hurnard, "The Jury of Presentment and the Assize of Clarendon," *English Historical Review* 56 (1941): 374–410; R. E. Latham and C.A.F. Meekings, "The Veredictum of Chippenham Hundred, 1281," in *Collectanea*, ed. N. J. Williams, Wiltshire Archaeological and Natural History Society, Records Branch, vol. 12 (Devizes, 1956): 50–128; R. C. Van Caenegem, "Public Prosecution of Crime in Twelfth-Century England," in *Church and Government in the Middle Ages: Essays Presented to C. R. Cheney*, ed. C.N.L. Brook, D. E. Luscombe, G. H. Martin, and D. M. Owen (Cambridge, 1976), pp. 41–76; C.A.F. Meekings, *The 1235 Surrey Eyre*, 2 vols., Surrey Record Society, vols. 31–32 (Guildford, 1979–83), vol. 1, pp. 94–116; Roger D. Groot, "The Jury of Presentment before 1215," *American Journal of Legal History* 26 (1982): 1–24; Thomas A. Green, *Verdict According to Conscience. Perspectives on the Criminal Trial Jury 1200–1800* (Chicago, 1985), pp. 4–13; Anthony Musson, "Twelve Good Men and True? The Character of Early Fourteenth-Century Juries," *Law and History Review* 15 (1997), pp. 115–26; J. G. Bellamy, *The Criminal Trial in Later Medieval England* (Toronto, 1998), pp. 19–56.
3. There were, however, a few exceptions to the rule. In manorial courts, for example, presentment was often tantamount to conviction without further process.
4. Pollock and Maitland, *History of English Law*, vol. 1, p. 144.
5. Hurnard, "Jury of Presentment"; Patrick Wormald, "Maitland and Anglo-Saxon Law: Beyond Domesday Book," in *The History of English Law. Centenary Essays on "Pollock and Maitland,"* ed. John Hudson, *Proceedings of the British Academy* 89 (Oxford, 1996), pp. 10–13.
6. Text in William Stubbs, *Select Charters from the Beginning to 1307*, 9th ed., ed. H.W.C. Davis (Oxford, 1913), pp. 170–73, 179–81; translation in *English Historical Documents*, vol. 2, 1042–1189, ed. David C. Douglas and George Greenaway (London, 1953), pp. 407–10.
7. Text in Stubbs, *Select Charters*, pp. 179–81; translation in *English Historical Documents*, vol.2, pp. 411–13.
8. Bellamy, *Criminal Trial in Later Medieval England*, chap. 1; Daniel Klerman, "Settlement and the Decline of Private Prosecution in Thirteenth-Century England," *Law and History Review* 19 (2001): 1–65.
9. On the development of the eyre, see Ralph Turner, *The King and His Courts* (Ithaca, 1968); Alan Harding, *The Law Courts of Medieval England* (London, 1973); David Crook, *Records of the General Eyre*, Public Record Office Handbooks Number 20 (London, 1982); Paul Brand, *The Origins of the English Legal Profession* (Oxford, 1992), chap. 2.
10. Irwin L. Langbein, "The Jury of Presentment and the Coroner,"

Columbia Law Review 33 (1933): 1329–1365. The quotation is on p. 1331.

11. See the works by Meekings cited in note 2 for an account of secret presentment.

12. As early as 1219, a presentment jury was challenged for making a presentment on a matter about which it had no direct knowledge. *Curia Regis Rolls*, ed. C. T. Flower and Paul Brand, 19 vols. (London, 1922–), vol. 8, pp. 9–10. Bracton gives an interesting account of how suspicion might arise and how justices ought to deal with presentments based on rumor: Henry de Bracton, *On the Laws and Customs of England*, trans. Samuel E. Thorne, 4 vols. (Cambridge, MA, 1968-), vol. 2, pp. 403–4. Legal historians have sometimes defined indictments as accusations substantiated by supporting evidence and presentments as accusations based on rumor, but the distinction appears relatively late in the period investigated in this book.

13. R. F. Hunnisett, *The Medieval Coroner,* Cambridge Studies in English Legal History (Cambridge, 1961).

14. Ibid., p. 96. Second presentment at the county court may have occurred in the first part of the thirteenth century. For examples of trials based directly on presentments made to coroners, see Wiltshire *Gaol Delivery and Trailbaston Trials 1275–1306*, ed. Ralph B. Pugh, Wiltshire Record Society, vol. 33 (Devizes, 1978), cases 383, 393, 402, 460, 468, 473; *A Cambridgeshire Gaol Delivery Roll, 1332–1334,* ed. Elisabeth G. Kimball, Cambridge Antiquarian Records Society, vol. 4 (Cambridge, 1978), p. 22 and cases cited there.

15. Harding, *Law Courts of Medieval England* (London,1973), pp. 86–98; David Crook, "The Later Eyres," *English Historical Review* 383 (1982): 241–68.

16. Richard W. Kaeuper, *War, Justice and Public Order. France and England in the Later Middle Ages* (Oxford, 1988), pp. 134–83; Ralph Pugh, "Reflections of a Medieval Criminologist," *Proceedings of the British Academy* 59 (London, 1975), pp. 83–104. Some of the problems associated with factionalism and corruption are discussed in *The Eyre of Kent 6 & 7 Edward II,* ed. Frederic W. Maitland, Leveson Harcourt and William Bolland, Selden Society, vol. 24 (London, 1910), vol. 1, pp. lxxxiii – lxxxvii

17. Anthony Musson, *Public Order and Law Enforcement: The Local Administration of Criminal Justice, 1294–1350* (Woodbridge, Suffolk, 1996).

18. *Proceedings before the Justices of the Peace in the Fourteenth and Fifteenth Centuries, Edward III to Richard III,* ed. Bertha Haven Putnam, Ames Foundation, vol. 5 (London, 1938); Alan Harding, "The Origins and Early History of the Keeper of the Peace," *Transactions of the Royal Historical Society,* 5th ser., 10 (1960): 85–109; Anthony Musson and W. M. Ormrod, *The Evolution of English Justice: Law, Politics and Society in the Fourteenth Century* (Basingstoke, Hampshire, 1999); Anthony Musson, *Medieval Law in Context: The Growth of Legal Consciousness from Magna Carta to the Peasants' Revolt* (Manchester, 2001), pp. 149–54.

19. *Records of Some Sessions of the Peace in Lincolnshire, 1360–1375,* ed. Rosamund Sillem, Lincoln Record Society, vol. 30 (Hereford, 1936), pp. xxxv–xxxix; *Proceedings before the Justices of the Peace,* ed. Putnam, pp. xcix–ciii.
20. J. H. Baker, *An Introduction to English Legal History,* 3rd ed. (London, 1990), pp. 576–77; Bellamy, *Criminal Trial in Later Medieval England,* pp. 20–24.
21. Stubbs, *Select Charters,* p. 170.
22. Helen M. Cam, *Studies in the Hundred Rolls. Some Aspects of Thirteenth-Century Administration,* Oxford Studies in Social and Legal History, ed. Paul Vinogradoff, (Oxford, 1921), vol. 6, pp. 9–101; Musson, *Medieval Law in Context,* pp. 150–52. For similar lists in other court venues, see F.J.C. Hearnshaw, *Leet Jurisdiction in England,* Publications of the Southampton Record Society, vol. 5 (Southampton, 1908), pp. 43–64; John Beckerman, "The Articles of Presentment of a Court Leet and Court Baron, in English, c. 1400," *Bulletin of the Institute of Historical Research* 47 (1974): 230–234; Musson, *Medieval Law in Context,* pp. 150–52.
23. Cam, *Studies in the Hundred Rolls,* p. 88.
24. *Proceedings before Justices of the Peace,* ed. Putnam, pp. 10–25.
25. Bracton, *On the Laws and Customs of England,* vol. 2, p. 329.
26. *Proceedings before the Justices of the Peace,* ed. Putnam, p. xcviii.
27. *Royal Justice and the Medieval English Countryside: The Huntingdonshire Eyre of 1286, the Ramsey Abbey Banlieu Court of 1287, and the Assizes of 1287–88,* ed. Anne Reiber DeWindt and Edwin Brezette DeWindt, Pontifical Institute of Mediaeval Studies, Studies and Texts 57 (Toronto, 1981).
28. The major works are still those of Helen Cam: *Studies in the Hundred Rolls,* chap. 3; *The Hundred and the Hundred Rolls* (London, 1930).
29. Hearnshaw, *Leet Jurisdiction;* William Morris, *The Frankpledge System* (New York, 1910). On the functioning of presentment in non-frankpledge areas, see R. Stewart-Brown, *The Sergeants of the Peace in Medieval England and Wales* (Manchester, 1936), pp. 76–80, 99–104.
30. Barbara Hanawalt, "Community, Conflict and Social Control: Crime in the Ramsey Abbey Villages," *Medieval Studies* 39 (1977): 402–23; idem, *Crime and Conflict in English Communities 1300–1348* (Cambridge, MA, 1979).
31. *Select Pleas in Manorial and Other Seignorial Courts,* ed. F. W. Maitland, Selden Society, vol. 2 (London, 1889), pp. xxxi–xxxii; Hurnard, "Jury of Presentment," p. 407. Helen Cam suggested that the tourn began much earlier: Cam, *Hundred and the Hundred Rolls,* p. 118.
32. *Britton. An English Translation and Notes,* ed. F. M. Nichols (Washington, DC, 1901), pp. 146–52.
33. D. A. Crowley, "The Later History of Frankpledge," *Bulletin of the Institute of Historical Research* 48 (1975): 1–15; Phillip R. Schofield, "The Late Medieval View of Frankpledge and the Tithing System: An

Essex Case Study," in *Medieval Society and the Manor Court*, ed. Zvi Razi and Richard Smith (Oxford, 1996), pp. 408–49.

34. For a recent summation of these economic changes, see John Langdon and James Masschaele, "Commercial Activity and Population Growth in Medieval England," *Past & Present* 190 (2006): 35–81.

35. H.R.T. Summerson, "The Structure of Law Enforcement in Thirteenth Century England," *American Journal of Legal History* 23 (1979), pp. 325–27.

36. Mark Bailey, *The English Manor c.1200–c.1500* (Manchester, 2002), pp. 167–240; K. J. Stocks, "Manorial Courts in England in the Early Thirteenth Century," in *Thirteenth Century England*, vol. 8, ed. Michael Prestwich, Richard Britnell, and Robin Frame, (Woodbridge, Suffolk, 2001): 135–42.

37. *Select Pleas in Manorial Courts*, ed. Maitland, pp. xxvii-xxxvii; Hearnshaw, *Leet Jurisdiction*, pp. 43–71.

38. Kate Parkin, *Courts and the Community: Reconstructing the Fourteenth-Century Peasant Society of Wisbeach Hundred, Cambridgeshire from Manorial Court Rolls*, PhD thesis, University of Leicester (Leicester, 1998).

39. John Beckerman, "Procedural Innovation and Institutional Change in Medieval English Manorial Courts," *Law and History Review* 10 (1992): 197–252.

40. E. F. Jacob, *Studies in the Period of Baronial Reform and Rebellion, 1258–1267*, Oxford Studies in Social and Legal History, vol. 8 (Oxford, 1925), pp. 59–60.

41. *Rotuli hundredorum*, ed. W. Illingworth and J. Caley, 2 vols. (London, 1812–18), vol. 2, p. 307.

42. Anne Reiber DeWindt, "Local Government in a Small Town: A Medieval Leet Jury and Its Constituents," *Albion* 23 (1991): 627–54; Sherri Olson, *A Chronicle of All that Happens: Voices from the Village Court in Medieval England* (Toronto, 1996), pp. 125–61.

43. J. Ambrose Raftis, *Tenure and Mobility: Studies in the Social History of the Mediaeval English Village* (Toronto, 1964), pp. 111–27.

44. E.g., British Library, Additional Charter 39459; British Library, Additional Charter 34911; National Archives, Public Record Office, SC 2/179/5; *Select Pleas in Manorial Courts*, ed. Maitland, pp. 91–92.

45. On the issue of respect for local manorial traditions, see P. L. Larson, *Conflict and Compromise in the Late Medieval Countryside. Lords and Peasants in Durham, 1349–1400* (London, 2006). Also relevant is Christopher Dyer "The Social and Economic Background to the Rural Revolt of 1381," in *The English Rising of 1381*, ed. T. H. Aston and R. H. Hilton (Cambridge, 1984), pp. 9–24.

46. The connection between the politics of Henry's reign and his legal reforms is best articulated in W. L. Warren, *Henry II* (Berkeley, 1973), chap. 9.

47. Joseph Biancalana, "For Want of Justice: Legal Reforms of Henry II," *Columbia Law Review* 88 (1988): 433–536.

48. S.F.C. Milsom, *The Legal Framework of English Feudalism* (Cambridge, 1976), chap. 2.
49. Donald W. Sutherland, *The Assize of Novel Disseisin* (Oxford, 1973), pp. 13, 29–33, 135.
50. *Curia Regis Rolls,* ed. Flower and Brand, vol. 15, no. 145, pp. 33–4.
51. Ibid., vol. 7, pp. 136–37.
52. As the procedure took hold, the time limit was periodically updated, although the updates had a tendency to offer ever longer windows of opportunity and eventually became irrelevant to the procedure.
53. Sutherland, *Assize of Novel Disseisin,* pp. 5–8.
54. The author of the Bracton text wrote a few generations after the assize had been introduced that it was "thought out and invented through many wakeful nights." Bracton, *On the Laws and Customs of England,* vol. 3, p. 25, cited in Sutherland, *Assize of Novel Disseisin,* p. 6.
55. Warren, *Henry II,* p. 336.
56. Sutherland, *Assize of Novel Disseisin,* p. 74.
57. *Bracton's Note book. A Collection of Cases Decided in the King's Courts during the Reign of Henry the Third, Annotated by a Lawyer of that Time, Seemingly by Henry of Bracton,* ed. F. W. Maitland, 3 vols. (London, 1887), vol. 3, no. 1821 pp. 626–27.
58. In Yorkshire in 1183–84, for example, the sheriff accounted for four fines imposed for disseisin, two payments for assize verdicts (*recognitiones*), and one license of concord in an assize. Several other payments to have *recognitiones* in land pleas probably also refer to assize litigation. *The Great Roll of the Pipe for the Thirtieth Year of the Reign of King Henry the Second, A.D. 1183–1184,* n. a., The Publications of the Pipe Roll Society, vol. 33 (London, 1912), pp. 28–41.
59. Sutherland, *Assize of Novel Disseisin,* p. 43.
60. Brand notes, for example, that 49 membranes of parchment sufficed to record all business in the Bench in 1200 while 1,056 membranes were needed in 1300: Brand, "The Origins of the English Legal Profession," in idem, *The Making of the Common Law* (London, 1992), n. 61, p. 19.
61. Pollock and Maitland, *History of English Law,* vol. 2, p. 565. In Huntingdonshire, 45 possessory assizes are documented in the eyre of 1227 while 64 are documented in the eyre of 1272: *Royal Justice and the Medieval English Countryside,* ed. DeWindt and DeWindt, n. 39, n. 41, p. 20.
62. *Calendar of the General and Special Assize and General Gaol Delivery Commissions on the Dorses of the Patent Rolls, Richard II (1377–1399)* (London, 1977), pp. 1–9. In spite of the narrow chronological focus of the volume, the "Formulary," written by C.A.F. Meekings, traces the development of assize commissions from their beginning.
63. J. C. Holt, *Magna Carta,* 2nd ed. (Cambridge, 1992), p. 456–57. For an example of the pleas heard under the commission of 1225, see *Somersetshire Pleas (Civil and Criminal) From the Rolls of the Itinerant Justices*

(*Close of 12th Century–41 Henry III*), ed. Charles Chadwyck-Healey, Somerset Record Society, vol. 11 (London, 1897), pp. 26–110.

64. Subsequent versions of Magna Carta substituted a single annual session for the quarterly sessions stipulated in 1215. The change was probably due to the inability of royal government to administer sessions with the frequency envisioned in 1215.

65. Musson, *Public Order* chap. 4 and 5; Musson and Ormrod, *Evolution of English Justice* (Houndmills, Basingstoke, Hampshire and New York, 1999), chap. 3.

66. *Calendar of the General and Special Assize Commissions*, pp. 4–6; Musson, *Public Order*, p. 86; Mary Margaret Taylor, "The Justices of Assize," in *The English Government at Work, 1327–1336*, ed. James F. Willard, William A. Morris, and William H. Dunham, Jr. (Cambridge, MA, 1950), vol. 3, pp. 225–31.

67. Great Britain. House of Commons Sessional Papers, 1881–1889. Deputy Keepers Annual Reports, nos. 42–50. A finding list of the Deputy Keepers' Reports can be found in Charles Gross, *The Sources and Literature of English History*, 2nd ed. (London, 1915), p. 691.

68. Great Britain. House of Commons Sessional Papers 1881, vol. 54. The Forty-Second Annual Report. The Deputy Keeper of the Public Records. June 24, 1881. (London, 1881), p. 473.

69. Ibid.

70. Great Britain. House of Commons Sessional Papers 1887, vol. 31. The Forty-Eighth Annual Report of the Deputy Keeper of the Public Records. August 8, 1887. (London, 1887). I took soundings of every tenth page of the calendar to calculate the total number for that year.

71. In 6 Edward I (1278–79), 21 assize commissions occur on the Patent Rolls, eight of which can be found in extant assize rolls. In 7 Edward I (1279–80), 29 assize commissions were issued and nine cases can be found in the assize rolls. In 8 Edward I (1280–81), ten assize commissions were issued and three can be found in the assize rolls. The number of commissions is derived from Haydon's calendars. The cases are recorded in National Archives, Public Record Office, JUST 1/1241, 1244.

72. Musson, *Public Order*, p. 86.

73. The lower figure assumes that one-third of 2,000 cases made use of 12 jurors each; the higher that two-thirds of 3,000 cases did so.

74. Milsom, *Legal Framework*, p. 24: "The overwhelming majority of all early assizes seem to be brought in respect of peasant holdings."

75. Sutherland, *Assize of Novel Disseisin*, pp. 48–50.

76. Great Britain. House of Commons Sessional Papers 1887, vol. 44 Forty-Eighth Annual Report of the Deputy Keeper of the Public Records. (London, 1887), p. 92.

77. National Archives, Public Record Office, SC 2/179/5, 9, 10, 11. A Benigna Clere, possibly the same person, is recorded in the Hundred Rolls of 1279 as possessing two virgates of land from Ramsey: *Rotuli hundredorum*, ed. Illingworth and Caley, vol. 2, p. 601.

78. Pollock and Maitland, *History of English Law*, vol. 2, pp. 646–47; Langbein, "The Jury of Presentment and the Coroner," pp. 1329–1365.
79. S.F.C. Milson, "Trespass from Henry III to Edward III," *Law Quarterly Review*, 74 (1958): 195–224, 407–36, 561–90; Brand, *Making of the Common Law;* Robert C. Palmer, *English Law in the Age of the Black Death, 1348–1381* (Chapel Hill, NC, 1993); Musson and Ormrod, *Evolution of English Justice.*
80. Robert Bartlett, *Trial by Fire and Water. The Medieval Judicial Ordeal* (Oxford, 1986), p. 98.
81. Stephen D. White, "Proposing the Ordeal and Avoiding it: Strategy and Power in Western French Litigation, 1050 to 1110," in *Power and Society in the Twelfth Century*, ed. Thomas N. Bisson (Philadelphia, 1995), pp. 89–123.
82. Groot, "The Early Thirteenth-Century Criminal Jury," in *Twelve Good Men and True*, ed. J. S. Cockburn and Thomas A. Green (Princeton, 1998), pp. 3–35. Troubled political circumstances in the aftermath of Magna Carta and the death of King John no doubt also account for the uncertainty.
83. Roger D. Groot, "The Jury in Private Criminal Prosecutions before 1215," *American Journal of Legal History* 27 (1983): 113–141.
84. Roger D. Groot, "The Jury of Presentment before 1215," *American Journal of Legal History* 26 (1982): 1–24.
85. Hurnard, *King's Pardon for Homicide*, p. 342.
86. *Rolls of the Justices in Eyre*, ed. Doris Mary Stenton, Selden Society, vol.53 (London, 1934), pp. lxx-lxxi; Catherine Kappauf, *The Early Development of the Petty Jury in England: 1194–1221*, University of Illinois PhD thesis (1973), pp. 153–68. Additional examples can be found in the early Curia Regis rolls.
87. M. J. Russell, "Trial by Battle Procedure in Writs of Right and Criminal Appeals," *Tijdschrift voor rechtsgeschiedenis* 53 (1983): 124–34; Bartlett, *Trial by Fire and Water*, pp. 103–26.
88. *Placita Corone*, ed. J. M. Kaye, Selden Society, Supplementary Series, vol. 4 (London, 1966), p. 23.
89. R. H. Helmholz, "The Law of Compurgation," in idem, *The ius commune in England. Four Studies* (Oxford, 2001), pp. 82–134.
90. In Wales, for example, compurgation continued to play a much greater role in adjudication than in England. See Daffydd Jenkins, "Towards the Jury in Medieval Wales," in *The Dearest Birthright of the People of England: The Jury in the History of the Common Law*, ed. John W. Cairns and Grant McLeod (Oxford, 2002): 17–46.
91. Charles Gross, "Modes of Trial in the Medieval Boroughs of England," *Harvard Law Review* 15 (1902): 691–706.
92. *The London Eyre of 1276*, ed. Martin Weinbaum, London Record Society, vol. 12 (n.p., 1976), p. xix; *Borough Customs*, ed. Mary Bateson, Selden Society, vols. 18 and 21 (London, 1904–1906), vol. 1, pp. 36–52; vol. 2, pp. xxvii-xxx.

93. Helmholz, "Law of Compurgation."
94. Leona Gavel, *Benefit of Clergy in England in the Later Middle Ages*, Smith College Studies in History, (Northampton, MA, 1929; reprt. New York, 1969), vol. 14, pp. 36–39.
95. E.g., *Curia Regis Rolls*, ed. Flower and Brand, vol. 1, p. 258; vol. 2, p. 136; vol. 3, p. 117; vol. 7, p. 190.
96. Roger D. Groot, "Teaching Each Other: Judges, Clerks, Jurors and Malefactors Define the Guilt/Innocence Jury," in *Learning the Law. Teaching and the Transmission of English Law, 1150–1900*, ed. Jonathan A. Bush and Alain Wijffels (London, 1999), pp. 28–30.
97. David J. Seipp, "Crime in the Year Books," in *Law Reporting in England*, ed. Chantal Stebbings (London, 1995): 15–34.
98. *The Court Baron*, ed. Frederic W. Maitland and William P. Baildon, Selden Society, vol. 4 (London, 1891), p. 63.
99. *Year Books of the Reign of King Edward the First*, ed. Alfred J. Horwood, Rerum Britannicarum Medii Aevi Scriptores no. 31 (London, 1863), vol. 3, p. 530.
100. *Placita Corone*, ed. Kaye, pp. 23–24.
101. H.R.T. Summerson, "The Early Development of the Peine Forte et Dure," in *Law, Litigants, and the Legal Profession*, ed. E. W. Ives and A. H. Manchester (London, 1983), pp. 116–18; Groot, "Early Thirteenth-Century Criminal Jury," pp. 30–33.
102. Ralph B. Pugh, *Imprisonment in Medieval England* (Cambridge, 1968), pp. 24–25.
103. A good account of the long-term development of this procedure can be found in James Bradley Thayer, *A Preliminary Treatise on Evidence at the Common Law* (Boston, 1898), pp. 74–81.
104. J. H. Baker, *An Introduction to English Legal History*, 3rd ed. (London, 1990), pp. 580–81.
105. *The Eyre of Northamptonshire, 3–4 Edward III, A.D. 1329–1330*, ed. Donald W. Sutherland, 2 vols., Selden Society vols. 97, 98 (London, 1983), vol. 1, pp. 178, 179, 189.
106. *Year Books of King Edward the First*, ed. Horwood, vol. 3, p. 531.
107. Thayer, *Preliminary Treatise on Evidence*, p. 74.
108. John H. Langbein, *Torture and the Law of Proof. Europe and England in the Ancien Regime* (Chicago, 1977).
109. Paul R. Hyams, *Rancor and Reconciliation in Medieval England* (Ithaca, 2003), pp. 184–86.
110. Green, *Verdict According to Conscience*, pp. 9–11.
111. Thomas A. Green, "A Retrospective on the Criminal Trial Jury, 1200–1800," in *Twelve Good Men and True*, ed. Cockburn and Green, p. 366.
112. Bernard William McLane, "Juror Attitudes toward Local Disorder: The Evidence of the 1328 Lincolnshire Trailbaston Proceedings," in *Twelve Good Men and True*, ed. Cockburn and Green, p. 36.
113. Margaret H. Kerr, Richard D. Forsyth and Michael J. Plyley, "Cold Wa-

ter and Hot Iron: Trial by Ordeal in England," *Journal of Interdisciplinary History* 22 (1992), p. 578.

114. Ibid., p. 574.

115. Green, *Verdict According to Conscience,* p. 10.

116. Henry Summerson, "Attitudes to Capital Punishment in England, 1200–1350," in *Thirteenth Century England VIII,* ed. Michael Prestwich, Richard Britnell and Robin Frame (Woodbridge, Suffolk, 2001), pp. 123–32.

117. J. B. Post, "Local Jurisdictions and Judgment of Death in Later Medieval England," *Criminal Justice History* 4 (1983): 1–21.

118. *The Roll of the Shropshire Eyre of 1256,* ed. Alan Harding, Selden Society, vol. 96 (London, 1981), pp. xxxii–lxxiv.

119. *Proceedings before the Justices of the Peace,* ed. Putnam, pp. cxii–cxxviii; *Essex Sessions of the Peace 1351, 1377–1379,* ed. Elizabeth Furber (Colchester, 1953), pp. 38–60; *Some Sessions of the Peace in Cambridgeshire in the Fourteenth Century 1340, 1380–1383,* ed. Mary Margaret Taylor, Cambridge Antiquarian Society Octavo Publications, vol. 55 (Cambridge, 1942), pp. lvix–lxv. On the development of trespass in the fourteenth century, see Robert Palmer, *English Law in the Age of the Black Death* (Chapel Hill, NC, 1993), pt. 3.

CHAPTER 3

1. A Year Book case from 1382 notes that a sheriff's oath of office required him to take personal responsibility for the process of jury formation: *Medieval English Legal History. An Index and Paraphrase of Printed Year Book Reports, 1268–1535,* comp. David J. Seipp, Entry 1382.019am. http://www.bu.edu/law/faculty/scholarship/yearbooks/.

2. *Curia Regis Rolls,* ed. C. T. Flower and Paul Brand, 19 vols. (London, 1922-), vol. 14, no. 722, p. 145.

3. National Archives, Public Record Office JUST 3/23/3, m. 1.

4. *The Roll and Writ File of the Berkshire Eyre of 1248,* ed. M. T. Clanchy, Selden Society, vol. 90 (London, 1973), p. 427.

5. Robert Palmer, *The County Courts of Medieval England* (Princeton, 1982), p. 287; J. H. Baker, *An Introduction to English Legal History,* 3rd ed. (London, 1990), pp. 24–25. For some early examples of *nisi prius* verdicts, see *Curia Regis Rolls,* ed. Flower and Brand, vol. 9, p. 315 (AD 1220); Ibid., vol. 16, no. 2289 (AD 1242), p. 457.

6. Richard W. Kaeuper, "Law and Order in Fourteenth-Century England: The Evidence of Special Commissions of Oyer and Terminer," *Speculum* 54 (1979): 734–84.

7. *Roll and Writ File of the Berkshire Eyre,* ed. Clanchy, pp. cv–cvii; *The Stonor Letters and Papers 1290–1483,* ed. Charles L. Kingford, vol. 1, Camden 3rd ser., (London, 1919), vol. 29, p. 15; Mabel Mills, "The Medieval Shire House" in *Studies Presented to Sir Hilary Jenkinson,* ed. J. Conway Davies (London, 1957), p. 261.

8. National Archives, Public Record Office C145/37, no. 6. A calendar of the file can be found in *Calendar of Inquisitions Miscellaneous (Chancery) Preserved in the Public Record Office*, n. a., 7 vols. (London, 1916–69), vol. 1, no. 1150, p. 343. The letter to the bailiff is referred to but not calendared.

9. According to the statute of mortmain (*De viris religiosis*), enacted in the same year as this inquest, donors to the church had to retain enough land in their own hands to uphold their traditional obligations and responsibilities, which is why the issue in Christina's case revolved around the relative values of her bequest and her recent acquisition. William Stubbs, *Select Charters from the Beginning to 1307*, 9th ed., ed. H.W.C. Davis (Oxford, 1913), pp. 451–52.

10. *Roll and Writ File of the Berkshire Eyre*, ed. Clanchy, pp. lxxxi-lxxxix.

11. Examples of jury panels preserved as part of the formal record of a court or inquest include: *A Lincolnshire Assize Roll for 1298*, ed. Walter S. Thomson, Lincoln Record Society, 36 (Hereford, 1944), pp. 123–35; *Wiltshire Gaol Delivery and Trailbaston Trials 1275–1306*, ed. Ralph B. Pugh, Wiltshire Record Society, vol. 33 (Devizes, 1978), pp. 165–70. For a Year Book discussion of the formal status of the panel, see *Medieval English Legal History. An Index and Paraphrase of Printed Year Book Reports, 1268–1535*, comp. David J. Seipp. Entry 1352.084ass.

12. A panel related to a case heard at a Hampshire quarter session in 1474–75 listed 87 names. *Proceedings before the Justices of the Peace in the Fourteenth and Fifteenth Centuries, Edward III to Richard III*, ed. Bertha Haven Putnam, Ames Foundation, vol. 5 (London, 1938), p. 254.

13. *Statutes of the Realm*, ed. A. Luders, T. E. Tomlins, J. France, W. E. Taunton, and J. Raithby, 11 vols. (London, 1810–28), vol. 1, p. 89; *The Eyre of Northamptonshire, 3–4 Edward III, A.D. 1329–1330*, ed. Donald W. Sutherland, 2 vols., Selden Society, vols. 97, 98 (London, 1983), vol. 1, p. 376.

14. *Statutes of the Realm*, ed. Luders et al., vol. 1, pp. 89, 139.

15. *Select Cases in the Court of King's Bench under Edward III*, vol. 5, ed. G. O. Sayles, Selden Society, vol. 76 (London, 1958), pp. 66–69, case 28. Similar complaints can be found in G. H. Tupling, *South Lancashire in the Reign of Edward II*, Remains Historical and Literary Connected with the Palatine Counties of Lancaster and Cheshire, Chetham Society, 3rd ser., vol. 1 (Manchester, 1949), pp. lv-lvi.

16. *State Trials of the Reign of Edward the First, 1289–1293*, ed. T. F. Tout and Hilda Johnstone, Camden Society, 3rd ser. vol. 9 (London, 1906), p. 9.

17. *Statutes of the Realm*, ed. Luders et al., vol. 1, p. 389. In 1427, the commons petitioned in parliament to have panels available to litigants who wanted them eight days before the trial date. The king conceded that the panels should be available at least six days before the trial. *The Parliament Rolls of Medieval England 1275–1504*, vol. 10, Henry VI, 1422–1431, ed. Anne Curry (London, 2005), pp. 351–52.

18. In the proceedings of an assize recorded in a Year Book in 1337, a sheriff rejected the jurors returned by the bailiff of a franchise, claiming that the men chosen by the bailiff were "suspect". *Medieval English Legal History. An Index and Paraphrase of Printed Year Book Reports, 1268–1535,* comp. David J. Seipp. no. 1337.012rs. Similar examples can be found in ibid., no. 1356.120ass, 1357.010ass.

19. This assertion is based on a comparison of two courts with large numbers of extant jury panels: the Berkshire eyre of 1248 and the Cambridgeshire eyre of 1272. *Roll and Writ File of the Berkshire Eyre,* ed. Clanchy; National Archives, Public Record Office, JUST 1/84 and JUST 4/1/6.

20. E.g., National Archives, Public Record Office, JUST 3/29/2, m. 8, 10, 11.

21. National Archives, Public Record Office, JUST 3/29/2, m. 38, 61

22. National Archives, Public Record Office, JUST 1/84 and JUST 4/1/6. Numerous examples can be found by comparing these two records. On m. 39, for example, Ancelinus le Bray, Robert of Pentfield, Stephen Oliver, and Peter Camera are cited for failure to appear in an assize of novel disseisin pitting Thomas of Sawston against William le Kenteys and several others, and all have a cross beside their name on the corresponding jury panel.

23. This observation is based mainly on the descriptions of jury panels included in the calendars of miscellaneous inquisitions.

24. On the circumstances surrounding these trials, see *State Trials of the Reign of Edward the First,* ed. Tout and Johnstone; Paul Brand, *The Making of the Common Law* (London, 1992), pp. 103–12.

25. National Archives, Public Record Office, JUST 1/541B, m. 8.

26. The size of the fine entered on the panel differs from the one entered on the roll.

27. Post, "Jury Lists and Juries in the Late Fourteenth Century," in *Twelve Good Men and True. The Criminal Trial Jury in England, 1200–1800,* ed. J. S. Cockburn and Thomas A. Green (Princeton, 1988), pp. 65–77. The practice of drafting talesmen came in for discussion in a Year Book case recorded in 1328: *Medieval English Legal History. An Index and Paraphrase of Printed Year Book Reports, 1268–1535,* comp. David J. Seipp. no. 1328.068.

28. The number presupposed here excludes Ralph of Ditton and the person who is named before him on the list, who was probably added at the head of the list as a "talesman" like Ralph before it was determined that his services were not required.

29. *State Trials of the Reign of Edward the First,* ed. Tout and Johnstone, pp. 18–23.

30. For general surveys of this topic, see James C. Oldham, "The Origins of the Special Jury," *University of Chicago Law Review* 50 (1983): 137–221; Marianne Constable, *The Law of the Other: The Mixed Jury and Changing Concepts of Citizenship, Law, and Knowledge* (Chicago, 1994), pp. 96–102.

31. *Select Pleas, Starrs, and Other Records from the Rolls of the Exchequer of the Jews, AD 1220 to 1284,* ed. J. M. Rigg, Selden Society, vol. 15 (London, 1902), p. xxxviii; H. G. Richardson, *The English Jewry under Angevin Kings* (London, 1960), p. 114.

32. *Documents Illustrative of English History in the Thirteenth and Fourteenth Centuries,* ed. Henry Cole (London, 1844), pp. 297–98.

33. *Calendar of Inquisitions Miscellaneous,* vol. 1, no. 396, p. 133.

34. An inquisition *post mortem* held in London a few years earlier was both sealed and signed by the Jewish jurors. *Calendar of Inquisitions Post Mortem,* vol. 1, no. 747, p. 242.

35. *Calendar of Patent Rolls, 1281–1292,* p. 397.

36. *Curia Regis Rolls,* ed. Flower and Brand, vol. 11, no. 2644, pp. 529–30.

37. *Rotuli chartarum in turri londinensi asservati, 1199–1216,* ed. T. D. Hardy (London, 1837), p. 93.

38. Cynthia J. Neville, *Violence, Custom and Law: The Anglo-Scottish Border Lands in the Later Middle Ages* (Edinburgh, 1998), pp. 5–11, 16–19, 127–39; Natalie Fryde, "A Royal Enquiry into Abuses: Queen Eleanor's Ministers in North-East Wales, 1291–1292," *Welsh History Review* 5 (1971), p. 373; *Year Books of the Reign of King Edward the First: Years XX and XXI,* ed. Alfred J. Horwood, Rerum Britannicarum Medii Aevi Scriptores no. 31 (London, 1866), vol. 1, p. 184–86.

39. Oldham, "Origins of the Special Jury," p. 168; Oldham, "The Varied Life of the Self-Informing Jury," Selden Society Lecture, July, 2004 (London, 2005), pt. II; N.S.B. Gras, *The Early English Customs System* (Cambridge, MA, 1918), p. 261; *Statutes of the Realm,* ed. Luders et al., vol. 1, pp. 336, 348. For precedents, see *Close Rolls of the Reign of Henry III Preserved in the Public Record Office: 1247–1251,* pp. 523–24; *Borough Customs,* ed. Mary Bateson, 2 vols., Selden Society, vols. 18 and 21 (London, 1904–06), vol. 1, p. 201.

40. *Calendar of Inquisitions Miscellaneous,* vol. 2, no. 358, p. 89.

41. R. C. Van Caenegem, *Royal Writs in England from the Conquest to Glanvill,* Selden Society, vol. 77 (London, 1959), pp. 69–81. The Hampshire case is discussed on p. 74.

42. E.g. *Curia Regis Rolls,* ed. Flower and Brand, vol. 3, p. 204; Ibid., vol. 15, no. 1291, p. 323.

43. Ibid., vol. 6, p. 361.

44. *Calendar of the Close Rolls of the Reign of Henry III, 1227–1231,* p. 250.

45. *Curia Regis Rolls,* ed. Flower and Brand, vol. 3, pp. 109–10; Ibid., vol. 11, no. 1034, p. 208; *Calendar of Charter Rolls, 1257–1300,* p. 437; *Eyre of Northamptonshire,* ed. Sutherland, pp. 126–27.

46. *Curia Regis Rolls,* ed. Flower and Brand, vol. 5, pp. 132–33.

47. Ibid., vol. 11, no. 1034, p. 208.

48. *The Treatise on the Laws and Customs of the Realm of England Commonly Called Glanvill,* ed. G.D.G. Hall (Oxford, 1993), pp. 151–52.

49. Henry de Bracton, *On the Laws and Customs of England,* trans. Samuel E. Thorne, 4 vols. (Cambridge, MA, 1968-), vol. 2, pp. 208–27; *Matthew*

Paris's English History, trans. J. A. Giles, 3 vols. (London, 1852), vol. 1, pp. 291–94. Bracton treats the matter in the context of disputes between heiresses.

50. *Rolls of the Justices in Eyre,* ed. Doris Mary Stenton, Selden Society, vol. 53 (London, 1934), pp. 103–4; 128; 167–73.

51. *Curia Regis Rolls,* ed. Flower and Brand, vol. 14, no. 722, p. 145, vol. 16, no. 2477, pp. 490–91; *Calendar of Inquisitions Miscellaneous,* vol. 7, no. 82, p. 53.

52. Helen Cam, *The Hundred and the Hundred Rolls* (London, 1930), pp. 78–82, 158–60; Thomson, *Lincolnshire Assize Roll for 1298,* Lincoln Record Society, vol. 36 (Hereford, 1944), pp. lxxxviii-cxxvii; Richard Kaeuper, *War, Justice and Public Order. France and England in the Later Middle Ages* (Oxford, 1988), pp. 170–83.

53. Daniel Lord Smail, *The Consumption of Justice* (Ithaca, 2003), pp. 95–100.

54. Thomas Andrew Green, *Verdict According to Conscience. Perspectives on the Criminal Trial Jury 1200–1800* (Chicago, 1985), pp. 13–14; Anthony Musson, *Public Order and Law Enforcement: The Local Administration of Criminal Justice, 1294–1350,* (Woodbridge, Suffolk, 1996), pp. 197–98.

55. *Statutes of the Realm,* ed. Luders et al., vol. 1, p. 320; *Britton, An English Translation and Notes,* ed. F. M. Nichols (Washington, DC, 1901), p. 25.

56. Green, *Verdict According to Conscience.*

57. *The Eyre of Kent 6 and 7 Edward II,* ed. Frederic W. Maitland, Leveson W. V. Harcourt and William C. Bolland, 3 vols., Selden Society, vols. 24, 27, 29 (London, 1910–13), vol. 1, p. 8; *Four Thirteenth Century Law Tracts,* ed. George E. Woodbine (New Haven, 1910), pp. 141–42; *Select Cases of Procedure without Writ under Henry III,* ed. H. G. Richardson and G. O. Sayles, Selden Society, vol. 60 (London, 1941), p. cci; *Eyre of Northamptonshire,* ed. Sutherland, vol. 1, p. 31.

58. Stubbs, *Select Charters,* p. 252.

59. *Curia Regis Rolls,* ed. Flower and Brand, vol. 15, no. 1285, pp. 319–20. On the issue of damage to preexisting market franchises, see R. H. Britnell, "King John's Early Grants of Markets and Fairs," *English Historical Review* 370 (1979): 90–96; James Masschaele, *Peasants, Merchants, and Markets: Inland Trade in Medieval England, 1150–1350* (New York, 1997), chap. 3.

60. *The Parliament Rolls of Medieval England 1275–1504,* vol. 1, Edward I 1275–1294, ed. Paul Brand (London, 2005), pp. 176–83.

61. Ibid., n.10, p. 254.

62. A few years later, in 1305, King Edward I issued a statute requiring his representatives at inquests to offer reasons for their challenges, and gave authority over how to deal with challenges to the official who had been commissioned to hold the inquiry. *Statutes of the Realm,* ed. Luders et al., vol. 1, p. 143. For an interesting Year Book case from 1316 that

sheds additional light on the use of challenges in inquest procedure, see *Year Books of the Reign of Edward II, vol. 20, 10 Edward II,* ed. M. Dominica Legge and Sir William Holdsworth, Selden Society, vol. 52 (London, 1934), no. 56, p. 152.

63. *Glanvill,* ed. Hall, p. 152.
64. Bracton, *On the Laws and Customs of England,* ed. Thorne, vol. 2, pp. 70–72.
65. E.g. *Curia Regis Rolls,* ed. Flower and Brand, vol. 1, p. 346; vol. 3, pp. 21, 67; vol. 5, pp. 33–34, 232; vol. 16, no. 2563, p. 504; *Eyre of Northamptonshire,* ed. Sutherland, vol. 2, pp. 749–50; G. Wrottesley, "Extracts from the Plea Rolls, 16 to 33 Edward III, Translated from the Original Rolls in the Public Record Office," *Collections for a History of Staffordshire Edited by the William Salt Archaeological Society* (London, 1891), vol. 12, p. 159; See also the following Year Book cases cited in *Medieval English Legal History. An Index and Paraphrase of Printed Year Book Reports, 1268–1535,* comp. David J. Seipp. nos. 1347.163, 1369.176ass, 1382.019am.
66. *Medieval English Legal History. An Index and Paraphrase of Printed Year Book Reports, 1268–1535,* comp. David J. Seipp. nos. 1339.231rs, 1343.160rs, 1345.252ass.
67. *Curia Regis Rolls,* ed. Flower and Brand, vol. 4, p. 140. Cf. *Eyre of Northamptonshire,* ed. Sutherland, vol. 1, p. 422–23.
68. "Extracts from the Plea Rolls," ed. Wrottesley, pp. 169–70.
69. Ibid., pp. 73, 120, 121.
70. N. Denholm-Young, *Seignorial Administration in England* (Oxford, 1937), pp. 116–18.
71. Percy Henry Winfield, *The History of Conspiracy and Abuse of Legal Procedure* (Cambridge, 1921), chap. 7; J. G. Bellamy, *Bastard Feudalism and the Law* (Portland, OR, 1989), pp. 27–29, 82–89, 123–29.
72. *The Parliament Rolls of Medieval England 1275–1504,* ed. Brand, p. 572.
73. Musson, *Public Order and Law Enforcement,* pp. 194–97; Idem, *Medieval Law in Context: The Growth of Legal Consciousness from Magna Carta to the Peasants' Revolt* (Manchester, 2001), pp. 99–100; J. G. Bellamy, *The Criminal Trial in Later Medieval England* (Toronto, 1998), pp. 100–101.
74. The frequency of challenges in criminal cases has given rise to conflicting opinions. Anthony Musson has argued that challenges in criminal cases were relatively common, but J. B. Post and J. G. Bellamy have described them as rare and of little consequence. Musson, *Public Order and Law Enforcement,* pp. 194–97; J. B. Post, "Jury Lists and Juries in the Late Fourteenth Century," pp. 65–77; Bellamy, *Criminal Trial,* pp. 100–101. Musson's suggestion that challenges became less common over time may help to reconcile the opposing views. But even in earlier periods they appear to have been significantly less common in criminal trials than in assizes.

75. *Britton*, ed. Nichols, p. 25 (crown pleas), pp. 277–81 (assizes).
76. Bracton, *On the Laws and Customs of England*, ed. Thorne, vol. 2, p. 405. The significance of the passage in which the account of challenges occurs is discussed in Daniel Klerman, "Was the Jury Ever Self-Informing?" in *The Trial in History, vol. 1, Judicial Tribunals in England and Europe, 1200–1700*, ed. Maureen Mulholland, Brian Pullan, and Anne Pullan (Manchester, 2003), pp. 64–65.
77. Bellamy, *Criminal Trial*, pp. 100–101; *Year Books of the Reign of King Edward the First*, ed. Horwood, Rerum Britannicarum Medii Aevi Scriptores, no. 31 (London, 1863), vol. 3, p. 530.
78. F. W. Maitland noted that he found no evidence for peremptory challenges in the court records of the thirteenth century. Pollock and Maitland, *History of English Law*, vol. 2, n. 5, p. 621. Possible examples of peremptory challenges in the first half of the fourteenth century can be found in *Eyre of Northamptonshire*, ed. Sutherland, vol. 1, p. 179; *A Cambridgeshire Gaol Delivery Roll, 1332–1334*, ed. Elisabeth G. Kimball, Cambridge Antiquarian Records Society, vol. 4 (Cambridge, 1978), no. 36, p. 55.
79. *Medieval English Legal History. An Index and Paraphrase of Printed Year Book Reports, 1268–1535*, comp. David J. Seipp. no. 1378.018am.
80. Sir John Fortescue, *On the Laws and Governance of England*, ed. Shelley Lockwood (Cambridge, 1997), p. 40. Cf. James Fitzjames Stephen, *A History of the Criminal Law of England*, 3 vols. (London, 1883), vol. 1, pp. 301–2; Musson, *Public Order and Law Enforcement*, p. 195. The number of peremptory challenges cited by Fortescue (35) also occurs in a case recorded in a Year Book in 1406: *Medieval English Legal History an Index and Paraphrase of Printed Year Book Reports, 1268–1535*, comp. David J. Seipp. no. 1406.022.
81. Parliament similarly insisted in 1341 that trial jurors should be removable if challenged solely on the grounds that they had also served on the presentment jury: *The Parliament Rolls of Medieval England 1275–1504*, vol. 4, Edward III, 1327–1348, ed. Seymour Phillips and Mark Ormrod (London, 2005), p. 323.
82. *Britton*, ed. Nichols, p. 25.
83. Musson, *Public Order and Law Enforcement*, p. 196.
84. *Year Books of the Reign of King Edward the First*, ed. Horwood, Rerum Britannicarum Medii Aevi Scriptores, no. 31, vol. 3, p. 528–29. See also James Bradley Thayer, *A Preliminary Treatise on Evidence at the Common Law*, pp. 123–24.
85. *Select Cases in the Court of King's Bench under Richard II, Henry IV and Henry V*, vol. 7, ed. G. O. Sayles, Selden Society, vol. 88 (London, 1971), p. 81.
86. *Eyre of Northamptonshire*, ed. Sutherland, vol. 1, pp. 287–88.
87. Michael T. Clanchy, *"Law and Love in the Middle Ages,"* in *Disputes and Settlements: Law and Human Relations in the West*, ed. John Bossy (Cambridge, 1983), pp. 47–67; Phillippa C. Maddern, *Violence and*

Social Order. East Anglia 1422–1442 (Oxford, 1992), chap. 2. On the use of legal procedure as an extension of personal animosities in France, see Smail, *Consumption of Justice.*

88. George Fisher has argued that jurors' oaths served this same purpose, by backing decisions with divine sanction. Fisher, "The Jury's Rise as Lie Detector," *Yale Law Journal* 107, 3 (1997): 575–714.

89. Roger D. Groot, "Petit Larceny, Jury Lenity and Parliament," in "The Dearest Birthright of the People of England." *The Jury in the History of the Common Law,* ed. John W. Cairns and Grant McLeod (Oxford, 2002), pp. 47–61.

90. On the explosive growth of the legal system in this period, see Paul Brand, "*The Formation of the English Legal System, 1150–1400,*" in *Legislation and Justice,* ed. Antonio Padoa-Schioppa (Oxford, 1997), pp. 103–22.

CHAPTER 4

1. Patrick Wormald, *The Making of English Law: King Alfred to the Twelfth Century,* vol. 1: Legislation and Its Limits (Oxford, 1999).

2. C. T. Flower, *Introduction to the Curia Regis Rolls, 1199–1230,* Selden Society, vol. 62 (London, 1944), p. 434.

3. Anthony Musson, *Medieval Law in Context: The Growth of Legal Consciousness from Magna Carta to the Peasants' Revolt* (Manchester, 2001), p. 116.

4. Bernard William McLane, "Juror Attitudes toward Local Disorder: The Evidence of the 1328 Trailbaston Proceedings," in *Twelve Good Men and True. The Criminal Trial Jury in England, 1200–1800,* ed. J. S. Cockburn and Thomas A. Green (Princeton, 1988), pp. 36–64; J. B. Post, "Jury Lists and Juries in the Late Fourteenth Century," in ibid., pp. 65–78; Edward Powell, "Jury Trial at Gaol Delivery in the Late Middle Ages: The Midland Circuit, 1400–1429," in ibid., pp. 78–116.

5. McLane, "Juror Attitudes," p. 44.

6. Post, "Jury Lists," p. 71.

7. Powell, "Jury Trial at Gaol Delivery," p. 95.

8. R. B. Goheen, "Peasant Politics? Village Community and the Crown in Fifteenth-Century England," *American Historical Review* 96 (1991): 42–62.

9. Christopher Dyer, *An Age of Transition? Economy and Society in the Later Middle Ages* (Oxford, 2005).

10. Christine Carpenter, *The Wars of the Roses: Politics and the Constitution in England, c. 1437–1509* (Cambridge, 1997), p. 93. Carpenter went on to argue that the traditional view needed modification but supported the view that Henry's ineffectiveness spawned the crises that ultimately led to civil war.

11. Anthony Musson, *Public Order and Law Enforcement: The Local Ad-*

ministration of Criminal Justice, 1294–1350 (Woodbridge, Suffolk, 1996), pp. 189–92.

12. Anthony Musson, "Twelve Good Men and True? The Character of Early Fourteenth-Century Juries," *Law and History Review* 15 (1997): 115–44.

13. Writing about the meaning of *homo* in the eighteenth century, the jurist William Blackstone stated that "though a name common to both sexes, the female is however excluded. . . ." *Commentaries on the Laws of England,* 4 vols. (Oxford, 1765–69), vol. 3, p. 362, cited in Oldham, "Varied Life of the Self-Informing Jury," n.127, p. 32.

14. Some of the assumptions behind this exclusion are discussed in Judith Bennett, *Women in the Medieval English Countryside. Gender and Household in Brigstock before the Plague* (Oxford, 1987), pp. 22–26.

15. Louise J. Wilkinson, "Women as Sheriffs in Early Thirteenth Century England," in *English Government in the Thirteenth Century,* ed. Adrian Jobson (Woodbridge, 2004), pp. 111–24. On women as churchwardens, see Katherine L. French, *The People of the Parish. Community Life in a Late Medieval Diocese* (Philadelphia, 2001), pp. 77–88.

16. Henry de Bracton, *On the Laws and Customs of England,* trans. Samuel E. Thorne, 4 vols. (Cambridge, MA, 1968-), vol. 2, p. 416.

17. James C. Oldham, "On Pleading the Belly: A History of the Jury of Matrons," *Criminal Justice History* 6 (1985): 1–64; Maryanne Kowaleski, "Women's Work in a Market Town: Exeter in the Late Fourteenth Century," in *Women and Work in Preindustrial Europe,* ed. Barbara A. Hanawalt (Bloomington, 1986), n. 43, p. 162; T. R. Forbes, "A Jury of Matrons," *Medical History* 32 (1988): 23–33. The early history of the writ *de ventre inspiciendo* is described in *Select Cases of Procedure Without Writ Under Henry III,* ed. H. G. Richardson and G. O. Sayles, Selden Society, vol. 60 (London, 1941), pp. cliii-clv.

18. For brief descriptions of the required physical examination see *Bracton's Note Book. A Collection of Cases Decided in the King's Courts during the Reign of Henry the Third, Annotated by a Lawyer of that Time, Seemingly by Henry of Bracton,* ed. F. W. Maitland, 3 vols. (London, 1887), vol. 3, no. 1605, p. 473; *Curia Regis Rolls,* ed. C. T. Flower and Paul Brand, 19 vols. (London, 1922-), vol. 15, no. 121, pp. 30–31.

19. Barbara Hanawalt, *Crime and Conflict in English Communities 1300–1348* (Cambridge, MA, 1979), p. 43; Ralph B. Pugh, *Imprisonment in Medieval England* (Cambridge, 1968), p. 24.

20. *Bracton's Note Book,* ed. Maitland, vol. 3, no. 1503, pp. 417–18.

21. Bracton, *On the Laws and Customs of England,* vol. 2, pp. 202–3.

22. *Curia Regis Rolls,* ed. Flower and Brand, vol. 17, no. 121, pp. 30–31; *Bracton's Note Book,* ed. Maitland, no. 1605, pp. 473–74.

23. *Curia Regis Rolls,* ed. Flower and Brand, vol. 4, p. 212.

24. National Archives, Public Record Office, JUST 3/35B, m.38. This reference was kindly given to me by Caroline Dunn.

25. Bracton, *On the Laws and Customs of England,* vol. 2, p. 416.

26. Charles E. Odegaard, *"Legalis Homo," Speculum* 15 (1940): 186–93. For comparable use of the concept on the continent, see Robert Bartlett, *Trial by Fire and Water. The Medieval Judicial Ordeal* (Oxford, 1986), pp. 112, 130–31; Daniel Lord Smail, *The Consumption of Justice* (Ithaca, 2003), pp. 129–30.

27. S. H. Rigby's argument that medieval women defined their status in terms of family and household rather than in terms of gender is relevant here. Rigby, *English Society in the Later Middle Ages. Class, Status and Gender* (New York, 1995), chap. 7.

28. E.g., *Calendar of Inquisitions Miscellaneous (Chancery) Preserved in the Public Record Office,* n. a., 7 vols. (London, 1916–69), vol. 4, no. 190, pp. 107–8.

29. Thomas Smith, *De Republica Anglorum: A Discourse on the Commonwealth of England,* ed. L. Alston (Cambridge, 1906), p. 42, cited in James C. Oldham, "The Origins of the Special Jury," *University of Chicago Law Review* 50 (1983), p. 149.

30. *Early Treatises on the Practice of the Justices of the Peace in the Fifteenth and Sixteenth Centuries,* ed. Bertha Haven Putnam, Oxford Studies in Social and Legal History, ed. Paul Vinogradoff (Oxford, 1924), vol. 7 p. 366.

31. *Britton. An English Translation and Notes,* ed. F. M. Nichols (Washington, DC, 1901), p. 52.

32. *The Treatise on the Laws and Customs of the Realm of England Commonly Called Glanvill,* ed. G.D.G. Hall (Oxford, 1993), pp. 25, 36.

33. Odegaard, *"Legalis Homo,"* p. 188.

34. Bracton, *On the Laws and Customs of England,* vol. 3, p. 71.

35. On the centrality of reputation in medieval society, see the essays in *Fama: The Politics of Talk and Reputation in Medieval Europe,* ed. Thelma Fenster and Daniel Lord Smail (Ithaca, 2003).

36. *Curia Regis Rolls,* ed. Flower and Brand, vol. 6, pp. 338–39.

37. In a private letter sent from Jerusalem in 1160, for example, a pilgrim stipulated that his bequest to the Priory of Llanthony should be supervised by "lawful men." David Walker, "A Letter from the Holy Land," *English Historical Review* 72 (1957), p. 665.

38. Paul Hyams, *Kings, Lords, and Peasants in Medieval England: The Common Law of Villeinage in the Twelfth and Thirteenth Centuries* (Oxford, 1980), p. 153. See also Goheen, "Peasant Politics?," pp. 56–58.

39. *Curia Regis Rolls,* ed. Flower and Brand, vol. 7, p. 288; vol. 12, no. 1456, p. 297; vol. 14, no. 2349, pp. 506–7.

40. *The Great Roll of the Pipe for the Thirty-Second Year of the Reign of King Henry the Second A. D. 1185–1186,* n. a., The Publications of the Pipe Roll Society, vol. 36 (London, 1914), p. 157; *Curia Regis Rolls,* ed. Flower and Brand, vol. 3, p. 276; *Medieval English Legal History. An Index and Paraphrase of Printed Year Book Reports, 1268–1535,* comp. David J. Seipp. http://www.bu.edu/law/faculty/scholarship/yearbooks/, no. 1352.092ass.

41. *The Eyre of Northamptonshire, 3–4 Edward III,* A.D. *1329–1330,* ed.

Donald W. Sutherland, 2 vols., Selden Society, vols. 97, 98 (London, 1983), vol. 1, p. 149.

42. Richard M. Smith, " 'Modernization' and the Corporate Medieval Village Community in England: Some Skeptical Reflections," in *Explorations in Historical Geography*, ed. Alan Baker and D. Gregory (Cambridge, 1984), p. 172; Anthony Musson and Mark Ormrod, *The Evolution of English Justice: Law, Politics and Society in the Fourteenth Century* (Basingstoke, Hampshire, 1999), p. 131; Judith M. Bennett, *A Medieval Life: Cecilia Penifader of Brigstock, c.1295–1344* (Boston, 1999), p. 4; Bruce M. S. Campbell, "The Agrarian Problem in the Early Fourteenth Century," *Past and Present* 188 (2005), pp. 24–37.

43. On the operation of merchet, see Judith M. Bennett, "Medieval Peasant Marriage: An Examination of Marriage License Fines in the *Liber Gersumarum*," in *Pathways to Medieval Peasants*, ed. J. A. Raftis (Toronto, 1981), pp. 193–246.

44. Helen M. Cam, "Pedigrees of Villeins and Free Men in the Thirteenth Century," in Idem, *Liberties and Communities in Medieval England. Collected Studies in Local Administration and Topography* (London, 1963), pp. 124–35; Hyams, *Kings, Lords, and Peasants*, pp. 173–76.

45. Ibid., pp. 176–80.

46. *A Lincolnshire Assize Roll for 1298*, ed. Walter S. Thomson, The Publications of the Lincoln Record Society, vol. 36 (Hereford, 1944), no. 323, p. 74.

47. *Curia Regis Rolls*, ed. Flower and Brand, vol. 12, no. 1031, pp. 208–9.

48. Hyams, *Kings, Lords, and Peasants*, p. 154; *Britton*, ed. Nichols, p. 172.

49. *Select Pleas in Manorial and Other Seignorial Courts*, ed. F. W. Maitland, Selden Society, vol. 2 (London, 1889), p. 94; Ada Elizabeth Levett, *Studies in Manorial History* (Oxford, 1938), pp. 146–47.

50. Frances M. Page, *The Estates of Crowland Abbey. A Study in Manorial Organization* (Cambridge, 1934), pp. 31–58.

51. Edwin Brezette DeWindt, *Land and People in Holywell-cum-Needingworth. Structures of Tenure and Patterns of Social Organization in an East Midlands Village 1252–1457* (Toronto, 1971), pp. 218–20.

52. National Archives, Public Record Office, JUST 1/48 m. 51, cited in *Roll and Writ File of the Berkshire Eyre of 1248*, ed. M. T. Clanchy, Selden Society, vol. 90 (London, 1973), n. 6, p. xl.

53. *Statutes of the Realm*, ed. A. Luders, T. E. Tomlins, J. France, W. E. Taunton, and J. Raithby, 11 vols. (London, 1810–28), vol. 1, pp. 210–12.

54. On the application of the statute, see R. F. Hunnisett, *The Medieval Coroner*, Cambridge Studies in English Legal History (Cambridge, 1961), p. 119.

55. F. M. Nichols, "Original Documents Illustrative of the Administration of the Criminal Law in the Time of Edward I," *Archaeologia* 40 (1866), pp. 96, 103. The references are drawn from Article 9 of the "Articles of Lincoln" that defined the commission of trailbaston justices.

56. *Yorkshire Inquisitions of the Reigns of Henry III and Edward I,* ed. William Brown, 4 vols., The Yorkshire Archaeological Society Record Series, vols. 12, 23, 31, 37 (n.p., 1892–1906), vol. 3 (1902), no. LXVI, pp. 95–6.

57. *The Court Baron,* ed. Frederic William Maitland and William Paley Baildon, Selden Society, vol. 4 (London, 1891), p. 97.

58. *Calendar of Inquisitions Miscellaneous,* vol. 6, no. 281, p. 138; no. 284, p. 146; nos. 290, 292, pp. 150–151.

59. National Archives, Public Record Office, C145/41, no. 2.

60. *Calendar of Inquisitions Miscellaneous,* vol. 2, no. 1230, pp. 301–2.

61. Ibid., vol. 2, no. 1215, p. 298.

62. Anne Reiber DeWindt and Edwin Brezette DeWindt, *Ramsey: The Lives of an English Fenland Town* (Washington, DC, 2006), chap. 5; Page, *Estates of Crowland Abbey,* chap. 6; J. Ambrose Raftis, *Tenure and Mobility: Studies in the Social History of the Mediaeval English Village* (Toronto, 1964), chap. 4; Goheen, "Peasant Politics?" pp. 42–62; Sherri Olson, *A Chronicle of All that Happens: Voices from the Village Court in Medieval England* (Toronto, 1996), chap. 3.

63. *Eyre of Northamptonshire,* ed. Sutherland, vol. 1, p. 74; J. B. Post, "Local Jurisdictions and Judgment of Death in Later Medieval England," *Criminal Justice History* 4 (1983): 1–21.

64. Stubbs, *Select Charters from the Beginning to 1307,* 9th ed., ed. H.W.C. Davis (Oxford, 1913), p. 249; *Statutes of the Realm,* ed. Luders et al., vol. 1, p. 211; *Fleta,* ed. H. G. Richardson and G. O. Sayles, vol. 2, Selden Society, vol. 72 (London, 1955), p. 41–42.

65. Sir John Fortescue, *On the Laws and Governance of England,* ed. Shelley Lockwood (Cambridge, 1997), p. 43.

66. Conveniently summarized in Oldham, "Origins of the Special Jury," pp. 214–21.

67. *Statutes of the Realm,* ed. Luders et al., vol. 1, p. 89.

68. Similar abuses were condemned in a parliamentary petition of 1341: *The Parliament Rolls of Medieval England 1275–1504,* vol. 4, Edward III, 1327–1348, ed. Seymour Phillips and Mark Ormrod (London, 2005), p. 323.

69. *Statutes of the Realm,* ed. Luders et al., vol. 1, p. 113.

70. *The Parliament Rolls of Medieval England 1275–1504,* vol. 4, ed. Phillips and Ormrod, p.133. Interestingly, though, the petitioners said that jurors could be asked to serve outside the hundred only if they had lands worth 40 shillings or more.

71. *Medieval English Legal History. An Index and Paraphrase of Printed Year Book Reports, 1268–1535,* comp. David J. Seipp. no. 1333.076.

72. *The Parliament Rolls of Medieval England 1275–1504,* vol. 9, Henry V, 1413–1422, ed. Chris Given-Wilson (London, 2005), p. 105; *Statutes of the Realm,* ed. Luders et al., vol. 2, p. 188, chap. 3.

73. Oldham, "Origins of the Special Jury," p. 145.

74. *Proceedings before the Justices of the Peace in the Fourteenth and Fifteenth Centuries, Edward III to Richard III,* ed. Bertha Haven Putnam, Ames

Foundation, vol. 5 (London, 1938), pp. 276–77; *Statutes of the Realm,* ed. Luders et al., vol. 2, p. 297, chap. 5.

75. *Statutes of the Realm,* ed. Luders et al., vol. 2, p. 479, chap. 4.

76. *Statutes of the Realm,* ed. Luders et al., vol. 2, p. 243, chap. 7; Ludwig Riess, *The History of English Electoral Law in the Middle Ages,* trans. K. L. Wood-Legh (Cambridge, 1940), pp. 81–82.

77. N. Denholm-Young, *Collected Papers of N. Denholm-Young* (Cardiff, 1969), p. 91; Michael Powicke, *Military Obligation in Medieval England. A Study in Liberty and Duty* (Oxford, 1962), pp. 73, 76, 78, 104–5, 109, 141, 149.

78. *Statutes of the Realm,* ed. Luders et al., vol. 2, p. 309, chap. 11.

79. Stubbs, *Select Charters,* pp. 183–84. For a discussion of the assize and its subsequent history, see Powicke, *Military Obligation.*

80. *Statutes of the Realm,* ed. Luders et al., vol. 1, pp. 97–8, chap. 6. A good updated translation is available in *English Historical Documents 1189–1327,* ed. Harry Rothwell (Oxford, 1975), pp. 460–62.

81. Olson, *A Chronicle of All that Happens,* p. 126 ("super-villager"); J. Ambrose Raftis, "The Concentration of Responsibility in Five Villages," *Mediaeval Studies* 28 (1966): 92–118; Edward Britton, *The Community of the Vill: A Study in the History of the Family and Village Life in Fourteenth-Century England* (Toronto, 1977).

82. Edward Miller and John Hatcher, *Medieval England. Rural Society and Economic Change 1086–1348* (London, 1978), pp. 45–46

83. *Accounts and Surveys of the Wiltshire Lands of Adam de Stratton,* ed. M. W. Farr, Wiltshire Archeological and Natural History Society, Records Branch, vol. 14 (1959), pp. 1–30; E. Stone, "Profit-and-Loss Accountancy at Norwich Cathedral Priory," *Transactions of the Royal Historical Society,* 5th ser., 12 (1962), p. 42; J. A. Raftis, *Assart Data and Land Values. Two Studies in the East Midlands 1200–1350* (Toronto, 1974), pp. 19–48; *Agrarian History of England and Wales,* 1042–1350, ed. H. E. Hallam (Cambridge, 1988), vol. 2, pp. 344, 666.

84. M. M. Postan, *The Medieval Economy and Society* (London, 1972), pp. 121–42; Rodney Hilton, *The English Peasantry in the Later Middle Ages* (Oxford, 1975), p. 39; Christopher Dyer, *Making a Living in the Middle Ages* (New Haven, 2002), p. 8.

85. *Historia et cartularium monasterii sancti Petri gloucestriae,* ed. William Henry Hart, Rerum Britannicarum Medii Aevi Scriptores, no. 33 (London, 1867) vol. 3.

86. *Walter of Henley and Other Treatises of Estate Management and Accounting,* ed. Dorothea Oschinsky (Oxford, 1971), p. 471.

87. Christopher Dyer, *Standards of Living in the Later Middle Ages. Social Change in England c. 1200–1520* (Cambridge, 1989), pp. 110–16.

88. Examples of dismissals of entire juries: *Curia Regis Rolls,* ed. Flower and Brand, vol. 5, pp. 68–69; vol. 6, p. 300, vol. 9, p.156; vol. 13, no. 709, p. 159; vol. 15, no. 532, pp. 111–12.

89. Ibid., vol. 13, no. 709, p. 159; vol. 15, no. 548, p. 115; vol. 16, no. 148F, p. 45.

90. Ibid., vol. 15, no. 568, pp. 120–21. See also ibid., vol. 6, p. 30.

91. Ibid., vol. 10, no. 1353, p. 235; vol. 14, p. 286.

92. J. Quick, "The Number and Distribution of Knights in Thirteenth Century England: The Evidence of the Grand Assize Lists," in *Thirteenth Century England,* ed. P. R. Coss and S. D. Lloyd (Woodbridge, Suffolk, 1986), vol. 1, pp. 114–19; Peter Coss, *The Origins of the English Gentry* (Cambridge, 2003), p. 91.

93. *Curia Regis Rolls,* ed. Flower and Brand, vol. 12, no. 1456, pp. 297–98.

94. *Curia Regis Rolls,* ed. Flower and Brand, vol. 3, p. 276; vol. 7, pp. 26, 288. See also Hyams, *Kings, Lords, and Peasants,* p. 153.

95. *Curia Regis Rolls,* ed. Flower and Brand, vol. 14, no. 2349, pp. 506–7.

96. Ibid., vol. 12, no. 1852, p. 377.

97. Ibid., vol. 2, p. 121.

98. *Year Books of the Reign of Edward II,* vol. 2, 2 and 3 Edward II, ed. F. W. Maitland, Selden Society, vol. 19 (London, 1904), no. 137, p. 69.

99. Helen M. Cam, *Studies in the Hundred Rolls. Some Aspects of Thirteenth-Century Administration,* Oxford Studies in Social and Legal History, ed. Paul Vinogradoff, (Oxford, 1921), vol. 6 pp. 160–61.

100. *Rotuli hundredorum,* ed. W. Illingworth and J. Caley, 2 vols. (London, 1812–18), vol. 1, p. 246.

101. Ibid., vol. 1, pp. 376, 462.

102. Ibid., vol. 2, p. 305.

103. *Year Books of the Reign of King Edward the First,* ed. Alfred J. Horwood, Rerum Britannicarum Medii Aevi Scriptores, no. 31 (London, 1863), vol. 3, p. 534.

104. *Yorkshire Inquisitions,* ed. Brown, vol. 2, no. 104, pp. 119–20.

105. *The Parliament Rolls of Medieval England 1275–1504,* vol. 1, Edward I, 1275–1294, ed. Paul Brand (London, 2005), pp. 550–51.

106. *Thomas Wright's Political Songs of England from the Reign of John to that of Edward II,* ed. Peter Coss (Cambridge, 1996), p. 228.

107. Scott Waugh, "Reluctant Knights and Jurors: Respites, Exemptions, and Public Obligations in the Reign of Henry III," *Speculum* 58 (1983), p. 966.

108. Richard W. Kaeuper, "Law and Order in Fourteenth-Century England: The Evidence of Special Commissions of Oyer and Terminer," *Speculum* 54 (1979), p. 753; Alan Harding, *England in the Thirteenth Century* (Cambridge, 1993), pp. 210–19; Coss, *Origins of the English Gentry,* pp. 146–64.

Chapter 5

1. See, for example, the comments in Timothy Reuter, "The Medieval Nobility in Twentieth-Century Historiography," in *Companion to Historiography,* ed. Michael Bentley (London, 1997), pp. 184–89.

2. Edwin B. DeWindt, *Land and People in Holywell-cum-Needingworth: Structures of Tenure and Patterns of Social Organization in an East Midlands Village 1252–1457* (Toronto, 1971); J. Ambrose Raftis, *Warboys: Two Hundred Years in the Life of an English Mediaeval Village* (Toronto, 1974); Edward Britton, *The Community of the Vill: A Study in the History of the Family and Village Life in Fourteenth-Century England* (Toronto, 1977); Zvi Razi, *Life, Marriage and Death in a Medieval Parish: Economy, Society and Demography in Halesowen* (Cambridge, 1980); Maryanne Kowaleski, *Local Markets and Regional Trade in Medieval Exeter* (Cambridge, 1995); Sherri Olson, *A Chronicle of All that Happens: Voices From the Village Court in Medieval England* (Toronto, 1996).

3. Hubert Hall, *A Formula Book of English Official Historical Documents. Part II, Ministerial and Judicial Records* (Cambridge, 1909).

4. These are discussed in *Wiltshire Gaol Delivery and Trailbaston Trials 1275–1306*, ed. Ralph B. Pugh, Wiltshire Record Society, vol. 33 (Devizes, 1978), pp. 17–29

5. Edward Powell, "Jury Trial at Gaol Delivery in the Late Middle Ages," in *Twelve Good Men and True. The Criminal Trial Jury in England, 1200–1800*, ed. J. S. Cockburn and Thomas A. Green (Princeton, 1988), pp. 83–85.

6. *The Roll and Writ File of the Berkshire Eyre of 1248*, ed. M. T. Clanchy, Selden Society, vol. 90 (London, 1973).

7. *Kent Keepers of the Peace, 1316–1317*, ed. Bertha Haven Putnam, Kent Archaeological Society Records Branch, vol. 13 (Ashford, 1933), pp. xxix-xxiv; *Rolls of Northamptonshire Sessions of the Peace*, ed. Marguerite Gollancz, The Publications of the Northamptonshire Record Society, vol. 11 (Kettering, 1940), p. xxxvi; *Some Sessions of the Peace in Cambridgeshire in the Fourteenth Century, 1340, 1380–1383*, ed. Mary Margaret Taylor, Cambridge Antiquarian Society Octavo Publications, No. 55 (Cambridge, 1942), pp. li-lii; *Essex Sessions of the Peace 1351, 1377–1379*, ed. Elizabeth Chapin Furber, Essex Archaeological Society Occasional Publications No. 3 (Colchester, 1953), pp. 32–37; *Wiltshire Gaol Delivery and Trailbaston Trials*, ed. Pugh, pp. 17–29.

8. *Royal Justice and the Medieval English Countryside: the Huntingdonshire Eyre of 1286, the Ramsey Abbey Banlieu Court of 1287, and the Assizes of 1287–88*, ed. Anne Reiber DeWindt and Edwin Brezette DeWindt, Pontifical Institute of Mediaeval Studies, Studies and Texts, vol. 57 (Toronto, 1981).

9. Ibid., p. 73.

10. Sandra Raban, *A Second Domesday? The Hundred Rolls of 1279–1280* (Oxford, 2004), pp. 118–43.

11. James Field Willard, *Parliamentary Taxes on Personal Property 1290 to 1334* (Cambridge, MA, 1934), pp. 68–72.

12. Michael J. Bennett, *Community, Class, and Careerism. Cheshire and Lancashire Society in the Age of Sir Gawain and the Green Knight* (Cambridge, 1983), p. 82.

13. *Inquisitions and Assessments Relating To Feudal Aids,* A.D. *1284–1431,* ed. A. S. Maskelyne, C. Johnson, A. E. Stamp, and J. V. Lyle, 6 vols. (London, 1889–1920), vol. 6, pp. 462–64. The subsidy was to have been taken from individuals with lands or rents worth more than £20, but the assessors in Huntingdonshire included lesser landholders and assigned each a share of the total calculated for the entire county based on their assessable wealth.

14. Nigel Saul, "The Social Status of Chaucer's Franklin: A Reconsideration," *Medium Aevum* 52 (1983), p. 15. See also Peter Coss, "An Age of Deference," in *A Social History of Medieval England, 1200–1500,* ed. Rosemary Horrox and W. Mark Ormrod, (Cambridge, 2006), pp. 62–66.

15. *Early Huntingdonshire Lay Subsidy Rolls,* ed. J. A. Raftis and M. P. Hogan (Toronto, 1976), p. 23, Table III. My calculation includes individuals described by the authors as belonging to presumptive families occurring in the court records.

16. *The Taxation of 1297. A Translation of the Local Rolls of Assessment for Barford, Biggleswade and Flitt Hundreds, and for Bedford, Dunstable, Leighton Buzzard and Luton,* ed. A. T. Gaydon,The Publications of the Bedfordshire Historical Record Society, vol. 39 (Streatley, Beds, 1959), Appendix B, pp. 104–8.

17. National Archives, Public Record Office, E143/1/5, no. 25.

18. Further details of their social prominence are available in the biographical register in *Royal Justice and the Medieval English Countryside,* ed. DeWindt and DeWindt.

19. National Archives, Public Record Office, C143/199, no. 20.

20. *Early Huntingdonshire Lay Subsidy Rolls,* ed. Raftis and Hogan.

21. Britton, *Community of the Vill,* p. 19, 29.

22. Ellen Wedemeyer Moore, *The Fairs of Medieval England: An Introductory Study* (Toronto 1985), p. 331.

23. National Archives, Public Record Office, SC 2/179/10–26. His subsidy assessment occurs in the neighboring village of Hemmingford Abbots.

24. *Court Rolls of the Abbey of Ramsey and of the Honor of Clare,* ed. Warren Ortman Ault (New Haven, 1928), pp. 241, 250, 251, 256.

25. *Rotuli hundredorum,* ed. W. Illingworth and J. Caley. 2 vols. (London, 1812–18), vol. 2, p. 680.

26. National Archives, Public Record Office, E143/1/5, no. 9.

27. *Rotuli hundredorum,* ed. Illingworth and Caley, vol. 2, pp. 706–709.

28. The size of the virgate in Oxfordshire is discussed in *Agrarian History of England and Wales,* vol. 2, 1042–1350, ed. H. E. Hallam (Cambridge, 1988), p. 668, and P.D.A.Harvey, *A Medieval Oxfordshire Village. Cuxham 1240 to 1400* (Oxford, 1965), p. 130.

29. See E. A. Kosminsky, *Studies in the Agrarian History of England in the Thirteenth Century,* trans. Ruth Kisch (Oxford, 1956), pp. 16–17.

30. *Rotuli hundredorum,* ed. Illingworth and Caley, vol. 1, pp. 403–33.
31. Ibid., vol. 1, pp. 423b-424b.
32. Ibid., vol. 2, p. 412a.
33. *Kent Keepers of the Peace,* ed. Putnam, pp. xi-xxii.
34. Printed in ibid., pp. 80–104.
35. Ibid., p. xxx.
36. Ibid., p. xxxi.
37. *Royal Justice and the Medieval English Countryside,* ed. DeWindt and DeWindt.
38. Ibid., pp. 419–21.
39. Unless otherwise indicated, the material on which this paragraph is based is drawn from the biographical register in ibid.
40. Richard le Fraunceys married the widow of Nicholas Hildegar.
41. Moore, *Fairs of Medieval England,* p. 311.
42. *Rotuli hundredorum,* ed. Illingworth and Caley, vol. 2, p. 601a. Half of his virgate was rented to a subtenant.
43. Britton, *Community of the Vill,* pp. 29, 128, 205.
44. *Rotuli hundredorum,* ed. Illingworth and Caley, vol. 2, p. 607a.
45. "Roll of the Bedfordshire Supervisors of the Peace, 1314," ed. Joyce Godber, *The Publications of the Bedfordshire Historical Record Society,* vol. 12 (Aspley Guise, 1928): 27–70. The jury lists are printed on pp. 35–39.
46. In most districts a bailiff was sworn and entered at the head of the list, but I assume that he was not a member of the jury. On the role of triers, see David Crook, "Triers and the Origin of the Grand Jury," *Journal of Legal History* 12 (1991): 103–16.
47. *Two Bedfordshire Subsidy Lists. 1309 and 1332 with Map,* [ed. Sydenham Henry Augustus Hervey], Suffolk Green Books no. 18 (Bury St. Edmunds, 1925).
48. *Two Bedfordshire Subsidy Lists,* p. ix; *Inquisitions and Assessments Relating to Feudal Aids,* vol. 1, p. 19.
49. *Two Bedfordshire Subsidy Lists,* p. 101.
50. *Inquisitions and Assessments Relating To Feudal Aids,* vol. 1, p. 19.
51. *Calendar of Inquisitions Post Mortem and Other Analogous Documents Preserved in the Public Record Office, 23 vols. (London, 1904-),* vol. 4, Edward I (29–35 Edward I) no. 169, p. 111.
52. National Archives, Public Record Office, JUST 4/1/6.
53. National Archives, Public Record Office, JUST 1/85.
54. William Farrer. *Feudal Cambridgeshire* (Cambridge, 1920), p. 179.
55. Ibid., p. 157.
56. *Rotuli hundredorum,* ed. Illingworth and Caley, vol. 2, p. 528b.
57. National Archives, Public Record Office, JUST 1/84, m. 5.
58. National Archives, Public Record Office, JUST 4/16, no. 444.
59. *Rotuli hundredorum,* ed. Illingworth and Caley, vol. 2, p. 525a.
60. Ibid., vol. 2, pp. 539b (transcribed as Elias de Gledeseye), 527a.

61. Ibid., vol. 2, pp. 513a, 518a-b, 519a, 520a.

62. Ibid., vol. 2, p. 524b.

63. Ibid., vol. 2, pp. 537a (Albert); 526a (Elys); 541a-b (Smith); 536a-b, 537b (Campiun).

64. Farrer, *Feudal Cambridgeshire,* pp. 56–57, 107, 113, 136, 146, 214–15.

65. National Archives, Public Record Office, JUST 1/84, m. 12.

66. National Archives, Public Record Office, JUST 4/1/6, no. 413.

67. *Rotuli hundredorum,* ed. Illingworth and Caley, vol. 2, pp. 564a (Bretun), 556b, 557a-b, 558a (Sterne). The juror William de Bans of Wimpole does not appear in the Hundred Rolls, but Robert, son of William de Bans of Wimpole is recorded in an inquisition post mortem as holding one-half of a knight's fee in the same village in 1297, so it seems reasonable to assume that the juror William held this same property. Farrer, *Feudal Cambridgeshire,* p. 253. John de Wraccewurye held more than 80 acres and had eight tenants in the Hundred Roll entry for Wimpole; I assume that the juror Walter de Wraccewurye held this land in 1272.

68. *Rotuli hundredorum,* ed. Illingworth and Caley, vol. 2, pp. 565b (le Eyre), 556b, 557a-b (Clerk), 543a, 544a (Marshal). The entry concerning Ralph le Eyre's holding notes that his ancestors had traditionally owed suit to the county court and that Ralph now paid suit to the honor court of Richmond. One can speculate that he was appointed to the jury on account of his prior court experience.

69. *Rotuli hundredorum,* ed. Illingworth and Caley, vol. 2, pp. 429b, 430b, 569b.

70. Ibid., vol. 2, pp. 568b, 569a-b.

71. National Archives, Public Record Office, JUST 1/84, m. 30.

72. National Archives, Public Record Office, JUST 4/1/6, no. 298.

73. *Rotuli hundredorum,* ed. Illingworth and Caley, vol. 2, p. 427b.

74. Ibid., vol. 2, pp. 421a, 422a.

75. Ibid., vol. 2, pp. 421a-b, 422a.

76. National Archives, Public Record Office, JUST 1/84, m. 10.

77. *Rotuli hundredorum,* ed. Illingworth and Caley, vol. 2, p. 574b.

78. Ibid., vol. 2, p. 573b.

79. National Archives, Public Record Office, JUST 4/1/6, no. 120.

80. *Rotuli hundredorum,* ed. Illingworth and Caley, vol. 2, pp. 413b, 414b (le Blund); 415b (Safrey); 568a (Tristram).

81. Ibid., vol. 2, pp. 576a-b, 577a.

82. Ibid., vol. 2, p. 588a-b.

83. Ibid., vol. 2, pp. 576a, 577b, 578b.

84. *Statutes of the Realm,* ed. Luders et al., vol. 1, p. 320.

85. *Royal Justice and the Medieval English Countryside,* ed. DeWindt and DeWindt, nos. 642 (Buleheved), 457 (Rode), 567 (Mowyn); National Archives, Public Record Office, JUST 3/86. The gaol delivery roll has two other cases linked to eyre presentments, but manuscript damage prevents identification of all jurors in the cases.

86. I have assigned status following details provided in the biographical

register in *Royal Justice and the Medieval English Countryside,* ed. DeWindt and DeWindt. The one peasant was Richard de Stoneley, who served on the jury that presented Roger Mowyn. He held the equivalent of a virgate in Alconbury Weston. Philip Deaules, or Daules of Brampton was not included in the biographical register. He held five virgates in Brampton and has accordingly been treated here as a member of the gentry: *Rotuli hundredorum,* ed. Illingworth and Caley, vol. 2, p. 608a.

87. *Hertfordshire Lay Subsidy Rolls 1307 and 1334,* ed. Janice Brooker and Susan Flood, Hertfordshire Record Publications, vol. 14 (Hertford, 1998).

88. National Archives, Public Record Office, JUST 3/23/2, m. 3.

89. National Archives, Public Record Office, JUST 3/23/3, m. 3.

90. National Archives, Public Record Office, JUST 3/2/2, m. 5.

91. *Two Bedfordshire Subsidy Lists,* ed. Hervey, pp. 48, 53, 65.

92. Ibid., p. 27.

93. National Archives, Public Record Office, JUST 3/2/2, m. 7.

94. Cf. *Wiltshire Gaol Delivery and Trailbaston Trials,* ed. Pugh, pp. 165–68.

95. *Two Bedfordshire Subsidy Lists,* ed. Hervey, p. 58.

96. National Archives, Public Record Office, JUST 3/2/2, m. 10.

97. *Two Bedfordshire Subsidy Lists,* ed. Hervey, p. 101.

98. *Taxation of 1297,* ed. A. T. Gaydon, p. 28.

99. *Two Bedfordshire Subsidy Lists,* ed. Hervey, p. 10. Hervey mistranscribed the name as Walter Beman.

100. *Court Roll of Chalgrave Manor 1278–1313,* ed. Marian K. Dale, The Publications of the Bedfordshire Historical Record Society, vol. 28 (Streatley, Beds, 1950).

101. I differ from Dale's reading of the word *servisiam* in the court of December 8, 1304. Dale understood it to mean that Goman led his neighbors out of the village to find employment (i.e. *servitium*). I read it to be an alternate spelling of the common word for ale (*cervisia*). The alternate spelling is attested in the period, whereas a feminine form of *servitium* is not.

102. *Court Roll of Chalgrave Manor,* ed. Dale, p. 57.

103. The distinction between professional and non-professional attorneys is discussed in Paul Brand, *The Origins of the English Legal Profession* (Oxford, 1992), pp. 69, 73, 83–85.

CONCLUSION

1. *The Parliament Rolls of Medieval England, 1275–1504,* vol. 3, Edward II, 1307–1327, ed. Seymour Phillips (London, 2005), p. 101.

2. *The Parliament Rolls of Medieval England, 1275–1504,* vol. 4, Edward III, 1327–1348, ed. Seymour Phillips and Mark Ormrod (London, 2005), p. 344.

3. *The Parliament Rolls of Medieval England, 1275–1504,* vol. 3, ed. Phillips, p. 100.

4. Christine Carpenter, *Locality and Polity. A Study of Warwickshire Landed Society, 1401–1499* (Cambridge, 1992), chap. 8.

5. David J. Seipp, "Jurors, Evidence, and the Tempest of 1499," in *The Dearest Birthright of the People of England. The Jury in the History of the Common Law,* ed. John Cairns and Grant McLeod (Oxford, 2002), p. 75.

6. *The Treatise on the Laws and Customs of the Realm of England Commonly Called Glanvill,* ed. G.D.G. Hall (Oxford, 1993), pp. 35–36; Sir John Fortescue, *On the Laws and Governance of England,* ed. Shelley Lockwood (Cambridge, 1997), p. 39; Percy Henry Winfield, *The History of Conspiracy and Abuse of Legal Procedure* (Cambridge, 1921), pp. 194–95.

7. Henry Summerson, "Attitudes to Capital Punishment in England, 1200–1350," in *Thirteenth Century England VIII,* ed. Michael Prestwich, Richard Britnell and Robin Frame (Woodbridge, Suffolk, 2001), p. 125.

8. National Archives, Public Record Office, C144/16, no. 28.

9. Medieval English Legal History. An Index and Paraphrase of Printed Year Book Reports, 1268–1535, comp. David J. Seipp. http://www.bu.edu/law/faculty/scholarship/yearbooks/. Seipp number 1353.169ass.

10. *Thomas Wright's Political Songs of England from the Reign of John to that of Edward II,* ed. Peter Coss (Cambridge, 1996), p. 228.

11. *Rotuli hundredorum,* ed. W. Illingworth and J. Caley, 2 vols. (London, 1812–18), vol. 1, p. 296.

12. *The Parliament Rolls of Medieval England, 1275–1504,* vol. 1, Edward I, 1275–1294, ed. Paul Brand (London, 2005), p. 411.

13. *Glanvill,* ed. Hall, p. 28.

14. Fortescue, *On the Laws and Governance of England,* ed. Lockwood, pp. 36–47.

15. *Liber Albus: The White Book of the City of London,* trans. Henry Thomas Riley (London, 1861), pp. 332–33.

16. *The Roll and Writ File of the Berkshire Eyre of 1248,* ed. M. T. Clanchy, Selden Society vol. 90 (London, 1973), p. cvi.

17. *Rolls of Northamptonshire Sessions of the Peace,* ed. Marguerite Gollancz, The Publications of the Northamptonshire Record Society, vol. 11 (Kettering, Northampthonshire, 1940), p. 9.

18. *Curia Regis Rolls,* ed. C. T. Flower and Paul Brand, 19 vols. (London, 1922-), vol. 1, pp. 315–16.

19. Based on a phrase search of Harvard Law School Library's edition of Bracton Online: http://140.247.226.46/bracton//index.htm.

BIBLIOGRAPHY

MANUSCRIPT SOURCES

British Library:
Additional Charter 39459.
Additional Charter 34911.
Harley Charter 58.E.40, 41.
The National Archives, Public Record Office (London):
C47: Chancery Miscellanea.
C143: Inquisitions *ad quod damnum*.
C144: Criminal Inquisitions.
C145: Miscellaneous Inquisitions.
E106: Extents of Alien Priories.
E142: Ancient Extents.
E143: Extents and Inquisitions.
E146: Forest Proceedings.
E199: Sheriffs' Accounts.
JUST 1: Eyre and Assize Rolls.
JUST 3: Gaol Delivery Rolls.
JUST 4: Eyre and Assize Writ Files.
SC 2: Court Rolls.

PRINTED PRIMARY SOURCES

Accounts and Surveys of the Wiltshire Lands of Adam de Stratton, ed. M. W. Farr. Wiltshire Archeological and Natural History Society, Records Branch, vol. 14 (1959).

Borough Customs, ed. Mary Bateson. Selden Society, vols. 18 and 21. London, 1904–1906.

Bracton, Henry de. *On the Laws and Customs of England.* trans. Samuel E. Thorne. 4 vols. Cambridge, MA. 1968-.

Bracton's Note Book. A Collection of Cases Decided in the King's Courts during the Reign of Henry the Third, Annotated by a Lawyer of that Time, Seemingly by Henry of Bracton, ed. F. W. Maitland. 3 vols. London, 1887.

Britton. An English Translation and Notes, ed. F. M. Nichols. Washington, DC, 1901.

Calendar of the Charter Rolls Preserved in the Public Record Office. n. a., 6 vols. London, 1903–27.

Calendar of the Close Rolls Preserved in the Public Record Office. n. a., 47 vols. London, 1892–1963.

Calendar of Inquisitions Miscellaneous (Chancery) Preserved in the Public Record Office. n. a., 7 vols. London, 1916–69.

Calendar of Inquisitions Post Mortem and Other Analogous Documents Preserved in the Public Record Office. 23 vols. London, 1904-.

Calendar of the Patent Rolls Preserved in the Public Record Office, n. a., 64 vols. London, 1891–1966.

Calendar of the General and Special Assize and General Gaol Delivery Commissions on the Dorses of the Patent Rolls, Richard II (1377–1399). n. a. London, 1977.

A Cambridgeshire Gaol Delivery Roll, 1332–1334, ed. Elisabeth G. Kimball. Cambridge Antiquarian Records Society, vol. 4. Cambridge, 1978.

Chronica magistri rogeri de hovedene, ed. William Stubbs. Rerum Britannicarum Medii Aevi Scriptores (Rolls Series) no. 51. London, 1869.

Close Rolls of the Reign of Henry III Preserved in the Public Record Office, n. a., 14 vols. London, 1902–38.

The Court Baron, ed. Frederic William Maitland and William Paley Baildon. Selden Society, vol. 4. London, 1891.

Court Roll of Chalgrave Manor 1278–1313, ed. Marian K. Dale. The Publications of the Bedfordshire Historical Record Society, vol. 28. Streatley, Beds., 1950.

Court Rolls of the Abbey of Ramsey and of the Honor of Clare, ed. Warren Ortman Ault. New Haven, 1928.

Curia Regis Rolls, ed. C. T. Flower and Paul Brand. 19 vols. London, 1922-.

Documents Illustrative of English History in the Thirteenth and Fourteenth Centuries, ed. Henry Cole. London, 1844.

Domesday-Book seu Liber Censualis Willelmi Primi Regis Angliae, ed. Abraham Farley. Record Commission. London, 1783.

Early Huntingdonshire Lay Subsidy Rolls, ed. J. A. Raftis and M. P. Hogan. Toronto, 1976.

Early Treatises on the Practice of the Justices of the Peace in the Fifteenth and Sixteenth Centuries, ed. Bertha Haven Putnam. Oxford Studies in Social and Legal History ed. Paul Vinogradoff, vol. 7. Oxford, 1924.

English Historical Documents. Vol. 2, 1042–1189, ed. David C. Douglas and George Greenaway. London, 1953.

English Historical Documents. Vol. 3, 1189–1327, ed. Harry Rothwell. Oxford, 1975.

Essex Sessions of the Peace 1351, 1377–1379, ed. Elizabeth Chapin Furber. Essex Archaeological Society Occasional Publications No. 3. Colchester, 1953.

"Extracts from the Plea Rolls, 16 to 33 Edward III, Translated from the Original Rolls in the Public Record Office," ed. G. Wrottesley. *Collections for a History of Staffordshire Edited by the William Salt Archaeological Society,* vol.12. London, 1891.

The Eyre of Kent 6 & 7 Edward II, ed. Frederic W. Maitland, Leveson W. V.

Harcourt and William C. Bolland. 3 vols. Selden Society, vols. 24, 27, 29. London, 1910–13.

The Eyre of Northamptonshire, 3–4 Edward III, A.D. 1329–1330, ed. Donald W. Sutherland, 2 vols. Selden Society, vols. 97, 98. London, 1983.

Fleta, ed. H. G. Richardson and G. O. Sayles. Vol. 2. Selden Society, vol. 72. London, 1955.

A Formula Book of English Official Historical Documents. Part II, Ministerial and Judicial Records, ed. Hubert Hall. Cambridge, 1909.

Fortescue, Sir John. *On the Laws and Governance of England,* ed. Shelley Lockwood. Cambridge, 1997.

Four Thirteenth Century Law Tracts, ed. George E. Woodbine. New Haven, 1910.

Great Britain. House of Commons. Sessional Papers, 1881–1889. Deputy Keepers Annual Reports, nos. 42–50.

The Great Roll of the Pipe for the Thirtieth Year of the Reign of King Henry the Second, A.D. 1183–1184. n. a. The Publications of the Pipe Roll Society, vol. 33. London, 1912.

The Great Roll of the Pipe for the Thirty-Second Year of the Reign of King Henry the Second A. D. 1185–1186. n. a. The Publications of the Pipe Roll Society, vol. 36. (1914).

Hertfordshire Lay Subsidy Rolls 1307 and 1334, ed. Janice Brooker and Susan Flood. Hertfordshire Record Publications, vol. 14. Hertford, 1998.

Historia et cartularium monasterii sancti Petri gloucestriae, ed. William Henry Hart. Rerum Britannicarum Medii Aevi Scriptores, no. 33. London, 1867.

Inquisitions and Assessments Relating to Feudal Aids, with other analogous Documents Preserved in the Public Record Office; A.D. 1284–1431, ed. A. S. Maskelyne, C. Johnson, A. E. Stamp, and J. V. Lyle. 6 vols. London, 1899–1920.

Kent Keepers of the Peace, 1316–1317, ed. Bertha Haven Putnam. Kent Archaological Society Records Branch, vol. 13. Ashford, 1933.

Liber Albus: The White Book of the City of London. trans. Henry Thomas Riley. London, 1861.

Liber Feodorum. The Book of Fees Commonly Called Testa de Nevill, Part One, AD1198–1242. n. a., London, 1920.

A Lincolnshire Assize Roll for 1298, ed. Walter S. Thomson. The Publications of the Lincoln Record Society, vol. 36. Hereford, 1944.

List of Inquisitions ad Quod Damnum Preserved in the Public Record Office. List and Index Society no. 17. London, 1904.

The London Eyre of 1276, ed. Martin Weinbaum. London Record Society, vol. 12. n. p., 1976.

Matthew Paris's English History, trans. J. A. Giles. 3 vols. London, 1852.

Medieval English Legal History. An Index and Paraphrase of Printed Year Book Reports, 1268–1535, comp. David J. Seipp. http://www.bu.edu/law/faculty/scholarship/yearbooks/.

Nonarum Inquisitiones in Curia Scaccarii Temp. Regis Edwardi III, ed. G. Vanderzee. London, 1807.

"Original Documents Illustrative of the Administration of the Criminal Law in the Time of Edward I," ed. F. M. Nichols. *Archaeologia* 40 (1866).

The Parliament Rolls of Medieval England1275–1504, vol. 1, Edward I 1275–1294, ed. Paul Brand. London, 2005.

The Parliament Rolls of Medieval England, 1275–1504, vol. 3, Edward II, 1307–1327, ed. Seymour Phillips. London, 2005.

The Parliament Rolls of Medieval England1275–1504, vol. 4, Edward III, 1327–1348, ed. Seymour Phillips and Mark Ormrod. London, 2005.

The Parliament Rolls of Medieval England1275–1504, vol. 9, Henry V, 1413–1422, ed. Chris Given-Wilson. London, 2005.

The Parliament Rolls of Medieval England1275–1504, vol. 10, Henry VI, 1422–1431, ed. Anne Curry. London, 2005.

Placita Corone, ed. J. M. Kaye. Selden Society Supplementary Series, vol. 4. London, 1966.

Proceedings before the Justices of the Peace in the Fourteenth and Fifteenth Centuries, Edward III to Richard III, ed. Bertha Haven Putnam. Ames Foundation, vol. 5. London, 1938.

Records of Some Sessions of the Peace in Lincolnshire, 1360–1375, ed. Rosamund Sillem. Lincoln Record Society, vol. 30. Hereford, 1936.

Records of the Templars in England in the Twelfth Century, ed. Beatrice Lees. Records of the Social and Economic History of England and Wales, vol. 9. London, 1935.

Red Book of the Exchequer, ed. Hubert Hall. Rerum Britannicarum Medii Aevi Scriptores (Rolls Series) no. 99. London, 1897.

Regesta Regum Anglo-Normannorum1066–1154, ed. H.W.C. Davis, Charles Johnson and R. J. Whitwell. 4 vols. Oxford, 1913–68.

The Roll and Writ File of the Berkshire Eyre of 1248, ed. M. T. Clanchy, Selden Society vol. 90. London, 1973.

"Roll of the Bedfordshire Supervisors of the Peace, 1314," ed. Joyce Godber. *The Publications of the Bedfordshire Historical Record Society*, vol. 12. Aspley Guise, 1928.

The Roll of the Shropshire Eyre of 1256, ed. Alan Harding, Selden Society vol. 96. London, 1981.

Rolls of the Justices in Eyre, ed. Doris Mary Stenton, Selden Society vol. 53. London, 1934.

Rolls of Northamptonshire Sessions of the Peace, ed. Marguerite Gollancz. The Publications of the Northamptonshire Record Society, vol. 11. Kettering, Northampthonshire, 1940.

Rotuli chartarum in turri londinensi asservati, 1199–1216, ed. T. D. Hardy. London, 1837.

Rotuli de dominabus et pueris et puellis de XII comitatibus [*1185*], ed. John H. Round. The Publications of the Pipe Roll Society, vol. 35. London, 1913.

Rotuli hundredorum, ed. W. Illingworth and J. Caley. 2 vols. London, 1812–18.

Royal Justice and the Medieval English Countryside: The Huntingdonshire Eyre of 1286, the Ramsey Abbey Banlieu Court of 1287, and the Assizes of1287–88, ed. Anne Reiber DeWindt and Edwin Brezette DeWindt. Pontifical Institute of Mediaeval Studies, Studies and Texts vol. 57. Toronto, 1981.

Select Cases in the Court of King's Bench under Edward III, vol. 5, ed. G. O. Sayles. Selden Society vol. 76. London, 1958.

Select Cases in the Court of King's Bench under Richard II, Henry IV and Henry V, vol. 7, ed. G. O. Sayles. Selden Society, vol. 88. London, 1971.

Select Cases of Procedure without Writ under Henry III, ed. H. G. Richardson and G. O. Sayles. Selden Society vol. 60. London, 1941.

Select Pleas in Manorial and Other Seignorial Courts, ed. F. W. Maitland. Selden Society, vol. 2. London, 1889.

Select Pleas, Starrs, and Other Records from the Rolls of the Exchequer of the Jews, AD 1220 to 1284, ed. J. M. Rigg. Selden Society vol. 15. London, 1902.

Smith, Thomas. *De Republica Anglorum: A Discourse on the Commonwealth of England*, ed. L. Alston. Cambridge, 1906.

Some Sessions of the Peace in Cambridgeshire in the Fourteenth Century. 1340, 1380–83, ed. Mary Margaret Taylor. Cambridge Antiquarian Society Octavo Publications No. 55. Cambridge, 1942.

Somersetshire Pleas (Civil and Criminal) From the Rolls of the Itinerant Justices (Close of 12th Century–41 Henry III), ed. Charles Chadwyck-Healey, Somerset Record Society, vol. 11. London, 1897: 26–110.

State Trials of the Reign of Edward the First, 1289–1293, ed. T. F. Tout and Hilda Johnstone. Camden Society, 3rd ser., vol. 9. London, 1906.

Statutes of the Realm, ed. A. Luders, T. E. Tomlins, J. France, W. E. Taunton, and J. Raithby. 11 vols. London, 1810–28.

The Stonor Letters and Papers1290–1483, ed. Charles L. Kingford, vol. 1, Camden Third Series, vol. 29. London, 1919.

Stubbs, William. *Select Charters from the Beginning to 1307*, 9th ed., ed. H.W.C. Davis. Oxford, 1913.

The Taxation of 1297. A Translation of the Local Rolls of Assessment for Barford, Biggleswade and Flitt Hundreds, and for Bedford, Dunstable, Leighton Buzzard and Luton, ed. A. T. Gaydon. The Publications of the Bedfordshire Historical Record Society, vol. 39. Streatley, Beds, 1959.

Thomas Wright's Political Songs of England from the Reign of John to that of Edward II, ed. Peter Coss. Cambridge, 1996.

The Treatise on the Laws and Customs of the Realm of England Commonly Called Glanvill, ed. G.D.G. Hall. Oxford, 1993.

Two Bedfordshire Subsidy Lists. 1309 and 1332 with Map, ed. Sydenham Henry Augustus Hervey. Suffolk Green Books no. 18 Bury St. Edmunds, 1925.

Walter of Henley and Other Treatises of Estate Management and Accounting, ed. Dorothea Oschinsky. Oxford, 1971.

The Warwickshire Hundred Rolls of1279–80, ed. Trevor John. Records of Social and Economic History, n.s. vol. 19. Oxford, 1992.

Wiltshire Gaol Delivery and Trailbaston Trials 1275–1306, ed. Ralph B. Pugh. Wiltshire Record Society, vol. 33. Devizes, 1978.

Year Books of the Reign of Edward II, vol. 2, 2 & 3 Edward II, ed. F. W. Maitland, Selden Society, vol. 19. London, 1904.

Year Books of the Reign of Edward II, vol. 20, 10 Edward II, ed. M. Dominica Legge and Sir William Holdsworth. Selden Society vol. 52. London, 1934.

Year Books of the Reign of Edward II. vol. 12, 5 Edward 11, ed. William C. Bolland. Selden Society vol. 33. London, 1916.

Year Books of the Reign of King Edward the First: Years XX and XXI. ed. Alfred J. Horwood, Rerum Britannicarum Medii Aevi Scriptores, no. 31, 5 vols. London, 1863–1879.

Yorkshire Inquisitions of the Reigns of Henry III and Edward I. ed. William Brown, 4 vols., The Yorkshire Archaeological Society Record Series, vols. 12, 23, 31, 37. n.p., 1892–1906.

SECONDARY SOURCES

Agrarian History of England and Wales: vol. 2, 1042–1350, ed. H. E. Hallam. Cambridge, 1988.

Arnold, Morris S. "Law and Fact in the Medieval Jury Trial: Out of Sight, Out of Mind." *American Journal of Legal History* 18 (1974): 267–80.

Bailey, Mark. *The English Manor c.1200–c.1500.* Manchester, 2002.

Baker, J. H. *An Introduction to English Legal History.* 3rd ed. London, 1990.

Bartlett, Robert. *Trial by Fire and Water: The Medieval Judicial Ordeal.* Oxford, 1986.

———. *England under the Norman and Angevin Kings, 1075–1225.* Oxford, 2000.

Beckerman, John "The Articles of Presentment of a Court Leet and Court Baron, in English, c. 1400." *Bulletin of the Institute of Historical Research* 47 (1974): 230–234.

———. "Procedural Innovation and Institutional Change in Medieval English Manorial Courts." *Law and History Review* 10 (1992): 197–252.

Bellamy, J. G. *Bastard Feudalism and the Law.* Portland, Oregon, 1989.

———. *The Criminal Trial in Later Medieval England.* Toronto, 1998.

Bennett, Judith M. "Medieval Peasant Marriage: An Examination of Marriage License Fines in the *Liber Gersumarum.*" In *Pathways to Medieval Peasants,* ed. J. A. Raftis. Toronto, 1981: 193–246.

———. *Women in the Medieval English Countryside: Gender and Household in Brigstock before the Plague.* Oxford, 1987.

———. *A Medieval Life: Cecilia Penifader of Brigstock, c.1295–1344.* Boston, 1999.

Bennett, Michael J. *Community, Class, and Careerism: Cheshire and Lancashire Society in the Age of Sir Gawain and the Green Knight.* Cambridge, 1983.

Biancalana, Joseph. "For Want of Justice: Legal Reforms of Henry II." *Columbia Law Review* 88 (1988): 433–536.

———. "Widows at Common Law: The Development of Common Law Dower." *Irish Jurist* new series 23 (1988): 255–329.

Blackstone, William. *Commentaries on the Laws of England.* 4 vols. Oxford, 1765–69.

Blickle, Peter, ed. *Resistance, Representation, and Community.* Oxford, 1997.

Bloch, Marc. *The Historian's Craft,* trans. Peter Putnam. Manchester, 1992.

Brand, Paul. "Henry II and the Creation of the English Common Law." *Haskins Society Journal* 11 (1990): 197–222.

———. *The Making of the Common Law.* London, 1992.

———. *The Origins of the English Legal Profession.* Oxford, 1992.

———. "The Formation of the English Legal System, 1150–1400." In *Legislation and Justice,* ed. Antonio Padoa-Schioppa. Oxford, 1997: 103–22.

Britnell, R. H. "King John's Early Grants of Markets and Fairs." *English Historical Review* 370 (1979): 90–96.

———, ed. *Pragmatic Literacy East and West,1200–1330.* Woodbridge, Suffolk, 1997.

Britton, Edward. *The Community of the Vill. A Study in the History of the Family and Village Life in Fourteenth-Century England.* Toronto, 1977.

Brunner, Heinrich. *Die Entstehung der Schwurgericht.* Berlin, 1871.

Cam, Helen. *Studies in the Hundred Rolls. Some Aspects of Thirteenth-Century Administration.* Oxford Studies in Social and Legal History, ed. Paul Vinogradoff. Vol. 6. Oxford, 1921.

———. *The Hundred and the Hundred Rolls.* London, 1930.

———. "Pedigrees of Villeins and Free Men in the Thirteenth Century." In Idem, *Liberties and Communities in Medieval England: Collected Studies in Local Administration and Topography.* London, 1963: 124–35.

Campbell, Bruce M. S. "The Agrarian Problem in the Early Fourteenth Century." *Past and Present* 188 (2005): 3–70.

Campbell, James. *The Anglo-Saxon State.* London and New York, 2000.

Carpenter, Christine. *Locality and Polity. A Study of Warwickshire Landed Society, 1401–1499.* Cambridge, 1992.

———. *The Wars of the Roses. Politics and the Constitution in England, c. 1437–1509.* Cambridge, 1997.

Carpenter, David. *The Struggle for Mastery. The Penguin History of Britain 1066–1284.* London, 2004.

Clanchy, Michael. "Law and Love in the Middle Ages." In *Disputes and Settlements: Law and Human Relations in the West,* ed. John Bossy. Cambridge, 1983: 47–67.

———. *From Memory to Written Record. England 1066–1307.* 2nd ed. Oxford, 1993.

Constable, Marianne. *The Law of the Other: The Mixed Jury and Changing Concepts of Citizenship, Law, and Knowledge.* Chicago, 1994.

Contamine, Philippe, ed. *War and Competition Between States.* Oxford, 2000.

Coss, Peter. *The Origins of the English Gentry.* Cambridge, 2003.

———. "An Age of Deference." In *A Social History of Medieval England, 1200–1500,* ed. Rosemary Horrox and W. Mark Ormrod. Cambridge, 2006: 31–73.

Crook, David. "The Later Eyres." *English Historical Review* 383 (1982): 241–68.

———. *Records of the General Eyre*, Public Record Office Handbooks Number 20. London, 1982.

———. "Triers and the Origin of the Grand Jury." *Journal of Legal History* 12 (1991): 103–16.

Crowley, D. A. "The Later History of Frankpledge." *Bulletin of the Institute of Historical Research* 48 (1975): 1–15.

Denholm-Young, N. *Seignorial Administration in England*. Oxford, 1937.

———. *Collected Papers of N. Denholm-Young*. Cardiff, 1969.

DeWindt, Anne Reiber. "Local Government in a Small Town: A Medieval Leet Jury and Its Constituents." *Albion* 23 (1991): 627–54.

DeWindt, Edwin Brezette. *Land and People in Holywell-cum-Needingworth. Structures of Tenure and Patterns of Social Organization in an East Midlands Village 1252–1457*. Toronto, 1971.

DeWindt, Anne Reiber and Edwin Brezette, DeWindt. *Ramsey: The Lives of an English Fenland Town*. Washington, DC, 2006.

Dyer, Christopher. "The Social and Economic Background to the Rural Revolt of 1381." In *The English Rising of 1381*, ed. T. H. Aston and R. H. Hilton. Cambridge, 1984: 9–24.

———. *Standards of Living in the Later Middle Ages. Social Change in England c. 1200–1520*. Cambridge, 1989.

———. *Making a Living in the Middle Ages*. New Haven, 2002.

———. *An Age of Transition? Economy and Society in the Later Middle Ages*. Oxford, 2005.

Ertman, Thomas. *Birth of the Leviathon. Building States and Regimes in Medieval and Early Modern Europe*. Cambridge, 1997.

Farrer, William. *Feudal Cambridgeshire*. Cambridge, 1920.

Fenster, Thelma and Daniel Lord Smail, eds. *Fama: The Politics of Talk & Reputation in Medieval Europe*. Ithaca, 2003.

Fisher, George. "The Jury's Rise as Lie Detector." *Yale Law Journal* 107 (1997): 575–714.

Fleming, Robin. *Domesday Book and the Law: Society and Legal Custom in Early Medieval England*. Cambridge, 1998.

Flower, C. T. *Introduction to the Curia Regis Rolls, 1199–1230*. Selden Society 62. London, 1944.

Forbes, T. R. "A Jury of Matrons." *Medical History* 32 (1988): 23–33.

Fowler, R. C. "Legal Proofs of Age." *English Historical Review* 22 (1907): 101–03.

French, Katherine L. *The People of the Parish. Community Life in a Late Medieval Diocese*. Philadelphia, 2001.

Fryde, Natalie. "A Royal Enquiry into Abuses: Queen Eleanor's Ministers in North-East Wales, 1291–92." *Welsh History Review* 5 (1971): 366–76.

Gavel, Leona. *Benefit of Clergy in England in the Later Middle Ages,* Smith College Studies in History, vol. 14. Northampton, MA, 1929; reprt. New York, 1969.

Goheen, R. B. "Peasant Politics? Village Community and the Crown in Fifteenth-Century England." *American Historical Review* 96 (1991): 42–62.

Gras, N.S.B. *The Early English Customs System.* Cambridge, MA, 1918.

Green, Judith. *The Government of England under Henry I.* Cambridge, 1986.

Green, Thomas A. *Verdict According to Conscience. Perspectives on the Criminal Trial Jury1200–1800.* Chicago, 1985.

———."A Retrospective on the Criminal Trial Jury, 1200–1800." In *Twelve Good Men and True,* ed. J. S. Cockburn and Thomas A. Green. Princeton, 1998: 358–400.

Groot, Roger D. "The Jury of Presentment before 1215." *American Journal of Legal History* 26 (1982): 1–24.

———. "The Jury in Private Criminal Prosecutions before 1215." *The American Journal of Legal History* 27 (1983): 113–141.

———. "The Early Thirteenth-Century Criminal Jury." In *Twelve Good Men and True,* ed. J. S. Cockburn and Thomas A. Green. Princeton, 1998: 3–35.

———. "Teaching Each Other: Judges, Clerks, Jurors and Malefactors Define the Guilt/Innocence Jury." In *Learning the Law. Teaching and the Transmission of English Law, 1150–1900,* ed. Jonathan A. Bush and Alain Wijffels. London, 1999: 17–32.

———. "Petit Larceny, Jury Lenity and Parliament." In *"The Dearest Birthright of the People of England." The Jury in the History of the Common Law,* ed. John W. Cairns and Grant McLeod. Oxford, 2002: 47–61.

Gross, Charles. "Modes of Trial in the Medieval Boroughs of England." *Harvard Law Review* 15 (1902): 691–706.

———. *The Sources and Literature of English History.* 2nd ed. London, 1915.

Hall, Hubert. *A Formula Book of English Official Historical Documents.* Cambridge, 1908–09.

Hanawalt, Barbara. "Community, Conflict and Social Control: Crime in the Ramsey Abbey Villages." *Medieval Studies* 39 (1977): 402–23.

———. *Crime and Conflict in English Communities1300–1348.* Cambridge, MA, 1979.

Harding, Alan. "The Origins and Early History of the Keeper of the Peace." *Transactions of the Royal Historical Society,* 5th ser., 10 (1960): 85–109.

———. *The Law Courts of Medieval England.* London, 1973.

———. "Plaints and Bills in the History of English Law, Mainly in the Period1250–1350." In *Legal History Studies 1972,* ed. Dafydd Jenkins. Cardiff, 1975: 65–86.

———. *England in the Thirteenth Century.* Cambridge, 1993.

———. *Medieval Law and the Foundations of the State.* Oxford, 2002.

Harvey, P.D.A. *A Medieval Oxfordshire Village. Cuxham 1240 to 1400.* Oxford, 1965.

Haskins, Charles Homer. *Norman Institutions.* Cambridge, MA, 1918.

Hearnshaw, F.J.C. *Leet Jurisdiction in England.* Publications of the Southampton Record Society, vol. 5. Southampton, 1908.

Helmholz, R. H. "The Law of Compurgation." In idem, *The ius commune in England. Four Studies.* Oxford, 2001: 82–134.

Hilton, Rodney. *The English Peasantry in the Later Middle Ages*. Oxford, 1975.

Holt, J. C. *Magna Carta*. 2nd ed. Cambridge, 1992.

Hudson, John. *Land, Law, and Lordship in Anglo-Norman England*. Oxford, 1994.

Hunnisett, R. F. *The Medieval Coroner*. Cambridge Studies in English Legal History. Cambridge, 1961.

Hurnard, Naomi. "The Jury of Presentment and the Assize of Clarendon." *English Historical Review* 56 (1941): 374–410.

———. *The King's Pardon for Homicide before AD 1307*. Oxford, 1969.

Hyams, Paul R. *Kings, Lords, and Peasants in Medieval England: The Common Law of Villeinage in the Twelfth and Thirteenth Centuries*. Oxford, 1980.

———. *Rancor and Reconciliation in Medieval England*. Ithaca, 2003.

Jacob, E. F. *Studies in the Period of Baronial Reform and Rebellion, 1258–1267*. Oxford Studies in Social and Legal History. Vol. 8. Oxford, 1925.

Jenkins, Daffydd. "Towards the Jury in Medieval Wales." In *The Dearest Birthright of the People of England: The Jury in the History of the Common Law*, ed. John W. Cairns and Grant McLeod. Oxford, 2002: 17–46.

Jenks, Susanne. "Das Writ und die Exceptio de Odio et Atia." *Tijdschrift voor Rechtsgeschiedenis* 68 (2000): 455–77.

Kaeuper, Richard W. "Law and Order in Fourteenth-Century England: The Evidence of Special Commissions of Oyer and Terminer." *Speculum* 54 (1979): 734–84.

———. *War, Justice and Public Order: France and England in the Later Middle Ages*. Oxford, 1988.

Kappauf, Catherine. *The Early Development of the Petty Jury in England: 1194–1221*. University of Illinois PhD thesis, Urbana-Champagne, IL, 1973.

Kerr, Margaret H., Richard D. Forsyth, and Michael J. Plyley. "Cold Water and Hot Iron: Trial by Ordeal in England." *Journal of Interdisciplinary History* 22 (1992): 573–95.

Klerman, Daniel. "Settlement and the Decline of Private Prosecution in Thirteenth-Century England." *Law and History Review* 19 (2001): 1–65.

———. "Was the Jury Ever Self-Informing?" In *The Trial in History, vol. 1, Judicial Tribunals in England and Europe, 1200–1700*, ed. Maureen Mulholland, Brian Pullan, and Anne Pullan. Manchester, 2003: 58–80.

Kosminsky, E. A. *Studies in the Agrarian History of England in the Thirteenth Century*, trans. Ruth Kisch. Oxford, 1956.

Kowaleski, Maryanne. "Women's Work in a Market Town: Exeter in the Late Fourteenth Century." In *Women and Work in Preindustrial Europe*, ed. Barbara A. Hanawalt. Bloomington, 1986: 145–64.

———. *Local Markets and Regional Trade in Medieval Exeter*. Cambridge, 1995.

Langbein, Irwin, L. "The Jury of Presentment and the Coroner." *Columbia Law Review* 33 (1933): 1329–1365.

Langbein, John H. *Torture and the Law of Proof: Europe and England in the Ancien Regime.* Chicago, 1977.

Langdon, John and James Masschaele. "Commercial Activity and Population Growth in Medieval England." *Past & Present* 190 (2006): 35–81.

Larson, P. L. *Conflict and Compromise in the Late Medieval Countryside. Lords and Peasants in Durham,1349–1400.* New York, 2006.

Latham, R. E. and C.A.F. Meekings. "The Veredictum of Chippenham Hundred, 1281." In *Collectanea,* ed. N. J. Williams, Wiltshire Archaeological and Natural History Society, Records Branch, vol. 12. Devizes, 1956: 50–128.

Levett, Ada Elizabeth. *Studies in Manorial History.* Oxford, 1938.

Lewis, C. P. "The Domesday Jurors." *Haskins Society Journal* 5 (1993): 17–44.

Lindkvist, Thomas. "Law and the Making of the State in Medieval Sweden." In *Legislation and Justice,* ed. Antonio Padoa-Schioppa. Oxford, 1997: 211–28.

Loengard, Janet Senderowitz. "'Of the Gift of Her Husband': English Dower and its Consequences in the Year 1200." In *Women of the Medieval World. Essays in Honor of John H. Mundy,* ed. Julius Kirshner and Suzanne F. Wemple. Oxford, 1985: 215–55.

Macnair, Mike. "Vicinage and the Antecedents of the Jury." *Law and History Review* 17 (1999): 537–90.

Maddern, Phillippa C. *Violence and Social Order. East Anglia1422–1442.* Oxford, 1992.

Maddicott, J. R. *The English Peasantry and the Demands of the Crown. Past & Present* Supplement, no. 1. Oxford, 1975.

Martin, M. T. "Legal Proofs of Age." *English Historical Review* 22 (1907): 526–27.

Masschaele, James. *Peasants, Merchants, and Markets: Inland Trade in Medieval England,1150–1350.* New York, 1997.

———. "Economic Takeoff and the Rise of Markets." In *Blackwell Companion to the Middle Ages,* ed. Edward D. English and Carol L. Lansing. Oxford, forthcoming 2008.

McLane, Bernard William. "Juror Attitudes toward Local Disorder: The Evidence of the 1328 Lincolnshire Trailbaston Proceedings." In *Twelve Good Men and True,* ed. J. S. Cockburn and Thomas A. Green. Princeton, 1998: 36–64.

Meekings, C.A.F. *The 1235 Surrey Eyre.* 2 vols. Surrey Record Society 31–32. Guildford, 1979–83.

Miller, Edward and John Hatcher. *Medieval England. Rural Society and Economic Change1086–1348.* London, 1978.

Mills, Mabel. "The Medieval Shire House." In *Studies Presented to Sir Hilary Jenkinson,* ed. J. Conway Davies. London, 1957: 254–71.

Milsom, S.F.C. "Trespass from Henry III to Edward III." *The Law Quarterly Review* 74 (1958): 195–224, 407–36, 561–90.

———. *The Legal Framework of English Feudalism.* Cambridge, 1976.

Mitnick, John Marshall. "From Neighbor-Witness to Judge of Proofs: The

Transformation of the English Civil Juror." *American Journal of Legal History* 32 (1988): 201–35.

Moore, Ellen Wedemeyer. *The Fairs of Medieval England: An Introductory Study*. Toronto, 1985.

Morris, William. *The Frankpledge System*. New York, 1910.

Musson, Anthony. *Public Order and Law Enforcement: The Local Administration of Criminal Justice, 1294–1350*. Woodbridge, Suffolk, 1996.

———. "Twelve Good Men and True? The Character of Early Fourteenth-Century Juries." *Law and History Review* 15 (1997): 115–44.

———. *Medieval Law in Context: The Growth of Legal Consciousness from Magna Carta to the Peasants' Revolt*. Manchester, 2001.

———. "The Role of Amateur and Professional Judges in the Royal Courts of Late Medieval England." In *The Trial in History*. Vol. 1, *Judicial Tribunals in England and Europe, 1200–1700,* ed. Maureen Mulholland, Brian Pullan, and Anne Pullan. Manchester, 2003: 37–57.

Musson, Anthony and W. M. Ormrod. *The Evolution of English Justice. Law, Politics and Society in the Fourteenth Century*. Basingstoke, Hampshire, 1999.

Neville, Cynthia J. *Violence, Custom and Law: The Anglo-Scottish Border Lands in the Later Middle Ages*. Edinburgh, 1998.

Odegaard, Charles E. "*Legalis Homo.*" *Speculum* 15 (1940): 186–93.

Oldham, James C. "The Origins of the Special Jury." *University of Chicago Law Review* 50 (1983): 137–221.

———. "On Pleading the Belly: A History of the Jury of Matrons." *Criminal Justice History* 6 (1985): 1–64.

———. "The Varied Life of the Self-Informing Jury." Selden Society Lecture, July, 2004. London, 2005.

Olson, Sherri. *A Chronicle of All that Happens. Voices from the Village Court in Medieval England*. Toronto, 1996.

Page, Frances M. *The Estates of Crowland Abbey: A Study in Manorial Organization*. Cambridge, 1934.

Palgrave, Francis. *The Rise and Progress of the English Commonwealth*. 2 vols. London, 1832.

Palmer, Robert C. *The County Courts of Medieval England*. Princeton, 1982.

———. *English Law in the Age of the Black Death,1348–1381*. Chapel Hill, 1993.

Parkin, Kate. *Courts and the Community: Reconstructing the Fourteenth-Century Peasant Society of Wisbeach Hundred, Cambridgeshire from Manorial Court Rolls*. PhD thesis, University of Leicester. Leicester, 1998.

Pollock, Frederick and Frederic William Maitland. *The History of English Law before the Time of Edward I*. 2nd ed. 2 vols. Cambridge, 1898.

Post, J. B. "Local Jurisdictions and Judgment of Death in Later Medieval England." *Criminal Justice History* 4 (1983): 1–21.

———. "Jury Lists and Juries in the Late Fourteenth Century." In *Twelve Good Men and True: The Criminal Trial Jury in England, 1200–1800,* ed. J. S. Cockburn and Thomas A. Green. Princeton, 1988: 65–77.

Postan, M. M. *The Medieval Economy and Society*. London, 1972.

Powell, Edward. "Jury Trial at Gaol Delivery in the Late Middle Ages: The Midland Circuit, 1400–1429." In *Twelve Good Men and True: The Criminal Trial Jury in England, 1200–1800,* ed. J. S. Cockburn and Thomas A. Green. Princeton, 1988: 78–116.

———. *Kingship, Law, and Society. Criminal Justice in the Reign of Henry V.* Oxford, 1989.

Powicke, Michael. *Military Obligation in Medieval England: A Study in Liberty and Duty.* Oxford, 1962.

Pugh, Ralph B. *Imprisonment in Medieval England.* Cambridge, 1968.

———. "Reflections of a Medieval Criminologist." *Proceedings of the British Academy* 59. London, 1975: 83–104.

Quick, J. "The Number and Distribution of Knights in Thirteenth Century England: The Evidence of the Grand Assize Lists." In *Thirteenth Century England I,* ed. P. R. Coss and S. D. Lloyd. Woodbridge, Suffolk, 1986: 114–19.

Raban, Sandra. *A Second Domesday?: The Hundred Rolls of 1279–80.* Oxford, 2004.

Raftis, J. A. *Tenure and Mobility: Studies in the Social History of the Mediaeval English Village.* Toronto, 1964.

———. "The Concentration of Responsibility in Five Villages." *Mediaeval Studies* 28 (1966): 92–118.

———. *Assart Data and Land Values: Two Studies in the East Midlands,1200–1350.* Toronto, 1974.

———. *Warboys: Two Hundred Years in the Life of an English Mediaeval Village.* Toronto, 1974.

Razi, Zvi. *Life, Marriage and Death in a Medieval Parish: Economy, Society and Demography in Halesowen,1270–1400.* Cambridge, 1980.

Reuter, Timothy. "The Medieval Nobility in Twentieth-Century Historiography." In *Companion to Historiography,* ed. Michael Bentley. London, 1997: 177–202.

Reyerson, Kathryn L. "Commerce and Communications." In *The New Cambridge Medieval History.* Vol. 5, c.1198- c.1300, ed. David Abulafia. Cambridge, 1999: 50–70.

Reynolds, Susan. *Kingdoms and Communities in Western Europe, 900–1300.* Oxford, 1984.

Richardson, H. G. *The English Jewry under Angevin Kings.* London, 1960.

Riess, Ludwig. *The History of English Electoral Law in the Middle Ages,* trans. K. L. Wood-Legh. Cambridge, 1940.

Rigby, S. H. *English Society in the Later Middle Ages: Class, Status and Gender.* New York, 1995.

Roffe, David. "The Hundred Rolls and their Antecedents: Some Thoughts on the Inquisition in Thirteenth-Century England." *Haskins Society Journal* 7 (1995): 179–87.

———. *Domesday: The Inquest and the Book.* Oxford, 2000.

Rosenthal, Joel. *Telling Tales: Sources and Narration in Late Medieval England.* University Park, PA, 2003.

Russell, M. J. "Trial by Battle Procedure in Writs of Right and Criminal Appeals." *Tijdschrift voor Rechtsgeschiedenis* 53 (1983): 124–34.

Saul, Nigel. "The Social Status of Chaucer's Franklin: A Reconsideration." *Medium Aevum* 52 (1983): 10–26..

———. *Richard II.* New Haven, 1997.

Schofield, Phillip R. "The Late Medieval View of Frankpledge and the Tithing System: An Essex Case Study." In *Medieval Society and the Manor Court,* ed. Zvi Razi and Richard Smith. Oxford, 1996: 408–49.

Scott, James C. *Weapons of the Weak: Everyday Forms of Peasant Resistance.* New Haven, 1987.

Seipp, David J. "Crime in the Year Books." In *Law Reporting in England,* ed. Chantal Stebbings. London, 1995: 15–34.

———. "Jurors, Evidence, and the Tempest of 1499." In *The Dearest Birthright of the People of England: The Jury in the History of the Common Law,* ed. John Cairns and Grant McLeod. Oxford, 2002: 75–92.

Smail, Daniel Lord. *The Consumption of Justice.* Ithaca , 2003.

Smith, Richard M. " 'Modernization' and the Corporate Medieval Village Community in England: Some Skeptical Reflections." In *Explorations in Historical Geography,* ed. Alan Baker and D. Gregory. Cambridge, 1984: 140–79.

Spufford, Peter. *Power and Profit: The Merchant in Medieval Europe.* London, 2002.

Stamp, A. E. "Legal Proofs of Age." *English Historical Review* 29 (1914): 323–24.

Stenton, Doris M. *English Justice between the Norman Conquest and the Great Charter,1066–1215.* The Jayne Lectures for 1963. London, 1965.

Stephen, James Fitzjames. *A History of the Criminal Law of England.* 3 vols. London, 1883.

Stevenson, E. R. "The Escheator." In *The English Government at Work, 1327–1336.* Vol. 2, Fiscal Administration, ed. William A. Morris and Joseph R. Strayer. Cambridge, MA, 1947: 109–67.

Stewart-Brown, R. *The Sergeants of the Peace in Medieval England and Wales.* Manchester, 1936.

Stocks, K. J. "Manorial Courts in England in the Early Thirteenth Century." In *Thirteenth Century England VIII,* ed. Michael Prestwich, Richard Britnell, and Robin Frame. Woodbridge, Suffolk, 2001: 135–42.

Stone, E. "Profit-and-Loss Accountancy at Norwich Cathedral Priory." *Transactions of the Royal Historical Society,* 5th ser., 12 (1962): 25–48.

Strayer, Joseph. "The Writ of Novel Disseisin in Normandy at the End of the Thirteenth Century." In *Medieval Statecraft and the Perspectives of History.* Princeton, 1971: 3–13.

Stubbs, William. *The Constitutional History of England.* 3rd ed., 3 vols. Oxford, 1880.

Summerson, H.R.T. "The Structure of Law Enforcement in Thirteenth Century England." *American Journal of Legal History* 23 (1979): 313–27.

———. "The Early Development of the Peine Forte et Dure." In *Law,*

Litigants, and the Legal Profession, ed. E. W. Ives and A. H. Manchester. London, 1983: 116–25.

Summerson, Henry. "Attitudes to Capital Punishment in England, 1200–1350." In *Thirteenth Century England VIII,* ed. Michael Prestwich, Richard Britnell and Robin Frame. Woodbridge, Suffolk, 2001: 123–32.

Sutherland, Donald, W. *The Assize of Novel Disseisin.* Oxford, 1973.

Taylor, Mary Margaret. "The Justices of Assize." In *The English Government at Work, 1327–1336.* Vol. 3, ed. James F. Willard, William A. Morris, and William H. Dunham, Jr. Cambridge, MA, 1950: 219–57.

Thayer, James Bradley. *A Preliminary Treatise on Evidence at the Common Law.* Boston, 1898.

Tupling, G. H. *South Lancashire in the Reign of Edward II.* Remains Historical and Literary Connected with the Palatine Counties of Lancaster and Cheshire (Chetham Society). 3rd ser., vol. 1. Manchester, 1949.

Turner, Ralph. *The King and His Courts.* Ithaca, 1968.

Van Caenegem, R. C. *Royal Writs in England from the Conquest to Glanvill.* Selden Society, vol. 77. London, 1959.

———. "Public Prosecution of Crime in Twelfth-Century England." In *Church and Government in the Middle Ages: Essays Presented to C. R. Cheney,* ed. C.N.L. Brook, D. E. Luscombe, G. H. Martin, and D. M. Owen. Cambridge, 1976: 41–76.

———. *The Birth of the English Common Law.* 2nd ed. Cambridge, 1988.

Walker, David. "A Letter from the Holy Land." *English Historical Review* 72 (1957): 662–65.

Walker, Sue Sheridan, ed. *Wife and Widow in Medieval England.* Ann Arbor, 1993.

Warren, W. L. *Henry II.* Berkeley and Los Angeles, 1973.

———. "The Myth of Norman Administrative Efficiency." *Transactions of the Royal Historical Society.* 5th ser., 34 (1984): 123–32.

Waugh, Scott L. "Reluctant Knights and Jurors: Respites, Exemptions, and Public Obligations in the Reign of Henry III." *Speculum* 58 (1983): 937–86.

———. "The Origins and Development of the Articles of the Escheator," *Thirteenth Century England V,* ed. P. R. Coss and S. D. Lloyd. Woodbridge, Suffolk, 1995: 89–113.

White, Alfred B. *Self-Government at the King's Command.* Minneapolis, 1933.

White, Stephen D. "Proposing the Ordeal and Avoiding it: Strategy and Power in Western French Litigation, 1050 to 1110." In *Power and Society in the Twelfth Century,* ed. Thomas N. Bisson. Philadelphia, 1995: 89–123.

Wilkinson, Louise J. "Women as Sheriffs in Early Thirteenth Century England." In *English Government in the Thirteenth Century,* ed. Adrian Jobson. Woodbridge, Suffolk, 2004: 111–24.

Willard, James Field. *Parliamentary Taxes on Personal Property 1290 to 1334.* Cambridge, MA, 1934.

Willock, Ian Douglas. *The Origins and Development of the Jury in Scotland.* Stair Society, vol. 23. Edinburgh, 1966.

Winfield, Percy Henry. *The History of Conspiracy and Abuse of Legal Procedure.* Cambridge, 1921.

Wormald, Patrick. "Maitland and Anglo-Saxon Law: Beyond Domesday Book." In *The History of English Law: Centenary Essays on "Pollock and Maitland,"* ed. John Hudson. Proceedings of the British Academy 89. Oxford, 1996: 1–20.

———. *The Making of English Law: King Alfred to the Twelfth Century,* vol. 1: Legislation and Its Limits. Oxford, 1999.

Index